Travelling Players in Shakespeare's England

Travelling Players in Shakespeare's England

Siobhan Keenan
Lecturer in English
University of the West of England
Bristol

First published 2002 by
PALGRAVE MACMILLAN
Houndmills, Basingstoke, Hampshire RG21 6XS and
175 Fifth Avenue, New York, N.Y. 10010
Companies and representatives throughout the world

PALGRAVE MACMILLAN is the global academic imprint of the Palgrave
Macmillan division of St. Martin's Press, LLC and of Palgrave Macmillan Ltd.
Macmillan® is a registered trademark in the United States, United Kingdom
and other countries. Palgrave is a registered trademark in the European
Union and other countries.

ISBN 0–333–96820–4

This book is printed on paper suitable for recycling and
made from fully managed and sustained forest sources.

A catalogue record for this book is available
from the British Library.

Library of Congress Cataloging-in-Publication Data
Keenan, Siobhan, 1973–
    Travelling players in Shakespeare's England / Siobhan Keenan.
      p. cm.
    Includes bibliographical references and index.
    ISBN 0-333-96820-4
      1. Traveling theater–England–History–16th century. 2. Traveling
    theater–England–History–17th century. I. Title.
    PN2590.T7 K44 2002
    792'.022–dc21

                                                            2002019595

10   9   8   7   6   5   4   3   2   1
11   10   09   08   07   06   05   04   03   02

Printed and bound in Great Britain by
Antony Rowe Ltd, Chippenham and Eastbourne

For Mum and Dad

and

David

Contents

List of Tables

List of Illustrations

List of Abbreviations

BRO   Bristol Record Office, Bristol
ERO   Essex County Record Office, Chelmsford
HMC   Historical Manuscripts Commission
LRO   The Record Office for Leicestershire, Leicester & Rutland, Leicester
MRDE   *Medieval and Renaissance Drama in England*
MSC   *Malone Society Collections*
N&Q   *Notes & Queries*
PRO   Public Record Office, London
RCHM   Royal Commission on Historical Monuments
REED   *Records of Early English Drama*
RES   *Review of English Studies*
RORD   *Research Opportunities in Renaissance Drama*
SBTRO   Shakespeare Birthplace Trust Records Office, Stratford-upon-Avon
ShS   *Shakespeare Survey*
SQ   *Shakespeare Quarterly*
TN   *Theatre Notebook*
VCH   *Victoria County History*

<.>   Lost or illegible letters in original manuscript
[...]   Ellipsis of original material

Original spelling and punctuation are preserved in the author's transcriptions of early modern manuscripts. Contractions in the original manuscripts are expanded and shown in italics.

Acknowledgements

During the course of my research I have received help and advice from numerous people for which I am grateful. Professor J. R. Mulryne and Professor Peter Davidson offered generous assistance and encouragement during the early stages of my research, while Professor Andrew Gurr is to be thanked for his helpful comments and suggestions regarding my original thesis and subsequent samples of work. I also owe a special debt of thanks to Professor Alexandra F. Johnston, Dr Sally-Beth MacLean and their colleagues at the REED office in Toronto, for allowing me to visit, for assisting with my research amongst the project's unpublished archives, and for allowing me to use unpublished REED material collected by the late Alice B. Hamilton. I am grateful as well to all those editors of unpublished REED collections who have generously allowed me to draw on their work in the present study (Professor Anne Brannen, Professor John Coldewey, Dr Jane Cowling, Professor John Elliott Jr, Professor Peter Greenfield, Professor Alexandra F. Johnston, Professor Barbara Palmer and Professor John Wasson), and to Dr Eileen White for permission to quote from her doctoral thesis on drama in York. I have also profited from the assistance of staff in various regional archives, libraries and museums to all of whom I am grateful. For advice and help with specific queries I should like to thank Professor Bernard Capp, Bill Champion, Dr Peter Fleming, Dr Scott Fraser, L. J. Rich, and Professor Alan Somerset.

For permission to quote from early modern manuscripts transcribed by REED editors and myself thanks are owing to Berkshire Record Office, Reading; Bristol Record Office, Bristol; Cambridgeshire Archives Service, Cambridge; The Trustees of the Chatsworth Settlement, Chatsworth House; Durham Record Office, Durham; Essex County Record Office, Chelmsford; Lambeth Palace Library, London; Newark Museums, Newark; North Yorkshire County Record Office, Northallerton; Nottinghamshire Archives, Nottingham; Oxford City Council, Oxfordshire Record Office and Oxford University Archives, Oxford; the Public Record Office, London; the Record Office for Leicestershire, Leicester and Rutland, Leicester; the Shakespeare Centre, Stratford-upon-Avon; and the Wiltshire & Swindon Record Office, Trowbridge.

Thanks are also owed to those individuals and institutions that provided or permitted the use of illustrative material included in the book.

Most of the contemporary photographs are my own. Other photographs and illustrations have been supplied or are reproduced by kind permission of the following: (Cover illustration, 4°. L62 Art (12)) the Bodleian Library, University of Oxford; (Illustration 1) the North Devon Athenaeum, Barnstaple; (Illustration 5) the Shakespeare Birthplace Trust, Stratford-upon-Avon; (Illustration 9) the General Editor of the *Victoria County History*; (Illustration 11) Bolton Museum and Art Gallery, Bolton; (Illustration 10) Lancashire County Museum Service, Preston; (Illustration 12) the Marquess of Bath, Longleat House, Warminster, Wiltshire; (Illustration 14) Salisbury & South Wiltshire Museum, Salisbury; (Illustration 15) L. J. Rich and the Governors of Boston Grammar School, Boston; (Illustration 16) the Master and Fellows of Trinity College, Cambridge; (Illustrations 17 and 18) the Governing Body of Christ Church College, Oxford; (Illustration 19) Shropshire Records and Research Centre, Shrewsbury; and (Illustration 20, BL Roy. 18. D. III. f89) the British Library, London.

The completion of this book has been assisted by a period of research leave, granted by the Faculty of Humanities at UWE (Bristol), and a British Academy small research grant, for which I express my thanks to both institutions. My last and greatest debt of gratitude is to my husband, David Morley for his unfailing encouragement and support during the preparation of the book.

SIOBHAN KEENAN

Preface

Traditionally, studies of English Renaissance theatre have focused on the drama and playhouses of the capital. Thanks to the work of scholars involved in the Records of Early English Drama project (based at the University of Toronto, Canada) and the Malone Society this has begun to change. A growing body of evidence regarding regional theatre is now available in print and more attention is being paid to drama outside the Shakespearean capital. I wanted to contribute to this new work and therefore prepared a doctoral dissertation on 'Provincial Playing Places and Performances in Early Modern England, 1559–1625' (Warwick University, 2000). Since that time and encouraged by the ongoing work of the REED project I have continued to study early modern regional theatre, becoming especially interested in the activities of professional touring companies. *Travelling Players* emerges from this research and is the first extended published study of professional English theatre outside Elizabethan and Jacobean London. It draws on my own work in early modern archives and the impressive body of dramatic records already transcribed by REED and Malone Society scholars. The collections prepared by the latter are an invaluable resource for all scholars of medieval and Renaissance drama and I am indebted to their editors: without their collections it would not have been possible to compile the present study at this time.

The main aim of this book is to study the touring practices and performances of professional travelling players in Elizabethan and Jacobean England and the venues in which they performed. Chapter 1 discusses travelling players and touring in general. Subsequent chapters focus on professional playing practices and performances in representative spaces used as temporary theatres by touring players (such as town halls, churches and large country houses). These chapters are illustrated with studies of specific performances in known spaces, and with visual evidence of recorded playing venues. The final chapter looks at the decline in touring performances that occurred in the 1620s; it considers some of the reasons for this decrease and its significance in the history of early modern travelling theatre.

The dating system used in the book is generally modern. Dramatic records are dated as in REED and Malone Society Collections and evidence cited from these sources follows the dating used therein. Where possible, the specific year and date of a record is given, but in some cases records of players can only be dated approximately or to an individual accounting or legal year, years which did not run from January to January in the early modern period. Fiscal years most often ran from Michaelmas to Michaelmas, while the old legal year began in March. Split-dates (such as 1589–90) are used to describe dramatic records dated according to the fiscal or legal year in which they occurred, showing that they belong to a recording period that bridges two modern calendar years.

SIOBHAN KEENAN

1
Travelling Players and Performances in Shakespeare's England: 'How chances it they travel?' (*Hamlet*, 2.2.317)

Hamlet.	Why did you laugh, then, when I said 'Man delights not me'?
Rosencrantz.	To think, my lord, if you delight not in man what lenten entertainment the players shall receive from you. We coted them on the way, and hither are they coming to offer you service.[1]
Rosencrantz.	Tumblers are you?
Player.	We can give you a tumble if that's your taste, and times being what they are.... Otherwise, for a jingle of coin we can do you a selection of gory romances, full of fine cadence and corpses, pirated from the Italian.[2]

When Shakespeare introduced travelling players to the stage in *Hamlet* he was writing about a phenomenon which would have been familiar to contemporary audiences and which he, as a one-time actor and member of a playing troupe, had lived for real. London-based acting companies regularly toured the country in the Elizabethan and Jacobean periods, performing in many provincial communities and in a variety of spaces ranging from town halls and churches, to large country houses. Other professional acting troupes were regionally based, touring exclusively in the provinces.[3] Some players ventured even further afield, travelling and performing on the Continent at places such as Elsinore, the Danish court depicted in *Hamlet*.[4] Such men, as Tom Stoppard imagined them, were likely to have been adaptable, hard-nosed experts in their own and their troupe's professional survival. Indeed, some of the actual evidence of 'that wandringe trade' was recorded as a result of the aggressive stance players took to ensure the show, or *their* show, must go on.[5]

The tradition of professional actors periodically touring the country can be traced back at least as early as the fifteenth century and was well established by the sixteenth century.[6] It was not a practice that was confined to playing companies patronised by nobles or royalty. Gentlemen also patronised travelling players. In 1583, players claiming Sir Walter Waller's patronage described how they had played in Sussex and Kent '& other plac*es*'.[7] There is evidence of town companies touring regionally, too.[8] The passing of government regulations that sought to control players and their touring with growing rigour in the sixteenth century is one testimony to the fact that travelling had become a customary activity for actors. In 1559, Queen Elizabeth I issued a proclamation which forbade

> all maner interludes to be played either openly or privately, except the same be notified beforehand, and licensed within any city or towne corporate by the mayor or other chief officers of the same, and within any shire by such as shall be lieutenants for the Queen's majesty in the same shire, or by two of the justices of peace inhabiting within that part of the shire where any shall be played.[9]

The proclamation forced playing companies to seek civic permission to perform in any community they visited. The letter the Earl of Leicester's players wrote to their patron in 1572 confirms that touring was usual by this date. They requested the Earl's licence 'to certifye that we are your housshold servauntes when we shall have occasion to travayle amongst our frendes as we do usuallye once a yere, and as other noble-mens Players do and have done in tyme past'.[10]

That the tradition of touring persisted into the late sixteenth and early seventeenth centuries is striking. In late Elizabethan London the major playing companies had access to permanent, purpose-built theatres and larger audiences than any other town in the country could afford. Yet they continued to travel the country on a regular basis. And the plays and staging practices of companies such as the Lord Chamberlain's Men (of which Shakespeare was a member) were informed by the experience of having to perform for diverse audiences and in a variety of spaces when touring. Players needed to be fast on their feet and in their wits, and plays had to be adaptable for different venues. As Gurr points out, plays written before the late 1590s were generally 'designed to be staged anywhere', precisely because of the diverse auditoria companies might be required to use. He also notes the important influence of touring on Elizabethan theatre:

> Travelling dictated all the early playing practices. [. . .] Company organisation, the teamwork of sharing and using few extras besides the boy 'apprentices', the essential resources of playbooks and costumes, the plays themselves seen as things that could be carried from one place to another, and the related expectation that performances could be mounted at new venues at short notice, these were all features of early company life that never lost their place in company thinking.[11]

Previous studies of professional theatre in Elizabethan and Jacobean England have generally focused on performances and playhouses in London.[12] Yet if we are to have a richer understanding of the dramatic culture that fostered the talents of playwrights such as Shakespeare and that gave birth to England's first theatres, professional theatre outside Renaissance London needs to be taken into account. The lively, competitive world of travelling players is therefore the subject of this book.

I

The evidence

Exploring the world of professional English theatre outside Renaissance London requires detective work and patience. A number of sources of evidence are available, including records of payments to acting troupes in church, civic and private household accounts. But the information which they provide may not be complete and is rarely detailed. In many cases all that is preserved is the name of the acting company, the year of their visit and the amount they were paid.[13] Other less direct sources of evidence include secular and ecclesiastical court records. The documentation of unlicensed or controversial performances, and arrests following misdemeanours by actors or audience members, can be especially revealing. For instance, we learn that the Earl of Worcester's players performed at a Leicester inn in 1583–84 because they were involved in a dispute beforehand with the mayor which is reported in the town's Hall Papers; and were only permitted to play at their inn after they had craved the mayor's pardon. They wisely promised to offer an on-stage apology as a prologue to the performance.[14] There are also several contemporary descriptions of provincial performances. One of the best known is that of Robert Willis, recounting a performance of a morality play which he saw at Gloucester's town hall (*c*.1565–75). Actors' personal papers and publications sometimes afford an insight into touring life as well. In Richard Tarlton's *Jests* he alludes to several towns that he visited as a player; and the letters Edward Alleyn wrote while on tour illuminate the route of some of his peregrinations with Lord Strange's Men in 1593.[15] Dramatic allusions to provincial playing and performances are also to be found in a number of Elizabethan and Jacobean plays.

Reconstructing a detailed picture of professional travelling theatre from such sources is a painstaking process. It requires the sifting and synthesis of diverse forms of information and a healthy scepticism with regard to the accuracy of various imagined versions of Elizabethan touring actors (such as Marc Norman and Tom Stoppard's road-dusted returning players – led by Edward Alleyn – in *Shakespeare in Love*).[16] We must also be 'ready to extrapolate from the known to the unknown, and at the same time be cautious about doing so'.[17] But, a general account of professional regional theatre can be given, as the following sections in this chapter demonstrate.

II

Professional theatre in the provinces

Licence to travel

Most professional Shakespearean companies had a royal or noble patron. The players would travel under the name of their patron and were usually entitled to wear his or her livery. Although the players might not receive any payment from their patron and were not usually based in the patron's household they were regarded as his or her servants. For elite men and women patronage of players was one way of displaying their power and social position, while such patronage lent players status and respectability. Royal or noble patronage became even more valuable in 1572 with the passing of a new Act for the Punishment of Vagabonds and for Relief of the Poor and Impotent. This Act specified that all players

> not belonging to any Baron of this Realme or towardes any other honorable Personage of greater Degree; [...] whiche [...] shall wander abroad and have not Lycense of two Justices of the Peace at

the leaste, whereof one to be of the Quorum, when and in what Shier they shall happen to wander . . . shalbee taken and adjudged and deemed Roges Vacaboundes and Sturdy Beggers.[18]

In theory the Act restricted the right to patronise players to nobles and royalty. All other playing companies were obliged to seek a licence to perform from two justices of the peace, although when the Act was revised in 1598 the power to license players was removed from justices, too.[19]

In practice, acting companies without royal or noble patronage were not always scrupulous about seeking permission to perform in the communities they visited. And sometimes the consequences were as dramatic as the material awaiting their performance. In 1583, players claiming the patronage of Sir Walter Waller found themselves in trouble with Kentish justice of the peace, Thomas Potter, after proclaiming an interlude (on 13 May) at Brasted in Kent 'without sufficient warrant'.[20] The case is recorded in a series of documents brought before Sir Francis Walsingham and the Privy Council. Having heard about the players' alleged proclamation, Potter had 'sent for ye sayd players by ye constable' of the town, 'to knowe what warrant they had'. They answered that,

they had ye lycence of Sir Walter Waller but no other warrant, which your said supplyant [Potter] knowinge, not to be suffycyent in Lawe, shewed them, yt they [. . .] were come within ye daunger of ye statute of roges, & so forbadde them to play, requyringe them allso, to deale no more with that wandringe trade of lyffe, but to employ them-sellfes to some more comendable exercyse, offerynge to them allso, yt yf they woulde promys so to doe, your sayd supplyant would let them quyetly departe.[21]

The players reacted angrily, saying that 'they muche dysdayned to be called Roges', and pointed out that 'they had longe tyme vsed that wandringe trade' and 'neyther coulde nor woulde leave yt, for yt they had none other meanes to lyve by' unless Potter would give them a hundred pounds a year for their maintenance (PRO, SP 12/163/44). At this point Potter committed the five adult players to the constable's custody. They were threatened with the stocks, and argued with the constable, but were spared from imprisonment after 'temporising' with him, and 'offering to pawn their playing apparel while they made contact with their patron'.[22] Waller responded vigorously on the players' behalf. When notified of their predicament he sent for the constable and seeing his warrant for carrying the five men to jail said 'yt they were hys men all of them, & no rog*es* [. . .] and yt your supplyant [Potter] was a knave & a villayne & ye soon of a vyllayne & of a knave' (PRO, SP 12/163/44). Nonetheless, the players faced prosecution as rogues and vagabonds because they had not obtained a licence to perform at Brasted from two local justices of the peace, as they were legally obliged to do post-1572. The performance did not actually take place, however, as Waller pointed out in a letter to Sir Francis Walsingham and the players were eventually released into their patron's custody.[23] The incident and the ensuing dispute between Potter and Waller was brought before the Privy Council but 'did not become a Star Chamber matter'.[24]

The 1583 Brasted case is not necessarily representative. Not all players without a royal or noble patron (post-1572) are likely to have faced so close a scrutiny of their credentials. Potter was a justice with an 'axe' to grind. He was suspicious of travelling performers, holding their 'wandringe trade of lyffe' in low esteem, and was 'concerned to prosecute [. . .] the players under the act as rogues and not merely as vagabonds'.[25] Not all patrons are likely to have been ready to involve themselves as directly or passionately in the protection of their players as Waller proved to be, either. He may have had a particular interest in drama, as this is not the only occasion when people from the Shakespearean theatre world claimed his name as protection. In 1583 he was 'linked with John Brayne in the latter's legal suit with his brother-in-law and business partner, James Burbage'. Brayne 'and his co-defendant [. . .] who were greatly in debt, claimed they "had a protection under Sir Walter Waller, knight" '.[26] Waller's strident championing of his players' case may also have had a religious dimension. As an alleged Catholic sympathiser, Waller was unlikely to look kindly on Potter's puritanical treatment of people claiming his patronage or Potter's interference with the culture and traditions of the community. As Roberts suggests, the incident in Brasted 'was a psychodrama exposing the latent religious tensions in Kentish society, a clash of cultures as well as of personalities'.[27]

The flourishing world of professional Elizabethan theatre was not viewed favourably by everyone. Some Elizabethans – like Potter – were hostile to the theatre and held players in low estimation socially and morally. For them, players were pariahs. In the 1570s and 1580s several books and pamphlets were published that attacked plays and players. John Northbrooke condemned contemporary plays as morally corrupting in *Dicing, Dauncing, Vaine Playes, or Enterludes* (1577); while Stephen

Gosson, another famous critic of the theatre and author of *The Schoole of Abuse* (1579) and *Plays Confuted in Five Actions* (1582), characterised players as professional deceivers.[28] The 1572 Act's identification of players as a social group that could be classified as rogues and vagabonds could be interpreted as reflecting such anti-theatrical feeling. Philip Stubbes, author of the *Anatomie of Abuses* (1583), evidently interpreted the Act as equating travelling actors with rogues and vagrants: 'Are they not taken by the lawes of the Realm for rogues and vacabounds? I speak of such as travaile the cuntrie with playes & enterludes, making an occupation of it, and oght so to be punished, if they had their deserts'.[29]

But the Act was not apparently intended to stigmatise players *en masse*, and need not be interpreted as anti-theatrical in its provisions regarding actors. The order was not solely or primarily concerned with players, but with two social 'problems': vagrancy and poverty. Mobile, masterless men and the discontented poor were both perceived as potential threats to political security and stability in Elizabethan England, particularly following the rebellion of the Northern Earls in 1569; and the government was keen to deal with them more rigorously. This anxiety provided the major impetus for the promulgation of the new Act and its provisions for stricter regulation of lower-class itinerant social groups. Similarly, while there was much discussion about the Act's parameters of application and its phrasing (particularly in relation to players), parliamentary debate about the Bill 'was not characterised by Puritan hostility [. . .] to itinerant entertainers'; and the eventual Bill provided for 'an enlarged list of those eligible for licences'.[30] The Act had its benefits for those players who were able to obtain authorisation to perform, too. Licensed players were afforded legal recognition and protection. The Act may even have helped to establish acting more firmly as a 'profession'.[31]

The introduction of stricter licensing under the 1572 Act did not diminish the hostility of those opposed to professional theatre, nor does it seem to have led to a sharp decrease in touring. Many troupes continued to travel and the professional theatre world flourished, especially in London with the establishment of several permanent playhouses in the late Elizabethan period.[32] By 1595 it is estimated that the two leading companies, the Lord Admiral's Men and the Lord Chamberlain's Men, were attracting audiences of '15,000 people weekly' at The Rose and The Theatre, respectively.[33] The patronage extended to players by the Court and members of the royal family proved particularly important in safeguarding the leading companies from their anti-theatrical opponents. Queen Elizabeth I and King James (and his family) took an active interest in drama, inviting players to entertain them at court and lending their names to acting companies. In 1583 Sir Francis Walsingham authorised Edmund Tilney, the Master of the Revels, to form a new company of Queen's players. The troupe of twelve actors included the most famous players of the day and was the leading troupe in the country until the late 1580s.[34] When King James succeeded to the English throne in 1603 patronage of the three major playing companies (the Lord Chamberlain's Men, the Lord Admiral's Men, and the Earl of Worcester's Men) was assumed by members of the royal family, with James becoming the patron of Shakespeare's company.[35] By extending their patronage to playing companies (and thus licensing them to travel) members of the Court and the royal family also helped to protect the tradition of touring theatre.

In the capital the Court (as represented by the Privy Council) also protected the players against several civic attempts to suppress metropolitan theatrical activity in the late sixteenth and early seventeenth centuries; and individual courtiers and Privy Councillors requested the toleration of major playing companies on numerous occasions. In 1581, for example, the Privy Council asked the mayor of London to allow the players to perform again in the city following a period of plague-induced closure of the theatres, 'tendering the releife of theis poore men the players and their redinesse with conuenient matters for her highnes solace this next Christmas, which cannot be without their vsuall exercise therein'.[36]

Travelling routes

As with many metropolitan theatre groups of our day, the national travelling companies used established touring routes based on the then major road network. McMillin and MacLean identify seven customary touring circuits: East Anglia; the south-east 'through Canterbury to the Cinque Ports'; the south-west 'via the coast through Southampton and Dorset or along one of several inland roads to Bristol'; the Midlands, 'centering on Coventry'; the West Midlands; the north-east 'via the Great North Road or another important road through Leicester'; and the north-west 'most commonly reached across Coventry'.[37] Towns on these major routes might play host to a number of professional acting companies annually. For example, Exeter 'though somewhat remote from London, lay at the cross-roads of several important routes' and drew 'touring performers continuously from 1370–1630s'.[38] Troupes did venture into areas less well served by the road system as well, occasionally performing in smaller towns such as Pershore. Indeed, despite the lack of commodious or speedy transport travelling players are known to have reached even the most far-flung parts of the country. In September 1588 Lord Scrope wrote from Carlisle to William Asheby, the English ambassador in Scotland, to say that the Queen's players had been there for ten days, adding that he had 'sought them out' on the King's behalf 'from "the furthest parte of Langheshire" ', where they had been on tour.[39]

The reasons for planning tours based on the major road networks are 'obvious': 'important cities or market towns on main roads were more accessible and accommodating, with guaranteed audiences'. However, when selecting which of the traditional touring circuits to follow each year companies may have been guided by other motives. Troupes often appear to have favoured routes which passed through areas where their patron's name would carry greater weight and 'guarantee of reward'. Until 1565 the Earl of Oxford's players toured mainly in 'the south and east', for instance, the 'principal sphere of influence' of the Earl's family, the de Veres.[40] Companies may even have been instructed to pursue their travels along such routes by patrons seeking to use dramatic patronage to publicise their power in territories where they claimed some position. No surprise then that players patronised by royalty had the most 'extensive annual itineraries' and 'received the highest rewards and most generous performance conditions' in early modern England.[41] The wide-ranging tours of royal troupes can be seen as complementing the royal progresses, allowing the monarch's name and a symbol of royal power to be borne to parts of the country far from London and the Court.

Life on the road

In 1910 J. T. Murray estimated that at least thirty-seven Greater Men's companies, seventy-nine Lesser Men's companies, five Players' companies and twenty-seven Town companies were active outside London between 1559 and 1645. Subsequent research has identified many more and there are likely to have been others. Competition was keen, with London companies not only contending with each other, but with regionally based troupes for a share of the provincial theatre market.[42] Elizabethan players proved tenacious travellers despite such competition. The nature and quality of life on the road remains under investigation, but it could be dangerous and hard. There are records of players being attacked and robbed, and of their vehicles being damaged. One Foskew was presented 'for breikinge the peice and drawing blude vppon one of the Queenes plears' in Canterbury, for instance, in 1596–97;

while in 1608–09 Thomas Bradford was called before the Woodstock Portmouth Court having stolen money from one of Lord Chandos's Men, when the troupe visited 'Buck Towne'.[43] It could also be a life of physical privations and economic difficulties, as the Earl of Pembroke's players discovered in 1593. Straitened financial circumstances forced the troupe to disband and return to London, as Philip Henslowe recounted in a letter to his son-in-law, the actor Edward Alleyn, in September:

> As for my lorde a penbrockes wch you desier to knowe wheare they be they are all at home and hauffe ben t[his] v or sixe weackes for they cane not saue ther carges (charges) [w]th trauell as I heare & weare fayne to pane (pawn) the[r] parell for ther carges.[44]

Contemporary dramatic allusions generally emphasise the hardships of touring life. In Thomas Dekker's *News from Hell* (1606) a character speaks of 'a companie of country players, [. . .] that with strowling were brought to deaths door'; and in his *Lanthorne and Candlelight* (1608) 'Strowlers' are defined as 'country players that (without socks) trotte from towne to towne vpon the hard hoofe'.[45] These are literary descriptions and not necessarily accurate representations of touring life. Indeed, there is a note of exaggeration and stereotyping in each which suggests that their descriptions should not be taken at face value. But, the clichéd images of the touring actor that they present would not have been comic unless they contained at least an element of truth. Yet, many Elizabethan and Jacobean actors 'spent a good part of their lives upon the road' (and, in most cases, apparently by choice).[46] Travelling life was presumably not without its pleasures and rewards, therefore. Recent research by scholars such as John Wasson has drawn attention to some of the more rewarding aspects of touring life, especially when a company's itinerary included country house performances. When troupes visited such private houses they could often look forward to 'perks' such as free food, good, safe accommodation and generous rewards.

The London companies may not always have had a great deal of choice when deciding whether or not to tour, as the closure of the playhouses during plague periodically left them without employment.[47] Although there was a chance that regional towns would be similarly afflicted, touring was an obvious option for companies facing an indefinite suspension of their activities in the capital. But it would be a mistake to think the metropolitan troupes only toured during such times. Many companies toured annually even when there were not plague epidemics in the city.[48] The fierceness of competition and/or declining fortunes in the capital may also have prompted some of the London-based troupes to tour, as do 'the tragedians of the city' in *Hamlet* (2.2.317). Some contemporaries offered more cynical explanations for companies' decisions to tour. Donald Lupton described how players 'sometimes [. . .] fly into the country; but 'tis a suspicion that they are either poor or want clothes, or else company, or a new play; or do as some wandering sermonists, make one sermon travel and serve twenty churches'.[49] Touring certainly allowed players some rest from the intensive repertory systems of the metropolitan theatres; but actors may have enjoyed the challenge of adapting their performances for different stages and audiences as well.

The length of players' tours is generally unrecorded. Most are likely to have lasted for several months, but they could vary from brief trips to a particular region to virtually year-round perambulations. Similarly, while some tours may have involved visits to only a handful of places, a troupe's itinerary could include more than thirty stops. The Queen's Men visited at least twenty-seven different places and some more than once when touring in 1588–89.[50] However many venues they visited, travelling troupes would usually have been relying on their feet and, possibly, a horse and wagon, to transport themselves, their belongings, and their theatrical 'gear' between venues.[51]

Average company sizes on tour are, likewise, hard to calculate accurately as troupe numbers were rarely noted. Where they *were* recorded the evidence testifies to varied sizes. In 1569–70 the Earl of Sussex's company was described as consisting of six men at Ludlow, but Wasson argues that 'even at this late date the average size [. . .] seems to have been four', company sizes only growing 'significantly' after 1572.[52] Certainly, later sources point to the existence of larger acting troupes. The company Dekker satirises in *News from Hell* (1606) is described as 'being nine in number, one sharer and the rest journeymen'; and fourteen players made up the Lord Derby's troupe that visited Chatsworth House (Derbyshire) in 1611.[53] Even larger travelling companies may not have been unknown. A troupe that visited Norwich in 1635 apparently consisted of 'twenty-eight persons'. Although they may not all have been actors, this example still suggests 'that travelling companies, far from being small or reduced, might be of very great size'.[54]

There is some evidence that professional playing troupes collaborated occasionally when touring, too, receiving rewards for joint performances. In 1599 Leicester's Corporation rewarded 'The Erle of Derbyes players & The Erle of Dudleys players, ioyned (at this present) togeyther as one company'.[55] Whether these amalgamations were negotiated prior to touring – or were opportunistic collaborations – is usually impossible to determine, although one would imagine that some preparation time was required. Of necessity, one or both companies' players might have to learn a new play, and the plays to be performed jointly would need to be cast differently. In many cases the decision to mount joint performances may have been pragmatic. If two troupes were touring the same region or visiting the same town offering to perform together was one way of ensuring that both companies received rewards. Other collaborations could have been politically motivated and arranged at the wish of one or both patrons. In Faversham in 1589–90 'the Queenes players and the Erle of Essexe players' were paid twenty shillings, suggesting that they might have performed together. If there was a temporary amalgamation of the two companies, it might have been initiated by the Earl's Men (and at their patron's suggestion), the players' collaboration offering a symbolic means of associating the Earl with the Queen and her power at a time when he was seeking to promote his reputation and his chances of gaining higher military offices.[56]

Travelling players may have collaborated occasionally with troupes of musicians as well, the latter often being patronised by the same person. In 1577–78 the Earl of Warwick's 'musyssyons and plears' were paid ten shillings at Nottingham, while at Coventry the corporation rewarded Lord Berkeley's and Lord Dudley's 'players and musicions' in 1583.[57] Although these payments could simply mean that the troupes contained specialist musicians, the phrasing suggests the musicians were not considered to be part of the playing troupe; and there are records of patronised musicians travelling and performing independently. There is some evidence of Elizabethan playing companies occasionally joining forces with other entertainers, too. There is a series of records relating to a troupe of the Queen's players in 1589–90 that suggests it was travelling with an acrobat and included players skilled in tumbling. They performed acrobatic shows together in several regional towns.[58] The author of *Dr Taylor's History* of Shrewsbury offers an account of one of their joint performances, describing how on 24 July 1590 a scaffold was erected in the town's cornmarket on which, 'an hongarian and other of the queenes Maiesties players and tvmblars vsid and excersisid them selves in sutche maner of tvmblinge and tvrninge as the lick was never seene in shrewsburie before'.[59] The Hungarian or Turkish rope-dancer also performed with the Queen's Men at Norwich and Bristol in 1589–90. In Norwich the city paid the Queen's Men 'when the Turke wente vponn Roppes' at New Hall, while in Bristol the troupe was rewarded for tumbling 'at the ffree schole where was tumblinge shewen also by a Turcke vpon a Rope'.[60] These collaborations are especially intriguing because they demonstrate that Elizabethan players could be versatile performers and did not always or only perform plays on tour.

Plays

Precisely what texts were taken on tour and how many plays were to be found in a standard company's repertory is unknown.[61] Companies do not appear to have kept such records and the plays performed by visiting troupes are rarely named in contemporary notices. There are exceptions, but the number of named plays is few in proportion to the performances known to have occurred, and many of the plays mentioned do not survive. This is true of several plays named in Bristol's civic records between 1575 and 1579: *The Red Knight* (performed by the Lord Chamberlain's Men), *Myngo* (Leicester's players), *What mischief worketh in the mynd of man* (Lord Berkeley's players), *The Queen of Ethiopia* (Lord Howard's players), *The Court of Comfort* (Lord Sheffield's players), and *Quid Pro Quo* (Earl of Bath's Men) all appear to have been lost.[62] However, it is possible to identify plays likely to have constituted the touring repertories of the major metropolitan troupes, working from their known playhouse repertories. In some cases there is even stronger evidence for the inclusion of plays in a company's touring repertory, prompt copies apparently adapted for such performances surviving. The Chicago copy of *A Looking Glass for London and England* (modified as a prompt text) carries the name of Gilbert Reason in a stage direction and is, therefore, likely to have been used by Prince Charles' company some time between 1613 and 1625, when Reason is believed to have been the touring troupe's leading member.[63]

Some scholars have suggested that the texts chosen for touring were abridged. For instance, David George argues that the plays which the Earl of Pembroke's Men were obliged to sell to the publishers in 1594 after their bankruptcy in 1593 (including *Edward II* and *The Taming of a Shrew*) were 'shortened touring texts'.[64] Other scholars such as Gurr have challenged such arguments, noting that, in theory, adapted play texts would need to have been re-licensed by the Master of the Revels. Yet the Master's papers contain no evidence 'that he ever approved any texts that had been revised specifically for touring'. The so-called 'cut' texts (including those discussed by George) show no evidence of having been adapted for performance by smaller troupes either; nor would such reductions usually have been necessary as touring troupes appear to have differed little in size from companies working in London.[65]

Travelling companies did not necessarily work exclusively from manuscript prompt books. Many of the plays published in Renaissance England were prepared with the needs of playing companies in mind. Some include prefaces addressed to potential performers. The 1578 edition of *The Commody of the moste vertuous and Godlye Susanna* is accompanied by the note that 'Eyght persons may easyly play it'; while the title-page of *The Conflict of Conscience* (1572) gives 'The Actors names, deuided into six partes, most conuenient for such as be disposed, either to show this Comedie in priuate houses, or otherwise'.[66] As well as suggesting that troupes sometimes worked from printed texts, such addresses anticipate the adaptation of texts for different performances. Printed texts were sometimes used as prompt copies, although the practice may have been more common amongst amateur acting companies.[67] Thomas Middleton satirises the practice in *The Mayor of Queenborough*, the mayor of the play being robbed of his purse during a performance by roguish actors later reported to 'take the name of country comedians' only 'to abuse simple people / with a printed play or two, which they bought at Canterbury for six pence'.[68] There is some evidence of playing companies soliciting play texts from other players as well. In 1581 Thomas Bayly, 'one of Shrewsbury's players' wrote from Sheffield to 'Thomas Bawdewine', one of Leicester's players, 'asking for more play texts'.[69]

Professional troupes are likely to have used the same repertory for most of their public and private performances on tour, although some plays could have been written for specific private house performances and hosts may have occasionally provided travelling companies with whole plays or additions of their own composition (as occurs in *Hamlet*). A number of Elizabethan noblemen and women are known to have been passionate supporters of drama and to have indulged in dramatic writing, including William Stanley, the 6th Earl of Derby, Sir William Percy and Elizabeth Cary, Lady Falkland.[70] Stanley and Percy are even thought to have written for professional players. In 1599 the Earl of Derby was reported to be 'busy penning comedies for the common players', while several of Percy's plays have been linked with the chorister players of St Paul's and their indoor theatre.[71]

Playing 'gear'

The pragmatics of travelling limited the amount of costumes and props that professional players could carry with them on tour, but it seems that some provision was customary. The will made by actor Simon Jewell, shortly before his death in 1592, reveals that he 'was obliged to sell not only his "share for horses" [and] "waggen" ', but for ' "apparrell newe bought" ' (purchases probably intended for use on a forthcoming tour).[72] More explicit evidence that travelling companies used playing gear is found in the statements made following the affray at the Red Lion in Norwich which occurred during a performance by the Queen's Men (1583). One of the witnesses described how he saw three of the players run from the stage with 'there sword*es* in there handes'; another alluded to one of the players in 'his players apperrell with a players berd vppon his face'.[73] As well as using costumes, the Queen's Men clearly had access to a wardrobe which included beards and real weapons. It also appears to have been common to carry instruments on tour. In February 1600 Henslowe paid for a drum and two trumpets for the Lord Admiral's Men 'when to go into the country'.[74] Such instruments could be used to provide music and sound effects, and to attract local attention when players advertised performances in regional communities.

Playing spaces and permission to perform

On arriving in a new town it was usual for companies to present themselves and their warrant to travel to the mayor or his equivalent to request permission to perform.[75] The troupe might then perform a play before the mayor and council, often at the town hall. In towns such as Gloucester, citizens were also welcome at the 'mayor's play':

> if the Mayor like the Actors or would shew respect to their Lord and Master, he appoints them to play their first play before himselfe, and the aldermen and common Counsell of the City; and that is called the Mayor's play, where every one that will comes in without money.[76]

In other towns, there might be more than one civic performance.[77] Civic patronage of players was a way of displaying corporate wealth and power, while hosting performances allowed town officials to screen visiting players and their interludes. The need to 'vet' players and their productions arguably became less pressing, however, once the Master of the Revels became responsible for licensing all plays in 1581.[78]

Having performed for a town's mayor and/or received his licence to play, troupes had the opportunity to perform elsewhere in the locale, although in some cases further productions were staged in town halls.[79] Sometimes their services were requested for private performances; other performances might be staged at the inns in which troupes frequently stayed when touring. Plays might be staged in inn chambers or outdoors in inn-yards, as at the Red Lion in Norwich (1583).[80] Another occasional venue for professional performances was the local church or cathedral. There is some evidence of professional performances within church-yards and church houses, too. Queen Elizabeth's players performed in the churchyard at Gloucester Cathedral, and rented the Church House room at Sherborne.[81] Schoolhouses and university colleges were another potential venue, although the students themselves more often staged performances in academic buildings. It is also possible that professional companies used the few recorded provincial playhouses in Elizabethan and Jacobean England.[82]

Professional troupes did not confine their tours to urban venues; they also visited large country houses, as noted earlier. Sometimes they were specifically invited to play at provincial country houses. This might include performing at the country residence(s) of their patron for the entertainment of his or her special guests and/or being invited to perform at other country residences as part of wedding celebrations or seasonal festivities. In 1595 Sir John Harington arranged for a company of London players to visit and perform at his Rutland home, Burley-on-the-Hill, for the entertainment of his guests during the Christmas holidays.[83] Entertainment was 'regarded as a means of impressing social equals and social inferiors' and the country house provided the ideal arena for such display.[84]

Publicity

In order to maximise their audiences professional companies usually 'announced' their presence in a new town. Often this involved peram-bulating the main street(s), sounding their drum(s) and trumpets and advertising their intended performance, as occurred when a company of English players visited the Scottish capital in 1599: 'Upon Moonday, the 12th of November they gave warning by trumpets and drummes through the streets of Edinburgh, to all that pleased to come to the Blacke Friers' wynd to see the acting of their comedeis'.[85] On other occa-sions players might simply make a proclamation at a central location in the town, as occurs when Sir Oliver Owlet's Men plan to perform a play at the town hall in John Marston's *Histrio-mastix*, one of the players announcing the performance at the market cross.[86]

Professional players sometimes also employed a form of advertise-ment used to promote metropolitan playhouse productions, putting up notices announcing a forthcoming performance. A controversial example of this practice is afforded by an incident involving the royal troupe in Cambridge in 1592. The University's disapproval of professional players is well known; and in 1575 a letter from the Privy Council granted the University power to prevent such performances within five miles of its precincts.[87] Acting on this authority, the Vice-Chancellor led the local justices of the peace in refusing the Queen's Men permission to perform in Cambridge and neighbouring Chesterton. Undeterred, the company proceeded to play at Chesterton, and had the audacity to 'proclaime theire Enterludes' at the University, setting up playbills on 'College gat*es*'.[88]

Times and lengths of performances

The timing of professional civic performances appears to have varied between towns and over the course of time. In the early Elizabethan period plays were staged both in the afternoon and evening. In York in 1581 the Earl of Sussex's players were to perform in the Common Hall at 'two of the clocke', while a payment for 'lynkes to the play' in 1568 at Newcastle-upon-Tyne points to an evening performance.[89] Professional performances in the daytime and the evening are also recorded at private country houses. Sometimes two plays would be performed in one day, as was the case on one occasion at Knowsley House (Lancashire) in 1589: the 'quenes players played in the after none & my Lord off Essix at nyght'.[90] With the turn of the century, some corporations began to place restrictions upon night performances. At Chester playing was not to be allowed anywhere in the city or its liberties after six o' clock in the evening from 1615.[91] In other towns evening performances persisted unchecked well into the seventeenth century, as at Shrewsbury where Lady Elizabeth's players staged an evening performance in the Booth Hall in 1613.[92] But the introduction of restrictions by some corporations may have prompted companies to seek licences of the kind carried by Lady Elizabeth's Men when they visited Plymouth in 1618–19: it stated that they 'had the Kings hand for playing aswell by night as by day'.[93]

The duration of troupes' urban visits varied. In larger towns companies might spend a week or more performing. In 1588 Queen Elizabeth's players stayed in Carlisle for at least ten days; and in 1611 Queen Anne's players were authorised to play for a week in Norwich.[94] On other occasions troupes appear to have been happy to perform for one night only before proceeding to their next venue. The Lord Admiral's Men performed at Ipswich on 26 May 1587 and were in Aldeburgh on 28 May, suggesting that their visit to the former town was brief.[95] The increasing regulation of playing by city authorities in the late sixteenth century extended in some instances to the number of days visiting players were allowed to perform. In Norwich the authorities regularly authorised players to perform for limited periods, as in December 1596 when Lord Willoughby's and Lord Beauchamp's players were only authorised to 'playe within this Cittie vntill wensdaye next'.[96] The duration of travelling companies' visits to private country houses also varied. Visits lasting between one and at least four days are recorded, with the number of performances given varying between one and as many as five. A brief visit to Knowsley House is recorded in 1590: 'On Thurseday Sir Ihon Savadge mr dutton & the Qwiens players came, on frydaye the[y] departed'. When they had visited Lathom House (another Derby residence) in 1589, however, they had played 'ij severall nyghtes'. Lord Derby's own players visited the Earl of Cumberland's house at Londesborough in 1589 and stayed longer again. Their visit extended for three days, in which time they played three times.[97]

Rewards

In Thomas Dekker's *Belman of London* (1608) strolling players are described as travelling 'vpon the hard hoofe from village to village for chees & butter-milke'.[98] In reality, professional travelling players could not and did not rely solely upon such modest payments-in-kind. Troupes could often look forward to payments for their performances outside Shakespearean London. Civic and private rewards ranged from a few shillings to several pounds. Higher-status companies could generally expect higher rewards; and civic gifts, when made, tended to be greater on average than those given by individuals, although wealthier patrons of drama at their country houses, such as the Clifford family, presented troupes with monetary gifts comparable with (and sometimes larger than) those given by richer corporations. In 1595 Lord Willoughby's Men received thirty shillings for playing twice at Londesborough, and in 1610–11 both Lord Evers' players and the Earl of Derby's Men received three pounds for performing two plays.[99]

Corporate rewards for performances became less frequent in some towns in the Jacobean period. Other corporations introduced restrictions on the rewards given to players. In Leicester it was agreed in 1582 that the corporation and council members would only contribute in future to rewards for players patronised by the Queen or Lords of the Privy Council.[100] In other towns, civic rewards were given as a supplement to an audience collection, as at Lyme Regis in 1592–93, when the Earl of Worcester's players were given five shillings and four pence 'to furnish 4 s. 8 d. geuen', and 'the queenes plaiers the duttons' were given '12 s. 6 d. vnto 7 s. 6 d. gatherde'.[101] In the later sixteenth century some towns shifted towards a system closer to that of the London theatres, charging spectators for entry to the playing space. Leicester's corporate records for 1590–91 note that ten shillings was received 'att the hall door' when the Queen's players performed. Some towns even introduced charges for the use of their civic hall, as at Bath where players paid to use the town hall in 1616–17.[102]

What money could be raised through gatherings at other public performances is unknown, as is the manner in which companies divided their income. Profits may have been shared equally, as is suggested in *Ratsey's Ghost* (1606), where it is claimed that 'the very best' of provincial actors 'have sometimes beene content to go home with fifteene pence share apiece'.[103] Other evidence suggests that the money was distributed in a manner akin to practices within the metropolitan playhouses, the 'sharers' gaining a larger proportion of the profits. Junior company members may have simply received a weekly wage. When Henslowe contracted William Kendall to work for him as a player he agreed to pay him ten shillings a week in London and five shillings a week 'in ye Cuntrie.' The promise to pay Kendall when in the country (presumably on tour) could mean that Henslowe received some of the profits from provincial performances of the Lord Admiral's Men; while the lower scale of payment for such performances indicates that touring was generally less profitable than London playing. William Ingram's calculations reveal how difficult it might have been to make profits when touring. He estimates that an average company could have faced travelling expenses of ten shillings a day. If performing every other day, such troupes would need to 'take in twenty shillings at each performance just to break even'. This was a sizeable sum of money to raise.[104]

As well as receiving monetary rewards professional travelling players could often expect to be entertained as guests by regional civic and private hosts. Payments to companies in civic records are regularly followed by entries recording expenses on the players at a local drinking house. At Gloucester the reward to Lord Dudley's players in 1562 is accompanied by an entry for money spent on the players 'at the taverne'. Occasionally, companies were offered food as well, as at Dover in 1586–87 when the Queen's players visited. The town paid 'for drinckinge to welcome' them 'and for theire breakefaste at their depar-ture'. Sometimes towns even covered part of a company's expenses. In 1567–68 the New Romney authorities paid 'mistris ffann [. . .] for the expenc*es* of the quenes maiesties player*es*'; while civic money was spent on horse meat and beer for the Queen's Men when they visited Fordwich in 1591–92.[105] Visiting companies could expect to be well treated during their stay at noble and gentry households as well, being provided with regular meals and a safe, comfortable place of rest. The pantry accounts from the Clifford family houses (Londesborough, Hazlewood, and Skipton Castle) show that visiting players were generally provided with several meals during their stay. At Londesborough there are also payments indicating that players' animals were sometimes fed at the Lord's cost.[106]

Staging

Tucca's satirical portrait of touring performances in *Poetaster* characterises provincial playing as crudely simple. He describes the strolling player as one who stalks 'vpon boords and / barrell heads to an old crackt trumpet'.[107] But other evidence suggests that travelling players could stage relatively sophisticated productions. As well as owning costumes and at least a small stock of properties, the professional players who toured England's provinces were generally well-experienced performers. That they could be skilful in their staging practices even in poorly resourced venues should not be surprising. Brief allusions in surviving documents afford some tantalising insights into the staging practices of touring players. Some of the records of damage caused to town halls are particularly intriguing. Occasionally, the damage is described as being the result of disorderly or large audiences. A payment for the repair of the iron cramp 'which shuttyth the barr' of the Guildhall door in Bristol (1575–76) was said to have been necessary after the cramp was stretched 'with the presse of people' at a Guildhall play performance.[108] Players evidently caused other damage. Rothwell draws attention to money spent at Barnstaple in 1592–93 for 'amendynge the Seelynge in the Guildhall that the Enterlude player*es* had broken downe', and wonders whether the players had tried to rig up a throne that could be lowered onto the stage.[109] There is no evidence to support Rothwell's hypothesis, but the fact that the players managed to damage the ceiling could mean the play included some lively action and ambitious staging. Surviving illustrations indicate that the Hall was a first-floor chamber in which the ceiling may have been low (see Illustration 1). Any exuberant stage business or use of special effects (such as fireworks) would have risked impairing the roof of such a chamber.

In some cases players could look forward to assistance with their performance preparations. In Elizabethan Gloucester the town authorities paid for stages to be built for many of the visiting troupes that performed before the mayor and aldermen in the Booth Hall. In 1567–68 we gain an insight into the large size and make-up of the stages built, with carpenter John Batty receiving eight shillings for 'C& iij quart*eres* of elme bourd*es* for a skaffold for play*ors* to playe one'.[110] A similar wooden platform appears to have been set up for the Queen's players when they performed at Nottingham in 1571–72, payment being made 'for bordes that was borowed for to make a skaffold to the Halle' for the troupe. There is some evidence of Jacobean towns providing stages for touring players, too. An improvised wooden platform made from 'bordes and hogserd' was created for Queen Anne's players at Exeter, for instance, in 1605–06.[111]

Other records suggest that visiting companies were opportunistic in their staging practices, occasionally borrowing furniture on site. This may have occurred when the Earl of Worcester's players visited Plymouth in 1580–81. The town payment to the company includes a reference to 'bearinge of Bordes and other furniture', possibly for the performance.[112] Another example of borrowing may be found in Leicester's 1605 civic accounts. After a payment for the preparation of the town hall for Queen Anne's players there is one 'for mendinge the cheyre in the p*ar*ler at the hall more than was receyved of Raphe Edgeton w*hi*ch was broken by the playars'.[113] The players may have damaged the chair while using it in their performance. When performing in private country houses players may have had access not only to furniture but to a selection of apparel and instruments, as some patrons maintained their own costume wardrobes and instrument collections. When Alexander Houghton of Lea died in 1581 he left his brother Thomas Houghton of Brynscoles 'all my Instrument*es* belonginge to mewsyck*es*, & all man*er* of playe clothes'.[114]

Audience responses

However simple their means, travelling players' performances proved popular in many regional English communities, often attracting large audiences. Several contemporary accounts also testify to their ability to move and influence regional spectators. Thomas Heywood in his *Apology for Actors* (1612) recounts one well-known incident reported to have occurred at Elizabethan King's Lynn (Norfolk) during a performance by the Earl of Sussex's players. The troupe was performing a (lost) play called *Friar Francis* in which a young woman that has murdered her husband in order to be with her lover is haunted by her husband's ghost.

As this was acted, a townes-woman (till then of good estimation and report) finding her conscience [. . .] extremely troubled, suddenly skritched and cryed out Oh my husband, my husband! I see the ghost of my husband fiercely threatning and menacing me. At which shrill and vnexpected out-cry, the people about her, moou'd to a strange amazement, inquired the reason of her clamour, when presently vn-urged, she told them that seuen yeares ago, she, to be possest of such a Gentleman [. . .] had poysoned her husband, whose fearefull image personated itself in the shape of that ghost: whereupon the mur-dresse was apprehended.[115]

Bearing in mind the anecdotal nature of the story and the fact that Heywood is writing a defence of actors, the truth of the tale cannot be accepted without question; but, that he relates it as a believable inci-dent points to the general acceptance of drama's power to produce such an effect. Indeed, the tale is in keeping with a tradition of exemplary stories, demonstrating theatre's power to disclose vice and offer instruc-tion. Notably, Hamlet is familiar with such tales and hopes to use the performance of a travelling company to similar effect (*Hamlet*, 2.2.566). Shakespeare may even have been thinking of the King's Lynn story and others like it, when he included Hamlet's theatrical scheme for reveal-ing Claudius' guilt.[116] More direct evidence of the potential skill and per-suasive power of travelling actors' performances is provided by Robert Willis's eyewitness account of *The Cradle of Security* which he saw per-formed at Elizabethan Gloucester's town hall when he was a boy. Describing the harsh 'moral' conclusion of the play, in which the play's protagonist was carried away by devils as a punishment for leading a decadent life, he speaks of the way that this closing scene 'tooke such impression in me, that when I came towards mans estate, it was as fresh in my memory, as if I had seen it newly acted'.[117]

Conclusion

With potential hazards as well as attractions and rewards, the profes-sional players of Shakespearean England were always likely to find life on the road eventful. Nonetheless, the tradition of touring the country was not one that they readily abandoned. These opening pages have offered an introduction to the world of Shakespearean travelling players and their touring practices. The following chapters focus more closely on playing practices and performances in representative spaces used as temporary theatres by Elizabethan and Jacobean touring players. By studying the spaces and communities in which players performed we can begin to gain more insight into the varied world of touring theatre and into the dynamic relationship that existed between metropolitan and regional professional theatre in Shakespearean England. We start by looking at touring play productions in town halls, the theatre of civic government and the most frequently named location for professional regional performances in surviving records.

2
Playing the Town Halls

All they that can sing and say,
Come to the Towne-house and see a Play,
At three a clocke it shall beginne,
The finest play that e're was seene,
Yet there is one thing more in my minde,
Take heed you leave not your purses behinde.[1]

Urban performances were a staple part of most players' tours and an important money-spinner. The inhabitants of England's regional towns and cities provided ready audiences and 'purses'; and performances by visiting troupes were sponsored in many provincial communities by the local corporation (or ruling civic body) as well. Such productions might be staged within the mayor's house, but the more usual venue for civic-funded performances appears to have been the town hall or its equivalent.[2] Players sometimes used or hired civic halls for self-financed performances as well. At Linton (Cambridgeshire), players paid to use the Town House several times in the Elizabethan period, while in Bath the Queen's players paid for the use of the Town Hall in 1616–17.[3]

Our main evidence for play performances in civic buildings, and the popularity of town halls as playing venues, is found in corporate records. As John Wasson notes, 'virtually every borough town for which we have records identifies the guildhall as the normal playing place if any site is mentioned at all'.[4] In the fifteen REED collections published thus far there are over one hundred and sixty records of performances by patronised Elizabethan and Jacobean playing companies in named playing places; and in at least one hundred and twenty cases the place named is the local civic hall.[5] The corporate ordinances introduced in increasing numbers in the late sixteenth century, regulating theatrical

24

use of civic halls, provide further testimony to their popularity as playing venues. In Oxford an order passed in 1579–80 restricting future play performances at the Guildhall suggested they had been mounted there in the past, ordering that 'no Mayor of this Cytie or his deputie *from henceforth* shall geve leave to any players to playe within the Guilde hall or the Lower hall or in the Guilde hall courte' without the consent of the council (own emphasis). There are, in fact, two clear references to performances at the hall between 1559 and 1625, one pre-dating the order, confirming its use for playing prior to 1579–80. In 1561–62 the Earl of Warwick's Men 'playd in the guyld hall', and in 1585–86 the Earl of Essex's men were authorised to 'playe onlie at this tyme, in the Guylde Hall courte'.[6]

Confirmation that town halls were viewed as potential playing places is also found in court records. In a 1608 Star Chamber case against Matthew Chubb of Dorchester (Dorset), it was alleged that he tried to persuade the town bailiff and magistrates to permit 'Lo: Barkleys servants' to 'play in the comon hall on the sabath day'. The company was denied permission to perform at the hall and ended up playing at a 'Comon Inne' instead.[7] But the incident reveals that the Common Hall was considered an attractive venue, and it was used for playing at a later date. In 1623 Willian Whiteway records that 'Mr Cheeke acted two commedies at the sheere hall [. . .] by his schollers'.[8] The licences issued to royal and noble acting troupes, authorising them to tour, confirm the importance of town halls as provincial playing venues, routinely requesting that regional corporations allow the named companies use of civic halls. In 1609, Queen Anne's players were licensed to perform at the Red Bull and Curtain theatres in London and 'alsoe within anye Towne halles, Mouthalles and other convenient places' within any other community in the realm.[9]

I

Players in civic buildings: the context

Thanks to the pioneering research of Robert Tittler on early modern English town halls in *Architecture and Power: The Town Hall and the English Urban Community, c.1500–1640*, a large body of information relating to Elizabethan and Jacobean civic buildings is now readily available. This can be used to construct a contextualised account of dramatic performances in town halls.[10] Frequently equipped with a 'hall' chamber, provincial civic buildings lent themselves to performance use. This was particularly true in towns where the only other sizeable indoor venue was likely to be the local church. For many provincial communities the possession of a civic hall was a recent phenomenon, many acquiring or building a town hall for the first time during the sixteenth century. In fact, almost half of 'the approximately six to seven hundred towns in the realm at this time appear to have built, substantially rebuilt, or purchased and converted a town hall' between '1500 and 1640'.[11]

The towns building or adapting civic halls were not always prosperous. Stafford and Salisbury both appear 'to have been economically distressed when they built halls in the 1580s'.[12] That towns were prepared to build halls during periods of recession testifies to the importance with which communities regarded the possession of a distinct civic space and suggests that the proliferation of halls cannot be explained in purely economic terms. In many towns a growing civic consciousness was a more important factor in the decision to build a town hall. This municipal consciousness was promoted by the increased political autonomy of many communities, through their incorporation. In some towns the creation of a civic hall directly followed incorporation, as at Banbury, where the new town hall was built after the town received its corporate charter in 1555. In such cases the building of a hall was as much a symbolic as a practical gesture, not only affording a centre for local government but a way of displaying corporate power and identity, as Tittler suggests.[13]

The day-to-day usage of town halls revolved around the business of civic government. As well as playing host to council meetings, the town hall was frequently the site for local and regional court sessions and might also incorporate a schoolroom, prison cells, an armoury and storage rooms for communal grain reserves. In some towns the civic hall was intimately involved in local marketing as well, a role facilitated by its often central location.[14] The town hall was also usually the theatre for civic festivities. Corporate banquets were mounted in civic halls in celebration of various occasions, ranging from events of local municipal significance, such as civic elections, to those of national importance. In Leicester, for example, a 'great feast' was held at the new Guildhall in 1588 'to celebrate the defeat of the Armada'.[15] Civic-sponsored feasts might be prepared in the town hall in honour of visiting nobles or royalty, too. When Lady Elizabeth (King James's daughter) was in Coventry in 1604, she was entertained with a banquet at St Mary's Hall.[16] In such cases, towns were generally seeking to impress as well as to honour their guests: entertaining those who exercised power locally and nationally was one means of securing their favour and aid in forwarding matters of local importance. Corporations also occasionally hosted performances by visiting entertainers at their civic halls, including tumblers and acrobats, as well as players (see Chapter 1). In Shrewsbury, the Booth Hall was the location for more unusual forms of cultural display too, as in 1572–73 when 'the head of a monsterous cauffe which had iiij Eyes two mowthes iiij Eares and but one fyrme and playne head' was brought there.[17]

In many towns the civic hall arguably replaced the guild chapel, the parish church and the market place as 'a focal point for social and civic life'.[18] In some cases this replacement was literal as well as metaphorical, ecclesiastical and guild properties being converted for use as town halls. The Guildhall at Leicester was converted for civic use from buildings originally belonging to the town's powerful Corpus Christi Guild (see Illustration 2). The corporation had used the Guildhall as a meeting place as early as 1495 but only acquired the property for its exclusive use in 1563.[19] When players staged their plays in civic buildings they were symbolically performing at the heart of the community. That room was made for players, both literally and figuratively, within such important urban spaces is striking, suggesting that theatre was perceived to be culturally significant in many provincial communities.

Town halls

Most early modern town halls in England can be classified into two main types: ground-floor halls and first-floor halls.[20] Those halls created through the conversion of medieval ecclesiastical or guild properties were usually stone constructions, while halls purpose-built during the mid-sixteenth century boom were often at least partly timber-framed. Most of the halls erected in the earlier part of the century were simple in appearance and vernacular in style: their external stone or woodwork was generally unembellished by special decorations. Later corporations were more ambitious in the buildings or renovations that they commissioned. When Exeter's Corporation decided to improve their Guildhall between 1592 and 1594 the extension made at the front of the building was neo-classical in design and richly painted, at a cost of nearly £800 (see Illustration 3). (The paintwork is no longer visible.)[21]

Most civic buildings incorporated a hall chamber, and some consisted of no more than this room. This space might be used for council meetings and court sessions and is the space most frequently associated with civic entertainment and dramatic performances. Such spaces varied greatly in size, but could be commodious in their dimensions. Probably the largest civic hall chamber in the period is that still to be found at St Andrew's Hall, Norwich. The 'New Hall' (as it was then known) was converted from the nave of the Blackfriars monastic church after the corporation acquired the property (1540). The seven-bay hall measures 'an impressive 126 feet in length' and nearly 70 feet in width (including the north and south aisles), and has accommodated 'audiences of over 2000 people' during music festivals held at St Andrew's in the last two centuries. With its seven large windows and its high roof rising 'to approximately 65 feet' in the nave, the hall is an airy and well-lit theatre for plays, too. The spacious chancel of the ex-monastic church (measuring 'about 100 × 33 feet') was also converted for civic use, becoming the chapel of the New Hall.[22] The New Hall and Chapel afforded playing spaces comparable in size with the great halls of the royal palaces; and performances may have been staged in both spaces.[23]

The Common Hall used by several professional companies in Elizabethan York is also capacious, although smaller than the New Hall and Chapel at Norwich, measuring 93 by 43 feet and rising 'to 31 feet 1 inch' at the apex of its reconstructed roof. The six-bay hall was damaged during a Second World War air raid (1942) but has been faithfully restored, retaining 'its original dimensions and aisled plan'.[24] The guildhall chambers used by players at Stratford-upon-Avon and Leicester were of more modest dimensions, measuring approximately 70 feet by 18^1/$_2$ feet and 63 feet by 20 feet, respectively, but are comparable in length with metropolitan hall playhouses such as the Second Blackfriars theatre (66 feet by 46 feet).[25] Both halls survive well preserved. That at Stratford-upon-Avon is now part of the King Edward VI Grammar School (see Illustrations 4 and 5), while Leicester's Guildhall is a museum. A gallery and staircase have been added since the seventeenth century to the lower end of the latter's hall, but it remains the same size and retains its original 'stone floor, timber-framed walls and pitched cruck frame ceiling'.[26]

The average size of civic 'halls' was smaller again, most halls measuring between 20–25 feet in width and 45–50 feet in length, proportions similar to those described as standard for college halls in early modern Cambridge.[27] The meeting hall in Bath's lost Guildhall and the first-storey civic chamber at Aldeburgh's surviving Moot Hall are representative of such standard-sized halls, measuring approximately 45 feet by 24 feet, and 46 feet by 20 feet respectively.[28] Although smaller than the halls found at Norwich and York, the dimensions of such medium-sized 'halls' are similar to those of halls found in smaller country houses known to have been used for dramatic performances, such as

Gawthorpe (Lancashire), where the 'Great Hall' measures 30 feet by 20 feet 4¹/₂ inches.²⁹ Civic hall chambers could be much smaller. In Cambridge the Town Hall's upper chamber measured only 17¹/₂ feet by 25 feet, but its compact size did not prevent it from being used for playing. In 1557 Lord Norfolk's players played 'in ye hall'; and in 1606 Queen Anne's players were given civic permission to perform there.³⁰ In some town halls other rooms (such as council chambers, courtrooms and mayors' parlours) were also potentially available as performance spaces. They tended to be of compact dimensions, too. A record from Bristol suggests that players occasionally took advantage of such alternatives. When the Earl of Leicester's Men visited the town in 1573 a payment was made for taking down the table in the Mayor's Court and 'setting yt vp agayne after the said players were gonne', suggesting they might have performed in the courtroom.³¹

Whether players performed in a hall chamber or in another town hall room, they would usually have found the decoration simple in the early Elizabethan period. Sixteenth-century town halls were not necessarily painted or their windows glazed and the furniture to be found in them (and potentially available to players) was often basic.³² Chairs were rare being 'still very much "seats of honour" '.³³ Benches were more common and would have been found when companies visited civic halls such as the New Hall, Norwich. In other town halls even benches appear to have been available in limited numbers. When Lord Strange's Men played at Bristol's Guildhall in 1580–81 forms were borrowed from St George's Chapel.³⁴ Tables are only occasionally mentioned in early sixteenth-century corporate records (usually as magistrates' tables) and most are likely to have been trestle tables. The table taken down in Bristol's Mayor's Court when Leicester's Men visited (1573) was probably of this variety.³⁵

The late sixteenth and early seventeenth centuries witnessed a general improvement in the interior decoration and furnishing of many town halls, as corporations chose to enhance the appearance and comfort of their buildings. Numerous payments occur for internal paintwork, plastering and wainscoting. In richer corporations, hard and soft furnishings became more commonplace as well, many civic bodies commissioning new furniture and/or paying for the improvement of existing fittings.³⁶ The purchase of substantial pieces of furniture such as sturdier, ornately carved, oak tables and chairs was another way of displaying corporate wealth and power. It also increased the material resources potentially available for, and in danger of being damaged by, town hall play productions.

II

Professional plays at civic halls

Town hall performances held a number of attractions for professional acting companies. Not only were troupes provided with an indoor playing place protected by municipal officers, but they were usually guaranteed some reward, either from the town authorities and/or through audience collections, and might be offered assistance with their performance preparations. The fact that the civic hall had become the new centre of communal life in many towns was probably a further attraction, guaranteeing hall performances local attention. What motivated civic bodies to reward and sanction town hall performances requires more explanation. As representatives of the government, every corporation (or its equivalent) was responsible for ensuring the observance of royal proclamations and statutory laws relating to theatre. In the Elizabethan period this included enforcing the 1559 proclamation 'Prohibiting Unlicensed Interludes and Plays' and the 1572 Act for the Punishment of Vagabonds (see Chapter 1). The 1559 statute required the licensing of all play performances 'within any city or towne corporate by the mayor or other chief officers of the same'; while the 1572 Act stipulated that players were only authorised to travel as performers if they were licensed by two justices of the peace or had a royal or noble patron.[37]

In theory, travelling players were obliged to present themselves to the civic officers of any town they visited to gain permission to perform. Not all Elizabethan companies were scrupulous about seeking such authorisation; and, after 1581, the importance of civic licensing was arguably reduced, with the Master of the Revels assuming responsibility for licensing all plays.[38] But players who toed the line and sought permission to perform might be rewarded with a monetary gift and/or an invitation to perform a 'mayor's play' at the town's expense. These 'command performances' might be staged in a local church or inn but the town hall was the most obvious, appropriate arena for such civic-sponsored productions and was the usual venue. The preliminary performance of a 'mayor's play' within the town hall allowed the local authorities to monitor the material and behaviour of acting companies and audiences. It also provided an opportunity to 'place their own stamp upon' local entertainment.[39]

The role of local authorities in licensing players was further diminished in the Jacobean period with the Master of the Revels beginning to issue 'annual licences' to touring troupes after 'about 1616'.[40] Town authorities were no longer directly responsible for licensing the players that visited their communities, and there was perhaps not the same impetus to screen players and their performances first-hand. This may be one reason why 'mayor's plays' become less common in the Jacobean period. Yet many troupes continued to present themselves to civic officials to obtain permission to perform or to seek a gratuity; and the changing licensing system did not stop town authorities exercising control over visiting players, a fact that occasionally became a source of tension between players and civic officials.

In Norwich the corporation monitored the activities of players carefully in the early seventeenth century. They routinely licensed troupes to play for specified periods of time only and occasionally refused them permission to perform.[41] Their decisions and authority did not always go unchallenged. In 1624 Francis Wambus arrived at the Mayor's Court, representing Lady Elizabeth's players. He was shown a letter from the Privy Council (dated 27 May 1623) requiring the Mayor and Justices 'not to suffer any players to shewe or exercise any playes' in the city, 'wherevpon [. . .] wambus peremtorily affirmed that he would play in this City & would lay in prison here this Tweluemoneth but he would try whether the kinges Command or the Counselles be the greater'.[42] While Wambus's aggressive championing of the superior power of the royal command might have been genuine, one could be forgiven for wondering if it was simply opportunistic and self-interested. His troupe wanted to play in Norwich. For this to occur with the town's permission the Privy Council order needed to be overlooked. Wambus was not a player to be easily dissuaded from his position or the pursuit of his business. When challenged he, again, threatened to out-brave the authority of the Privy Council and corporation, insisting 'he would make tryall what he might doe by the kinges authority'.[43]

Wambus proceeded to advertise a troupe performance at the White Horse Inn, but was arrested before the play could take place. When questioned he continued to protest that the King's licence authorised him (and his fellow players) to perform irrespective of any Privy Council order: 'he would play whatsoeuer had bene saide to the contrary & accused mr Maior to his face that he contemned the kynges authority [. . .] & taxed mr Maior very falsely & scandalusly with vntruthes'.[44] Wambus did not confine his histrionic skills to the stage, it seems, although in this instance he sustained his 'brave' part rather too well, finding himself committed to the town prison for his pains. He was not the only Jacobean player who challenged the right of local authorities to refuse licensed troupes permission to perform. Nor was he the only player to find himself 'cooling his heels' in the local jail as a result of his outspoken behaviour (see below).[45]

Town authorities did not always reward companies of players, although royal and noble players were usually offered some gift. To treat such players with generosity was to demonstrate respect for their often powerful patrons, and, potentially, a way of procuring the patron's good favour. The size of the payments made to visiting companies also frequently varied according to the status of their patrons, a further sign that corporations were acting politically in their dramatic patronage. This was explicitly the case at Chester, where a graduated scheme for rewarding troupes was outlined in 1596–97, according to which the Queen's players were to be allowed twenty shillings when they visited, and noblemen's players six shillings and eight pence.[46] Town authorities were able to display their wealth and power through their largesse as dramatic patrons, and there is evidence that some municipal bodies welcomed the inclusion of drama in their calendar of civic celebrations, hosting plays on special occasions. In Kendal, for example, Lord Morley's players were paid for performing at a banquet when the auditor and receivers were there at 'martinmas', 1586.[47] City authorities may have been catering for the cultural needs of the community as well. The popularity of provincial performances is well attested, and there is evidence of a positive thirst for drama in some early modern towns.[48] The ceremonies and plays of the liturgical calendar had (perhaps) traditionally satisfied people's taste for drama and ritual in many communities. The Reformation swept away most of these 'official sanctioned ritualistic activities', leaving secular culture to fill the vacuum.[49] But secular entertainment afforded by touring performers was not only an alternative to the plays and rituals of the Catholic Church. In towns such as Exeter and Shrewsbury there is evidence of a civic appetite for touring performers and secular entertainment long before the Reformation, payments to visiting patronised entertainers occurring as early as the fourteenth century.[50]

Changing attitudes

In the late sixteenth and early seventeenth centuries, civic payments to players become less frequent and council orders regulating theatrical use of town halls more common. It has usually been supposed that these facts reflect a general change in attitudes to professional theatre in provincial towns. Andrew Gurr, for instance, argues that, 'the Puritanical hatred of playing was stronger and showing itself early outside

London, where the Court had less sway'.[51] But not all corporations regarded acting companies as an alien nuisance or sought to banish drama from their town halls. Occasional references to town hall performances are recorded across the country even late in the Jacobean period; and the regulatory orders passed by provincial corporations varied in the nature of the restrictions they placed on players' use of town halls.[52] Although some corporations had entirely prohibited playing in their town halls by the early decades of the seventeenth century, in other cases acting troupes were restricted only as to the number of performances permitted. An early regulation at York stated that players should play only twice in the Common Hall (1582).[53] Other towns simply confined players to daytime performances or to the use of certain parts of the hall. The ordinance passed in Worcester in 1622 provides an example of both forms of restriction, ordering,

> that noe playes bee had or made in the vpper end of the Twonehall [. . .] nor Councell Chamber vsed by anie players whatsoever, And that noe players bee had or made in Yeald by nyght tyme, And yf anie players bee admytted to play in the Yeald hall to be admytted to play in the lower end onelie.[54]

The town authorities in Hadleigh (Suffolk) chose to confine play performances at their Guildhall to the daytime in similar fashion in 1598 and stipulated that plays should not be staged at the hall without the written consent of six of the town's chief inhabitants.[55] In other towns access to civic halls became dependent on the status of one's patron. At Durham in 1608 the City ordered that 'the Maior for the time beinge shall not att anye time hereafter permitt or suffer anye plaiers whatsoeuer to plaie in the Tooleboothe. Except his Maiesties plaiers or such other as the saide Maior and Aldermen shall in there wisdomes and discretions thinke fitt to allow'.[56]

The passing of orders restricting town hall performances by players cannot be automatically equated with their observation. Some towns were obliged to issue subsequent orders in which the continuation of unauthorised performances is noted, as at Stratford-upon-Avon. In 1602 the town ordered that there be 'no pleys or enterlewdes playd in the chamber' or 'the guild hall'.[57] Yet, in 1612 the authorities were again 'seriouslie' considering 'the inconuenience of plaies', introducing a higher fine for breaking the original order. By implication, it had not been strictly observed in the interim.[58] Moves to bar players from town halls were not always inspired or supported by civic authorities either.

In at least one instance a civic official promoted a town hall performance in the face of powerful opposition. In 1606 Queen Anne's Men were authorised to perform at the town hall in Cambridge by the mayor. Yet, in granting the company permission to perform there he was acting contrary to the wishes of the University and transgressing a prohibition on professional play performances within five miles of the University, authorised by the Privy Council and King James.[59]

Even in towns where the corporation did seek to suppress town hall performances, they were not necessarily motivated by religious-inspired anti-theatricalism. When Lord Berkeley's Men were denied permission to perform in Dorchester's town hall in 1608 the main objection to the intended performance appears to have been its proposed occurrence on the Sabbath, Sunday playing having been forbidden by statute in 1603.[60] Not until the second decade of the seventeenth century is there any evidence that the Dorchester authorities assumed a more generally negative stance towards players. In 1615 the town's Recorder, Sir Francis Ashley, imprisoned Gilbert Reason of the Prince's Men, after Reason complained about being denied permission to perform. However, even in this instance when the actions of Ashley and his officers probably were partly inspired by opposition to drama, Reason's imprisonment appears to have been prompted more specifically by a concern to maintain order and uphold civic dignity. He was arrested only after accusing the chief bailiff of being 'little better than A Traitor for refusing to look on the Commission', and daring Ashley 'to laye him by the heeles with other fowle language'.[61]

The regulations passed by some towns cite the disruption frequently attendant on dramatic performances (such as disorderly crowd behaviour) and the expense surrounding them as their grounds for objecting to or regulating town hall playing. A combination of moral and socio-economic concerns appears to underpin the Chester civic order of 1615. The order also provides a hint that visiting players were well known for their canny, opportunistic ability to circumvent restrictions when determined to perform:

> Consideringe likewise the many disorders which by reason of Plaies acted in the night time doe often times happen and fall out to the discredit of the government of this Citie and to the greate disturbance of quiet and well disposed People, and beinge further informed that mens Servantes and apprentices neglectinge their Masters busines doe Resorte to Innehowses to behold such Plaies and there many times wastfullie spende thar Masters goodes ffor avoidinge of all which

inconveniences It is ordered that from hensforth noe Stage Plaiers
upon anie pretence or color whatsoever shalbe admitted or licensed
to set vp anye stage in the said Comon Hall or to acte anie tragedie
or Commedie or anie other Plaie [. . .] in the night time or after vje
of the Clocke in the eveninge.[62]

Other towns' regulatory orders appear to have been primarily motivated
by a desire to protect the fabric and furnishings of town halls from
the damage large gatherings often caused. When York's Corporation
excluded players from the Common Hall and St Anthony's Hall in 1592
they observed that, the 'doores, lockes, keyes, wyndowes, bordes,
benches & other building*es*' of the Common Hall are 'greatlye impared
and hurte and diverse of the same broken, shakne, Lowse and Ryven vp
by people reparinge thither to se and heare plays'.[63] In 1606–07 the civic
authorities in Sudbury (Suffolk) complained in like manner that the
Moot Hall 'hath byn broughte in muche ruyn and decaye by meanes of
diuers disordered and vnrulie per*s*ons resortinge thither to playes of
enterludes'. The mayor and aldermen decided that no more plays
should be allowed in the hall, as it had been 'nowe latelie repaired &
bewtified by the nowe Maior as well at the greate chardges of the Cor-
porac*i*on'.[64] As the Sudbury Council make clear, their primary aim was
to protect their civic building from damage; and the improvements
lately made at the hall provided the immediate impetus for the 1606–07
order. Many provincial town halls underwent similar renovations.
Having made such investment it is not surprising that councils were
anxious to avoid damage. Nonetheless, that the Sudbury order begins
by mentioning the ruin and decay caused by unruly crowds resorting
to the Moot Hall suggests they were as keen to exclude disorderly people
from the improved hall as to avoid damaging the building. This was
probably as symbolic as it was pragmatic. Damage and disorders could
be costly but they could also be thought to compromise the prestige of
the civic space and the dignity of civic authority.

III

Performing in town halls

In Chapter 1 we looked at some of the conventions surrounding town
hall performances. As noted there, players routinely advertised their
urban productions through public processions accompanied by drums
and trumpets (and, occasionally, with playbills), and might perform in

the daytime or evening. Most dramatic productions in town halls appear to have been staged in hall chambers, although performances in other civic spaces are not unheard of. Less is known about how much time and access playing companies were allowed to prepare these spaces. As travelling troupes only visited some towns for a day or two, preparation time would often have been limited. But references to the erection of stages and the removal of glass windows (as occurred prior to Queen Anne's players' planned performance at Cambridge Town Hall in 1606) suggest that some pre-performance access to the playing space was customary.[65]

How players used civic spaces is not well documented either. A number of possible playing areas would have been found in most hall chambers, but contemporary evidence suggests that plays were usually staged at the upper or lower end of halls. A lower end screen (or partition dividing the main body of the hall from the principal entrances) would, if available, afford a potentially attractive, adaptable backdrop. The two doorways with which such screens were usually fitted could be used as entry and exit points while the screens passage or an adjoining room (such as a kitchen) served as a changing space. If the screens passage was enclosed and supported a gallery, an upper playing level might be available. There was likely to be more status, however, in playing at the upper end of the hall. It might be fitted with a dais, affording a natural platform, too, while an adjacent room might serve as a tiring space. At Leicester Guildhall an upper end dais can still be seen and although new is thought to reflect the original position (see Illustration 6). Elizabethan players might have used it, while the neighbouring Mayor's Parlour would be a comfortable, convenient changing area.[66] The analogous evidence of performances in university college halls suggests that performing at the upper end of halls was more common and this may have been true, too, for civic halls. Some evidence to support this point is found in the 1622 corporate order passed in Worcester banning play performances at the upper end of the Town Hall; it suggests that this had been used – and was possibly the customary place – for playing there.[67]

Spectators at town hall performances could often expect to be seated on benches, while players might use a wooden stage. If troupes were lucky, the latter might be built at corporate expense, as occurred when the Queen's players visited Gloucester in 1559–60. The town paid two men for erecting a scaffold for them in the Booth Hall.[68] Professional companies generally travelled with a stock of playing gear; their town hall performances are therefore likely to have been costumed as well.

The use of lighting and props (some of which might be borrowed on-site) was, likewise, common. The chair broken by Queen Anne's players at Leicester Guildhall (1605–06) may have been a piece of furniture borrowed for a performance at the hall.[69] Some civic hall productions included music, too, players demonstrating their own musical skills or hiring specialist musicians. Audiences were not always appreciative of such accompaniment, as one troupe discovered when playing at Gloucester Booth Hall (1602–03). Spectator John Wilmot reportedly 'offered to goe vppon the same stage' and play on one of their instruments, having first boasted that he could play better than 'any of those stage players'.[70]

Wilmot may have been watching a 'mayor's play'. At Gloucester these civic-sponsored performances were freely open to the public.[71] Audiences for these and other town hall productions could be large and socially diverse. Indeed, in some cases the 'press' of spectators was so great that halls were damaged, as at Bristol in 1575–76 when the Lord Chamberlain's Men played at the Guildhall: the pressure of the crowd stretched the 'cramp of Iren which shuttyth the barre' of the hall door.[72] Town hall audiences could also be unruly. When two forms were broken during another play performance at Bristol's Guildhall (1579–80) the town records baldly note that the damage resulted from 'the disordre of the people'.[73] Even some would-be spectators found audiences boisterous. When Lady Elizabeth's players staged a Saturday night performance at Shrewsbury's Booth Hall in 1613 at least one spectator, Edward Cowper, left early 'bycause the company was vnruly'.[74]

The plays

Early modern civic accounts rarely preserve the titles of the plays staged in town halls, but other sources provide clues to the identity of some of those performed. In the case of London-based acting troupes, records of the plays they performed in the metropolis and at Court prior to travelling offer a guide to their subsequent touring repertory and to the plays they performed at town halls.[75] Occasionally, additional information is available, as in the case of the Earl of Pembroke's players' touring repertory in 1592–93. The career of the troupe (1591–93) was 'short-lived yet outstanding'. In their first season they were one of only two companies selected to perform at Court.[76] But the prolonged plague-induced closure of the theatres from June 1592 forced the company to commence a period of provincial touring that ended in bankruptcy in 1593.[77] The company's collapse and return to London was shortly followed by the appearance of several Pembroke's plays on the book market. Four plays, which the company had performed (according to the title pages), were printed as quartos between 1593 and 1595: *Edward II*, *Titus Andronicus*, *The Taming of a Shrew* and *The True Tragedy of Richard Duke Of York*. *The Contention of the Houses of York and Lancaster*, published in 1594, does not have any troupe's name on its title page but is probably another Pembroke's play. By implication, each of the plays had been in their repertory and might have been taken on the ill-fated tour.[78]

Indirect evidence could confirm the place of at least one of these plays in the 1592–93 stock of touring texts. The tour included a performance in Bath for which the company received sixteen shillings. In the same year, Bath's Chamberlain's Accounts include a receipt of two shillings from 'my Lord of Penbrokes plaiers for A bowe that was broken by them'.[79] Tittler suggests the damage occurred when the players broke into the Guildhall armoury.[80] There does not appear to be any proof that the troupe forced entry into the armoury and it is, perhaps, more likely that they asked to borrow the bow. Nonetheless, their access to at least one of the town weapons suggests that their civic-sponsored performance in Bath that year was staged at the Guildhall, where the armoury was close at hand.[81] A survey of Elizabethan drama reveals that weapons are most frequently required for history plays. The company's 1592–93 repertory included several such plays. However, the Bath records only refer to one rather unusual item, a 'bow', and while swords are frequently demanded in Elizabethan history plays, the same cannot be said of bows. There are at least two exceptions in plays associated with Pembroke's Men. In *Titus Andronicus* the protagonist and his companions enter in Act 4, scene 3 'with bows' and 'arrows with letters at the end of them', ready to fire to the gods; and in *The True Tragedy* King Henry is watched by two keepers in Act 3, scene 1 who are required to enter 'with bow and arrowes'.[82] Potentially, the bow could have been used (or intended for use) in a production of either play in the Guildhall. However, in recent years it has been suggested that *Titus* post-dates 1592–93, in which case the play performed by the troupe at Bath was more probably *The True Tragedy*.[83]

IV

Case study: the performance of *The Cradle of Security*

The most detailed contemporary account of a town hall performance is that provided by Robert Willis in *Mount Tabor. or Private Exercises of a Penitent Sinner* (1639). He describes a 'mayor's play' he watched as a child at Gloucester Booth Hall (*c*.1565–75).[84] The play told the story of a prince seduced and distracted from 'his graver Counsellors, hearing of Sermons, and listning to good counsell' by three ladies in his court; and culminated with a scene in which the women persuaded the protagonist to lie down in a cradle and transformed him into a swine. At this point two old men entered, one carrying a mace. They circled the stage until

> at last they came to the Cradle, when all the Court was in greatest jollity, and then the foremost old man with his Mace stroke a fearfull blow upon the Cradle; whereat all the Courtiers with the three Ladies [. . .] vanished; and the desolate Prince starting up bare faced, and finding himselfe thus sent for to judgement, made a lamentable complaint of his miserable case, and so was carried away by wicked spirits.[85]

Willis closes his account of the play with a fascinating explication of its meaning:

> This Prince did personate in the morall, the wicked of the world; the three Ladies, Pride, Covetousnesse, and Luxury, the two old men, the end of the world, and the last judgement. This sight tooke such impression in me, that when I came towards mans estate, it was as fresh in my memory, as if I had seen it newly acted.[86]

Willis does not name the players responsible for the performance, possibly because he did not know or remember the name of their patron, having seen the play as a child. But it is likely that they were professionals with a royal or noble patron since he prefaces his account with a description of the conventions observed when such players visited Gloucester. The company may have been a provincial rather than a metropolitan group, however, as the play performed appears to have belonged to a genre atypical of those performed by London-based actors in the Elizabethan period.[87] The play, identified by Willis as *The Cradle of Security*, is no longer extant and otherwise unknown, but his allegorical interpretation of its narrative and characters suggests that it was a morality drama.[88] Morality plays were the 'second major genre of religious drama' in the medieval period, typically featuring a central figure, representative of mankind being 'tempted by forces of evil and defended by forces of good'.[89] These symbolic, didactic plays were less common in the sixteenth century, particularly on the professional stage, as religious drama was superseded in importance and popularity by new varieties of secular drama.[90]

The location of *The Cradle of Security* performance is not explicitly mentioned by Willis but 'the Chamberlain's accounts indicate that the mayors' plays were invariably given in the Boothall'.[91] The building, which was located on the south side of Westgate Street, does not survive but contemporary records provide valuable information about its make-up.[92] The Booth Hall of the Elizabethan period was built in the early 1530s after the corporation decided to rebuild an earlier hall in 1529.[93] A 1569 indenture reveals that it contained, 'one large hall, a smaller one sometimes called the "shreeve hall", and at the top of the stairs, the election chamber'. From the early fourteenth century the site also apparently incorporated an inn. The town continued to improve and add to the Booth Hall: 'work carried out in the years 1593–4 involved building a "new hall"'; and in 1607 they 'rebuilt and enlarged' the entire building.[94] It was an important local space. As well as housing the wool and leather markets, the Hall was used for various town and county courts. From the mid-sixteenth century it was also a regular venue for plays, a use which it continued to serve in later centuries, plays being 'regularly staged there' in the eighteenth and early nineteenth centuries.[95] Willis does not describe which part of the Hall the players used, but the 'mayor's play', where 'every one that will comes in without money' would probably have required the large hall.[96] Whichever space was used, at least some spectators were accommodated on benches as Willis observes that his father made him stand between his legs, as 'he sate upon one of the benches'.[97] The audience was apparently socially diverse, too. Willis's own presence reveals that children as well as adults attended, and the free entry to 'mayor's plays' made them accessible to everyone in the town, irrespective of social status.

The performance

Willis's description of the performance is brief but revealing. He identifies a cast including a prince (or king), courtiers, three ladies (as 'Pride', 'Covetousness', and 'Luxury'), two old men (as the 'End of the World' and 'Last Judgement') and wicked spirits. A relatively small professional company of eight or nine players could have met these casting demands, with boys possibly taking the female roles. Playing gear was used, although Willis does not give detailed information about it. The only explicitly described outfits are those worn by the two old men: 'the one in blew with a Serjeant at Armes, his mace on his shoulder, the other in red with a drawn sword in his hand'.[98] By implication, their costumes and props were symbolic, the mace with its connotations of justice and law enforcement identifying the first old man as 'the last judgement', while the death-dealing sword of the second old man is in keeping with his symbolic representation of 'the end of the world'.

The wicked spirits who transport the prince from the stage are also likely to have worn symbolic apparel. They may have worn the 'ugly masks' characteristic of devils in Tudor interludes and black costumes 'painted with flames of fire' like those worn by damned souls in earlier plays.[99] There is also some suggestion that the three 'Ladies' were attired symbolically, allowing them to be identified as Pride, Covetousness and Luxury. Contemporary representations of allegorical figures may provide a guide to the apparel they wore. Pride's actor might have worn red and been richly dressed, as Pride is in Ripa's *Iconologia*.[100] The player might also have worn a wig of elaborately dressed hair, a style that Pride recommends to Mary in Wager's *Mary Magdalene* play.[101] 'Luxury' may have worn red as well, because of the colour's associations with the carnal; while 'Covetousness' could have worn a costume which incorporated items associated with personifications of envy and greed, such as moneybags.[102] Willis does not describe the costume of the play's protagonist but his recognition of the character's royal status suggests that the player wore regal garb and/or a crown. Extravagant clothing might also have been used to suggest his arrogance and sinfulness as the play's representative of 'the wicked of the world'. 'When sumptuary laws prevented, or at least condemned, excesses in apparel, it would be instantly perceived that a character in a feathered hat, slashed doublet, scalloped sleeves and (later) bombasted breeches was full of vanity and wickedness.'[103] Craik is discussing earlier fashions and the drama of interludes here, but his point about the significance of flamboyant clothing is equally applicable in the Elizabethan period, when sumptuary laws remained in place.

The players used several props during their Gloucester performance, including the sword and mace of the two old men, the cradle of the play's title, and the swine's mask used to transform the protagonist. The sword and the mace may have been real, although the latter is unlikely to have resembled the increasingly elaborate, decorative maces of provincial corporations, while the cradle may have been specially constructed for performances of the play. The prince was rocked in it so, presumably, it was large enough to accommodate a full-grown player. Willis's account provides fuller information about the mask and its construction, describing it as 'a vizard like a swines snout [. . .], with three wire chains fastned thereunto', the ends of which were held by the three

Ladies.[104] The three chains attached to the mask suggest that it was specially adapted or made for the performance, allowing the actors to hold it over the prince's face for the duration of the transformation scene.

The account of the play summarises the main points of the action; only the staging of key episodes is reported more fully. Willis describes the startling transformation scene in particular detail:

> these three Ladies joyning in a sweet song rocked him asleepe, that he snorted againe, and in the meane time closely conveyed under the cloaths where withall he was covered, a vizard like a swines snout upon his face, with three wire chaines fastned thereunto, the other end whereof being holden severally by those three Ladies, who fall to singing againe, and then discovered his face, that the spectators might see how they had transformed him.[105]

Willis's description of the mask and the sleight of hand by which it is fitted reveals how the prince's transformation was ingeniously effected. We also learn something about the players' acting style and their relationship with the audience, Willis suggesting that the ladies made a point of revealing the transformed prince to the spectators.

The entry of the two old men also receives more detailed description. In this case, Willis provides an insight into the company's use of stage space. He describes the entry of the two men from a door at 'the farthest end of the stage', suggesting that the cradle which they headed towards was located on the fore part of the stage and that the stage was set near or against a wall flanked by more than one door. The account of their procession 'in a soft pace round about the skirt of the Stage', until they reached the cradle is even more intriguing.[106] Their circuitous entry witnessed by the audience, but not the on-stage court, would seem to have been a means of generating dramatic suspense; but it is not clear whether Willis is describing a circuit upon the stage or a procession around the platform on the hall floor. The staging would be interesting in either instance, alternatively demonstrating the company's full use of the stage or their readiness to expand the playing area beyond the platform for dramatic effect. The allusion to the skirt of the stage could also be significant. While it might simply refer to the edge of the stage it could be a literal description, revealing that a skirt of cloth fringed the playing platform, as was apparently the case in some London playhouses.[107] A contemporary portrait of Mary Queen of Scots' execution scaffold (erected in the hall of Fotheringhay Castle in 1587) may give us some idea of the appearance of such skirted stages. The painting shows a railed platform, covered and fringed with black cloth.[108] The symbolic black colouring of the cloth draping the Fotheringhay stage would have been equally appropriate for *The Cradle of Security* performance.

The performance of the play's dramatic finale is recounted by Willis in similarly tantalising fashion. The old man's fierce blow upon the cradle suggests that the strike was either real (in which case the mace and cradle must have been of sturdy construction) or mimed convincingly, a sound effect perhaps giving the impression the blow was genuine. The disappearance of the courtiers and ladies could have involved an even more impressive feat of staging if the players did give the illusion that they vanished. But, it is more likely that they simply fled the stage, the ladies carrying the mask with them. Willis does not describe the protagonist's subsequent complaint, or the manner of its delivery. But, as the character is likely to have moralised upon the shortcomings of his life and the precautionary example offered the audience, the speech could have been delivered in a didactic manner directly to the spectators. The prince's final removal from the stage by wicked spirits reinforces the play's moral; and, judging by the profound impression made upon Willis, the episode was powerfully staged by the company at Gloucester. Possibly acted by players wearing demon costumes, it is not surprising the scene proved frightening and memorable.[109] Unless his father explained the 'moral' of the drama to him or the significance of the play was expounded during the performance, Willis's closing explication of its meaning suggests the drama's allegorical lesson was explicit enough to be understood by children and adults alike, although it could equally be a testimony to the familiarity of early modern spectators with allegories and their interpretation, and proof that provincial audiences could be adept interpreters of visual dramatic language.

Conclusion

There are more references to performances being staged in town halls (between 1559 and 1625) than there are to productions in any other provincial venue. As well as reflecting the fact that civic halls lent themselves to use as temporary theatres, often affording large indoor spaces, the favouring of town halls as provincial playing venues provides further evidence of drama's popularity and perceived cultural importance in many regional communities in early modern England. Town halls were increasingly viewed as being at the heart of the social space in provincial towns. To be allowed to perform within these locally significant buildings was thus to occupy a prestigious social arena.

Town hall playing was to decline, however, in the Jacobean period and some towns passed orders explicitly prohibiting plays in their civic buildings. The reasons for introducing such legislation were varied and not necessarily anti-theatrical. Town halls perhaps became less attractive playing venues, too, as corporations introduced tighter restrictions on their use and became less likely to sponsor performances. The possibility of being charged to use them may also have deterred companies from using some towns' civic buildings. At the same time, alternative, more readily available venues emerged in some communities, encouraging troupes to abandon town halls as their first choice of venue. Bristol had two playhouses in the early seventeenth century, and in Salisbury players were required to use the George Inn for plays from 1624.[110] The tradition of staging plays in town halls was not one that died out easily or rapidly, however, and plays continued to be performed in civic halls in towns such as Blandford Forum throughout the Jacobean period.[111]

3
Playing to the Gods:
Church as Theatre

Four hundred years ago churches were sometimes used as 'playhouses', just as they occasionally serve as theatres for plays and concerts today. Most of the performances staged at England's Renaissance churches were local, amateur productions; but church buildings were among the provincial spaces sometimes available as temporary playhouses for professional touring companies, too. Travelling players acted in various (mainly indoor) ecclesiastical spaces in early modern England, including parish and cathedral churches and church houses.[1] The Earl of Leicester's Men performed in the parish church at Aldeburgh in 1573–74, for instance, while a professional cathedral production is recorded at Norwich in 1590.[2] Other touring players paid to use the church houses in Bridgwater, Sherborne, and Somerton.[3] Professional performances in churchyards appear to have been less common: only one clear record of a patronised troupe performing in a churchyard has been found so far between 1559 and 1625. In 1589–90 a troupe of the Queen's players performed in the 'Colledge Churche yarde' at Gloucester Cathedral.[4] But more examples may be found as research continues.

Until recently professional players' performances at Elizabethan and Jacobean churches had received comparatively little consideration, with scholars of provincial theatre tending to focus instead on performances 'within the multi-purpose hall' found in buildings such as town halls and noble houses.[5] Thanks to the work of editors involved in the REED project and the Malone Society it is now better recognised that churches were occasionally used by professional as well as amateur players and more attention is being paid to touring performances at churches. The tendency to overlook professional players' use of churches probably stems from the perception that plays would have been considered 'entirely inappropriate in the official institution of religious worship' in 'an age when the theatre was often viewed as a kind of anti-church'.[6] The reality was rather more complex. Some contemporaries *were* critical of playing in church. In 1580 Anthony Munday wrote angrily about professional players being 'priuledged to roame abroad, and permitted to publish their mametree in euerie Temple of God [. . .] so that now the Sanctuarie is become a plaiers stage, and a den of theeves and adulterers'.[7] But, as Munday's own account reveals, such criticism did not prevent playing at churches and his views were not widely held. Indeed, the 'impression that in late Medieval and Renaissance England the church was deemed unsuitable by conscientious clerics and lay men for anything other than religious worship' is 'distorted and historically inaccurate'.[8] In post-Reformation England churches remained important social spaces in which secular as well as religious events took place, as is revealed indirectly by the Church Canons of 1604. Order eighty-eight forbade 'plays, feasts, banquets, suppers, church ales, drinkings, temporal courts or leets, lay-juries, musters or any other profane usage, to be kept in the church, chapel or church yard'.[9] By implication, these were all activities known to occur in contemporary churches and their grounds. The ecclesiastical authorities may have decided that it was time such activities were barred, but many parishioners were presumably accustomed to – and saw no irregularity in – engaging in such secular pursuits on church ground.

Protestantism was not an inherently anti-theatrical religion either. The early Protestant Church used drama as a tool of religious instruction and propaganda. John Foxe spoke of 'players, printers and preachers' being 'set up against the triple crown of the Pope, to bring him down'.[10] And pioneering theologians such as John Bale produced Protestant plays to promote the new church. Even in the Elizabethan and Jacobean periods, when some religious reformers were critical of theatre, other Protestants were happy to watch or be involved in dramatic productions, including those staged at churches. The Earl of Leicester and Sir Francis Walsingham were both well-known patrons 'of Puritans and players'; and Leicester's players are known to have performed in several churches in the Elizabethan period. In 1573–74, for instance, they were rewarded when they played 'in ye churche' at Aldeburgh (Suffolk) and at Doncaster (Yorkshire).[11] In fact, almost half of the clear records of professional players performing in provincial churches in the Elizabethan dramatic records published by REED and the Malone Society are records of performances by Leicester's Men. This could mean they had a taste for, or had been encouraged to use, church venues.[12] If their playing repertory reflected Leicester's Protestant interests and values (as is possible), performing in churches was potentially an effective, symbolically appropriate way of proselytising on behalf of the new faith and their patron. Leicester would not have been the first Protestant to use his players as political and religious propagandists; and there is growing evidence to suggest that he was well-practised in the use of theatre 'to present his own political or religious viewpoint'.[13]

I

The evidence

The main source of evidence for professional play productions at Renaissance churches is the payments occasionally made for performances in surviving church and civic accounts. But clear evidence of professional church performances is comparatively rare even in these sources. There are only six records of professional players receiving church or civic rewards for productions explicitly described as occurring in or outside church buildings in the Elizabethan and Jacobean dramatic records published by REED and the Malone Society.[14] But church accounts do include indirect evidence of other professional performances. In several cases accounting entries make it clear that church officers rewarded players for performances but do not specify their location. While it is possible that ecclesiastical officials would sponsor plays in other local spaces the most likely venue for the recorded productions is the church (or church buildings). Hence, when St Eustace's churchwardens (Tavistock) paid the Earl of Warwick's players 'for a playe' in 1572–73, they were probably being rewarded for a performance at the parish church. Similarly, when the Dean and Chapter at Norwich Cathedral rewarded several professional troupes for performing before them in 1577–78, 1580–81 and 1581–82 the productions are likely to have taken place within the Cathedral precincts, even though this is not stated in the accounts.[15]

Other cathedral and parish churches that patronised professional players may also have hosted on-site performances although this is not stated in surviving records. It is possible, for instance, that at least some of the professional players rewarded by cathedral clerics in York and Chester performed within the precincts of the respective cathedrals. In Chester's records we may even find a clue to the location of such performances since in 1582–83 the Earl of Essex's players received two shillings from the Dean and Chapter 'when they woude haue played in

Mr Deanes howse'. It seems that the performance did not take place but the Dean's house had been identified as a potential playing venue and might have been used for performances staged when the Queen's players were rewarded by the Dean and Chapter in 1589–90, 1590–91 and 1591–92.[16] Evidence that some of the players rewarded by York's Dean and Chapter might also have performed within private cathedral lodgings may be found in 1598. A troupe of unnamed players was rewarded by the Cathedral for performing 'at Mr Doctor Bennittes'. Dr John Bennett was Chancellor of the diocese: the performance is therefore likely to have been staged in the Chancellor's house within the Minster Close.[17] Other visiting players might also have performed at the Chancellor's house and/or other houses in the close.

Ecclesiastical and secular court records also include occasional references to travelling play productions at churches. In these instances, the performances are generally recorded because they proved controversial. Hence, we know that a play was performed in 1584 'in the church' at Duns Tew (Oxfordshire) 'vpon a Saterdaye in the evening after service was donne' because the matter was raised at the Archdeacon's Court.[18] The two churchwardens were cited for 'keping enterludes and playes in the churche'. The wardens admitted that there had been a play 'in the churche of Dunstewe [. . .] but by whom they know not, nor whose men they weare'.[19] The wardens were perhaps being politic in their ignorance but the assumption that the players were somebody's men suggests that they were a patronised professional company. Denying to know the name of their patron was possibly a way of protecting the players (who may have had a local or powerful sponsor) and preventing the collection of further evidence against themselves.

In Norwich evidence of a performance by Lord Beauchamp's players at the Cathedral is preserved in the records of the Mayor's Court. On 10 June 1590 it is recorded that Lord Beauchamp's players 'did sett vpp bille*s* to P*r*ovoke men to com to their playe and did playe in ch*r*iste-churche' despite having been 'forbidden by mr maior to playe within the libe*r*ties of this Citie', and given a gift of twenty shillings. ('Christchurch' appears to have been another name for the Cathedral.)[20] In performing at the Cathedral Mufford and his fellow players may have hoped to evade civic punishment, the Cathedral precincts being an area traditionally exempt from the city's control. This was not to be the case. Mufford paid the price for the players' misdemeanour, finding himself committed to prison. Precisely where the players performed is unclear; and a number of spaces potentially adaptable for performance were available (including the Cathedral church and churchyard, and private

Cathedral residences). Since the players visited in June and appear to have expected a public audience (posting playbills to publicise it), an open-air performance in the churchyard might have been favoured. Here, they would have found one area specifically adapted for public gatherings. The 'preaching' or 'green yard' to the north of the Cathedral was fitted with seating for ecclesiastic and city dignitaries, as Sir Thomas Browne reported when he described the yard's use for public sermons prior to the Reformation:

> The mayor and aldermen, with their wives and officers, had a well-contrived place built against the wall of the Bishop's palace, covered with lead so that they were not offended by rain. Upon the north side of the church, places were built gallery wise, one above another, where the dean, prebendaries and their wives, gentlemen, and the better sort, very well heard the sermon: the rest either stood or sat in the green, upon long forms provided for them, paying a penny or half-penny a-piece.[21]

With its galleried seating and its open green the 'yard' was a ready-made theatre, suitable for public plays as well as public sermons. Whether the Cathedral would have permitted such a use of the preaching yard is more debatable, although the promise of a share in the 'takings' of the performance might have been a sufficient inducement to permit an alternative public use of the yard.

The information supplied by court records can be more revealing, socially and theatrically. In 1577 the churchwardens of West Ham, Essex (William Rokes and Vincent Hancottes) were presented at the Archdeacon's Court in April to answer the charge that

> theie suffered and caused in lent last past [. . .] ij playes [to be] kepte in the church by comon players the one vpon the sondaie before *our* Ladie and the other one on *our* Ladie daie laste paste and the people were suffered to stand vpon the commun*ion* table, diuerse of them.[22]

Although the actors are not identified their description as common players suggests they were professional rather than occasional amateur performers, while the latter charge includes tantalising evidence about the play's staging. If the people suffered to stand on the communion table were spectators (as seems likely) it could mean either that 'they were facing the nave where the action was taking place', or that the performance was mounted in or near the chancel, where the communion table was usually located.[23] The churchwardens did not deny the charge but explained why they apparently chose to tolerate the plays:

> the same Vincente hancottes and William Rokes confessed the same to be true, addinge that the same players were suffered for that theie had a poore man in decay and had some relef of the same players to the vse of the same poore man.[24]

The churchwardens' planned use of the players' contribution to alleviate a case of local poverty has its metropolitan parallels. In a number of London parishes, contributions from players were welcomed and used for the relief of the local poor in similar fashion in the late sixteenth century.[25]

Attractions of church playing

Ecclesiastical buildings and their grounds were an obvious venue for parish plays and other church-sponsored productions as they were a conventional place of assembly for parishioners, generally freely available and 'large enough to hold all the inhabitants'.[26] Their usual capacity to accommodate a town or village's community and their provision of indoor performance spaces and churchyards that might serve as open-air playing venues also made parish and cathedral churches potentially appealing venues for professional actors. This was especially true in towns where sizeable public venues were scarce. In some towns the church or church house may have been the 'best available' theatre for public play performances in the Elizabethan period.[27] In Plymouth, for instance, St Andrew's parish church where Lord Dudley's players performed in 1559–60 was possibly used by the company because it afforded the largest covered public space in the town, measuring 185 feet by 94 feet internally.[28] Dudley's players may have performed in Aldeburgh's parish church for similar reasons in 1573–74. The 'spacious' fourteenth century church exceeded the local Moot Hall in size and the nave was a traditional venue for large secular events such as ship auctions and public meetings. (It is a tradition continued today with the church occasionally hosting concerts.)[29]

Some ecclesiastical buildings may have had additional recommendations as theatres. Professional companies that visited churches with a tradition of performing parish plays might have been able to look forward to assistance with their preparations and to access to church-owned playing gear. In Chelmsford, St Mary's Church owned a stock of playing apparel that included general costumes (such as four gowns 'of red velvet', and eight jerkins without sleeves), and accessories (such as beards and wigs). Although the costumes were originally prepared for local religious plays, the churchwardens' accounts reveal that they were sometimes loaned to local and professional players, as in 1572 when 'John Walker of Hanfild' and the 'Earle of Sussex players' paid to hire the 'players garments'.[30] Travelling troupes that hired church houses might also have been able to borrow additional props and furniture on-site, many church houses maintaining a stock of domestic and parish equipment.[31]

Church spaces

Few English churches were built in the Renaissance. Consequently, churches or cathedrals of medieval or earlier origin served most Elizabethan and Jacobean communities. They varied in size and in the facilities they afforded players, but most were divided into two main areas, nave and chancel. Both areas could be large, although the naves and chancels of cathedral churches were generally more spacious than those of parish churches. In Hornchurch (Essex), the parish church of St Andrew's (the likely venue for the controversial 1566 church perfor-mance in which the players did 'playe and declare certayn things against the Ministers') has a nave measuring $40^1/_4$ feet by $16^1/_2$ feet, and a chancel of $33^1/_2$ feet by $18^1/_2$ feet. By contrast, at Gloucester Cathedral the nave alone measures 253 feet 9 inches long, and the total length of the building is 433 feet.[32] But parish churches could be much larger than that at Hornchurch, affording indoor spaces comparable with some of the largest halls found in town halls and country houses. At All Saints in West Ham, where the 'common' players are likely to have performed in 1577, the nave measures $88^1/_2$ feet by 22 feet, and the chancel 43 feet by 19 feet (see Illustration 7).[33] One of the most capacious parish churches to be found in the entire country in the Renaissance is that still to be found at Boston (Lincolnshire). St Botolph's 'is a giant among English parish churches', measuring 282 feet in length and having an area of 20,070 square feet. It is not hard to see why players might have wished to perform there, although they were theoretically prohibited from using the 'churche' (or parish nave) and 'Chauncell' from 1578.[34]

A wooden screen sometimes separated the nave and chancel in parish and cathedral churches.[35] These screens were often in two parts and might be elaborately carved and decorated: 'the upper part was con-structed of open panels or traceried panels, so that the high altar might be in view, the lower part was sometimes left more or less open [. . .];

much more frequently it was of solid panels, either carved, or, in rich parishes, painted'.[36] Access to the chancel was gained through one or more doorways in the screen, while a gallery or 'church loft' might be fitted above, reached by a staircase within the screen. These platforms 'were generally about six feet' in breadth but varied from five to as much as eight feet.[37] In medieval churches the loft might support the rood of Mary and John or reliquaries, but following the Reformation and the outlawing of roods, surviving lofts were more often bare and used as choir galleries or platforms for music. Sometimes the church organ was placed on the gallery.[38]

The association of galleries with artistic performance might account for the decision of 'players' to perform on the church loft at Great Marlow (*c*.1593–95).[39] The church of All Saints where the performance is likely to have occurred was pulled down in 1832, and it is not clear where the loft used by the players was located. The plan of the church prepared by Alfred Heneage Cocks shows several screens: a stone screen (between the Parish chancel and nave), an oak screen (in the neighbouring Town chancel or Lady Chapel) and a screen or parclose 'between the two aisles of the chancel'.[40] The term 'church loft' usually refers to the area above the rood screen so it is perhaps most likely that the players performed on the main screen between the chancel and nave, facing an audience accommodated in the latter.

When professional companies visited cathedral and parish churches, they may have been invited to perform occasionally in private ecclesiastical lodgings. Information about such private church residences is generally more limited. For instance, it is not clear whether the Dean's House where the Earl of Essex's players planned to perform at Chester (1582–83) survives.[41] But such private lodgings could have offered an attractive alternative to performing in public ecclesiastical buildings, often incorporating large well-fitted halls readily adaptable for performance use, as at Norwich Cathedral. Here, the professional players rewarded for performing before the dean and prebendaries might have acted in the large hall of the deanery – 'one of the grandest houses in the close' – or within the 'great chamber' of the even larger, more lavishly equipped Bishop's Palace.[42]

Evidence about parish 'church houses' and their use for drama is more plentiful. Most 'numerous in southern and south-western England', church houses were usually located 'close to the church' and 'erected or bought' by the church 'for the purpose of becoming the focus of the social life of the parish'.[43] Sometimes the houses were conversions of existing buildings, as at Wimborne where the church house (now lost) was converted from the Chapel of St Peter.[44] In other cases the house was specially built or rebuilt in the late sixteenth century. In Sherborne, the churchwardens 'rented a site in Half Moon Street from the master of Sherborne's almshouse' in 1530 and then built 'a long two-storey building' on the property which can still be seen today (see Illustration 8); while Somerton's parish house (hired by Lord Chandos's players in 1605–06) was rebuilt (1582–83) after being bought by the churchwardens (1581–82).[45]

As a result of their differing origins, church houses varied in size and layout. But most contained at least one room capable of accommodating a sizeable parish gathering. Often this room was on an upper floor, while the lower floor might be rented out annually. In Somerton the parish house had a first-floor hall reached by an external staircase from the churchyard, while the lower floor was used for a shop and kitchen. At Sherborne, the ground floor of the church house was divided in similar fashion 'into four shops and a kitchen', while the long upper storey room was available for parochial uses and private hire.[46] The latter afforded a spacious 'theatre', extending almost the whole of the church house's upper storey (measuring approximately 116 feet by 19 feet). It is also likely to have been open to the roof (measuring approximately $18^{1}/_{2}$ feet 'at the peak'). When players such as the Queen's Men performed there in 1597–98 and 1598–99, they would have found the upper room reasonably well lit as well, being fitted with 'fourteen windows, each with four vertical panes,' 41 inches high and 12 inches wide; while the fireplace in the 'east wall of the room' would have allowed the space to be heated. There was good, easily supervised access to the space too, the upper room being reached by a staircase 'with nine stone steps' at the west end of the room.[47]

Despite varying in size, church houses often shared similar facilities. As spaces intended for parish recreations, including parish ales, provision was sometimes made for baking and brewing on-site. There were kitchens below the church house rooms in Somerton and Sherborne. The latter was also supplied 'with iron racks and spits and a great brass pot' and, by 1574, with 'two dozen platters and a dozen pottingers'.[48] It was also usual for church houses to be supplied with trestles, forms and other domestic utensils. At Somerton we know there were forms because they had to be mended after a play performance at the parish house in 1607–08, and at Sherborne there were tables, 'benches by the walls, and forms and trestles'.[49] Such equipment could often be hired with the church house for private functions including plays. Some church houses were home to military ware and other more unusual equipment, such as fire-fighting tools, which was potentially available for hire by local people and playing troupes, too. The 1567–68 inventory for Sherborne's church house listed 'a corselet and pike' and 'a black jack'; and by the mid-1580s there were 'eight leather buckets, a shovel, a pickaxe, various ladders [. . .], as well as a bow and a sheaf of arrows'.[50] These were items that could prove useful props. The availability of assorted equipment and the association of church houses with parish recreation may have encouraged their use as playing venues, while the fact that professional players were prepared to pay for their use suggests that they were considered desirable playing spaces.[51]

Outdoor performances at churches were less common but might be staged in the churchyard within which parish and cathedral churches normally stood. Parish and cathedral churchyards often functioned partly as cemeteries, the latter sometimes being divided into two areas, a 'lay cemetery' and a graveyard for cathedral clerics, as at Gloucester Cathedral. Here, a wall 'extended south from the corner of the south transept, dividing the area on the south side of the church into the inner or monks' cemetery, lying on the east side of the wall, and the lay ceme-tery on the west side of the wall' (see Illustration 9).[52] The performance by the Queen's Men in Gloucester's college churchyard in 1589–90 prob-ably refers to a performance in the lay cemetery (or upper churchyard), or in the lower churchyard, also known as College Green.[53] It is less likely that the performance occurred in the monks' cemetery because access was restricted to this part of the churchyard. On this occasion the players may have expressed a preference for an open-air playing space. In 1589–90 one branch of the Queen's Men was on tour with a Turkish or Hungarian rope-dancer (see Chapter 1); and together, the players and rope-dancer staged several acrobatic shows.[54] Although such displays might be staged indoors, open-air venues were potentially better suited to such performances, and there is evidence of the troupe and acrobat performing at least one other open-air performance during the same tour in the cornmarket at Shrewsbury. The troupe may have planned to entertain the audience at Gloucester Cathedral with tum-bling as well as drama.[55]

The size of churchyards varied but they were generally large spaces. Notionally, the standard size for churchyards was an acre (in keeping with the conception of the churchyard as 'God's acre') but in reality some covered 'more than one acre and some less'.[56] Churchyards were also usually fairly open spaces. As David Dymond points out:

Before the seventeenth century, although thousands of burials had already accumulated in the average churchyard, it had fewer surface obstructions than today and was more of an open space. It [. . .] was not so cluttered with the large permanent fixtures which became common from the seventeenth century onwards.[57]

This was especially true of the north part of the churchyard, 'often known as the "wrong" or Devil's side' and 'regarded (incorrectly) as unconsecrated'. This area 'tended to be used only for the burial of suicides, executed criminals and those who were unbaptised and excommunicated' and 'often remained relatively empty until the nineteenth century'.[58] As uncluttered spaces, Elizabethan and Jacobean churchyards could be easily adapted for entertainment and were usually capable of accommodating large audiences. At Norwich Cathedral players would even have found seating for civic and ecclesiastic dignitaries in one part of the churchyard (the green yard).[59]

By the sixteenth century churchyards were also usually walled, people entering them through one or more gates.[60] If walled, entry to churchyard performances might be controlled, permitting a degree of audience regulation and facilitating the collection of money from spectators. In the case of the Queen's Men's performance at Gloucester Cathedral, entry to a performance in the lower churchyard would have been gained through St Mary's gate, while spectators for a performance in the lay cemetery would have entered through King Edward's gate and/or St Michael's gate. In either instance, entry through the gateways might have been regulated by gatekeepers who could have collected money, as occurred when professional Shakespearean troupes like the Queen's Men performed in other regional venues.[61] Until the late eighteenth century the gateways into Gloucester's close 'were maintained and manned by porters'. The players could have employed one or more of these individuals as their temporary gatekeepers.[62]

II

Performing at churches

Church performances by professional travelling troupes might occur at any time during the year. They were not occasional productions as a rule, although some troupes may have timed visits to particular towns and churches to coincide with known fair days and church holidays. Having arrived in a town or village, troupes wishing to perform at a local parish or cathedral church theoretically needed to gain permission to perform from the town's mayor and the church's officers. Civic and ecclesiastic permission to perform was not always granted. In Norwich

Lord Beauchamp's players were forbidden to perform anywhere in the town in 1590 (although they proceeded to perform at the Cathedral anyway), while in Syston 'Lord Mordens' men were paid 'because they should not play in the Church' in 1602.[63] Players did not always take the trouble to obtain permission to play at churches either. In some instances the support of parishioners appears to have been taken as sufficient authorisation to use the parish church as a playing venue. An interlude staged by unnamed players in the parish church at Winslow (Oxfordshire) in 1595 was facilitated in this fashion. When churchwarden William Leach was cited in the church courts for allowing the players to perform in the church, he described how local parishioners had interceded with him on their behalf. He denied letting the players

> go into the church to playe but he saith that some of the parishe ded promise him that they woulde beare him harmeles if any trouble shoulde happen unto him wherupon he this respondent ded delyver unto [. . .] [them] the key of the churche dore and that they ded let the players in viz. Mr Peter Fige Thomas Deverell and Nicholas Mychell William Spooner & William Gyles.[64]

Presumably, the parishioners' protection had not materialised or proved ineffective in the face of the power of the church.

Gaining authorisation from church officers could also be problematic because there was usually more than one official to deal with. At parish churches one churchwarden might authorise a performance without gaining the agreement of the other warden. This may have been the case at West Ham in 1577. Both churchwardens were charged with suffering plays to be 'kepte in the church by comon players', but one of the wardens claimed that he had not granted the troupe prior permission:

> William Rokes affirmed that he comminge into the Church perseved that the players went about to playe he speakinge to them declared that he wold not give his consent that theie shold not play there, and he wold not be blamed for them but he taried & hard the play & therein he consented to the play.[65]

As Rokes was fined only 'ij s vi d', while the other warden, Vincent Hancottes was fined five shillings, it is possible that Hancottes was responsible for allowing the players into the church in the first place.

If permission to perform was granted, and the church or town was to sponsor the performance, companies may have offered their patrons the opportunity to choose the play performed, as was customary when they visited noble houses. Civic and ecclesiastic rewards for church performances varied but could be generous, and comparable with the gifts received for performances at noble houses and town halls. When Lord Robert Dudley's players performed at the church in Plymouth in 1559–60 they were given twenty shillings by the corporation, while they received a pound from the town when they played in the church at Dartmouth (1569–70), and twenty shillings from St Andrew's churchwardens in Bewdley (1573–74).[66] Players may have made audience gatherings (or charged entry fees) as well. A collection of some sort was made when Dudley's players performed at Long Sutton in 1565–66, as the churchwardens reimbursed the vicar for money 'that he laied out more then coulde be gathered' when the troupe performed there. That the vicar felt obliged to supplement what was gathered could mean that the amount of money collected from the audience was not large. He may have thought it wise to reward the servants of the Queen's powerful favourite more generously.[67]

Public church performances are likely to have been advertised in similar fashion to other regional play productions. Players might perambulate the town or village with their drums announcing their intended performance and/or circulate playbills, as did Lord Beauchamp's players at Norwich (1590), while the commencement of performances may have been announced in some cases by ringing the church bells. Sounding the bells may even have been a way of summoning audiences, as it was a means of calling parishioners to church services. The players that 'towlde the Bell' in the chapel where they performed in the parish of Great Burstead (1579) may have been advertising their performance in this way. Such a misuse of the church bells and their power to rouse local attention was contrary to church injunctions and calculated to rile the ecclesiastical authorities, especially at a time when there was concern about people being distracted from church-going by secular recreations.[68]

The plays

The plays performed by Elizabethan and Jacobean touring players are generally unnamed in provincial records and this is true of their performances at churches. None of the professional church performances recorded so far in the period is identified. Contemporary secular works dominated the repertories of professional English companies in the

Renaissance.[69] Most of the professional play productions at Renaissance church buildings are therefore likely to have been secular. In the case of leading troupes such as Leicester's players and the Queen's Men, the plays performed on tour and at churches are likely to have derived from their metropolitan repertories. Information about the repertory of Leicester's Men is scarce and many of their known plays have been lost; but what information we have affords some insight into the kind of dramas they might have performed at churches. For instance, in 1573–74, the year they played in the church at Aldeburgh, they performed *Mamillia, Predor and Lucia, Panecia* and *Philmeon and Philecia* at Court, plays now lost but probably 'belonging to the classical and romantic veins associated with humanism'.[70] They might have entertained Aldeburgh's parishioners with one of the same plays, offering them a taste of the humanist culture important in academic and elite circles. When the Queen's Men performed at Gloucester Cathedral (1589–90) they would have been choosing a play from a repertory of generically more diverse works including contemporary dramas, and history plays (such as the *Three Lords and Three Ladies of London* and *The Famous Victories of Henry V*), as well as pastoral plays.[71]

Staging

Most professional plays mounted inside parish and cathedral churches are likely to have been staged in or near the nave since this was generally the largest part of the church, although performances may have occurred occasionally in areas such as the chancel as well.[72] The east end of the nave 'or what is sometimes referred to as the crossing in churches and cathedrals with transepts' lent itself to performance use since it was usually an open area. It also left the remainder of the nave free for the accommodation of spectators, a use to which it was well suited being the traditional place of assembly for lay congregations.[73] By the end of the sixteenth century, players could often expect to find the nave equipped with seating as well as at St Martin's, Leicester, where the church was fitted with 'moveable benches without backs' before 1569.[74] As the church space associated with parishioners, the nave lent itself to use for plays at a symbolic as well as a pragmatic level.[75] It was a communal space in which communal recreation as well as worship could take place.

In churches that retained a screen between the chancel and nave, the partition afforded a potential backdrop and entry and exit point(s). Leicester's players might have used the rood screen as their performance backdrop and temporary tiring house when they performed at St Saviour's Church in Dartmouth in 1569–70. The fifteenth-century screen – which can still be seen in the church – lies east of the fourth bay of the nave, leaving a large space before the possible performance area for spectators.[76] The church of St Mary Magdalen in Duns Tew, where the troupe of unnamed players is likely to have performed in 1584, was also fitted with a rood screen (until 1861) that might have served as a performance backdrop at the east end of the nave.[77] If the screen was galleried the players potentially had access to an upper playing area as well, facilities similar to those afforded by the tiring house and gallery of the London theatres in the late sixteenth century. The players who paid a fee for using the church loft in Great Marlow (*c.*1593–95) might have been using the loft as a second level for a performance staged before the screen in this way.[78]

Parclose screens dividing chancel aisles from the chancel or screening side-chapels afforded other staging possibilities. In St Saviour's (Dartmouth) the two parclose screens installed *c.*1567–68 created enclosed areas that might have served as temporary tiring houses as well as, or instead of the chancel, if Leicester's players performed before the rood screen there in 1569–70. Side chapels or the arms of transepts might have been used as temporary changing spaces or stage 'houses' in other churches in similar fashion.[79] The 'common' players that probably performed in All Saints Church, West Ham (1577) would have found two spacious chapels available for such use during a performance staged at the east end of the church, the north chapel measuring 44 feet by 20 feet and the south chapel 43 feet by 19 feet.[80]

Generalising about professional players' performances in other indoor church spaces, such as private cathedral lodgings and church houses, is more difficult because there is usually little evidence regarding such performances and information about the spaces used is frequently limited. When performing in private lodgings (such as deaneries) players are likely to have performed in the hall or great chamber typically found in large residences. These rooms could be spacious and well suited to recreational use. In chambers with distinctive upper and lower ends analogous evidence regarding hall performances in university colleges would suggest that troupes are more likely to have performed at the more prestigious upper end of the hall.[81] In church house rooms of the kind hired by players at Somerton and Sherborne, it was possibly also usual to perform at the upper end (where there was a distinction between the two ends), or opposite the main entrance of the chamber.

At Sherborne this probably meant performing at the east end of the long room, facing the 'elaborate staircase' leading to the upper chamber, while Lord Chandos's players are likely to have played at the far end of the first-floor hall in Somerton's church house, facing the entrance from the churchyard.[82]

Churchyard performances of the kind staged by the Queen's Men at Gloucester Cathedral were rare and evidence regarding their staging is scarce. In large churchyards a number of sizeable open areas might be adaptable for playing, but at parish churches the north part of the yard was possibly the most suitable playing area. This was often the emptiest part of the yard, and was viewed as slightly less sacred ground, as noted earlier.[83] However, when the Queen's Men performed at Gloucester Cathedral, it is more likely that they performed in the south-western upper or lower churchyards (the areas shown as the former lay cemetery and college green in Illustration 9). These were the largest spaces available in the churchyard and therefore the best suited for a performance aimed at a large audience. They may also have been the only spaces available for public use. Whether the Queen's players chose to play next to the church or churchyard wall, or to perform in a more open part of the yard is not recorded. But it is perhaps more likely that the troupe used a wall as a backdrop since late Elizabethan companies did not usually perform completely 'in the round'. We know from earlier records of amateur churchyard drama that performing against church walls was not unknown. In the early sixteenth century plays performed outside St Lawrence's Church, Reading were acted on 'a trestle stage built against the wall of the Benedictine Abbey in a space called the Forbury'.[84]

Whether professional church performances were mounted on stages is not usually mentioned in early modern records. Companies were accustomed to playing on stages in the Renaissance but there is no clear evidence for their construction in the churches professional players visited in the Elizabethan and Jacobean periods. This could mean that the productions were performed without stages or that actors provided their own scaffolds, possibly creating improvised platforms from locally borrowed materials and/or furniture such as boards and benches. It would not have been unusual to use stages in or outside church buildings. Playing platforms were erected for at least some of the amateur plays performed at Renaissance England's churches. In Sherborne there is evidence of players performing in the Abbey Church on an improvised wooden platform in 1543–44, the churchwardens paying two pence for carrying away 'bordes that the players plaid vppon in the churche'. A similar temporary stage may have been erected for players in St Saviour's (Dartmouth), the church that later hosted a performance by Leicester's Men. In 1567–68 payment was made for 'caryng of bordes to the churche for the players'.[85] As professional Shakespearean players generally performed in costume and employed props in their performances it is also likely that their plays in and outside church buildings were staged in costume and with at least some stage furniture.

Audiences

When travelling players visited cathedrals they may have sometimes performed privately before a select body of cathedral clerics and officers, but almost all parish church and church house productions are likely to have been public, and the audiences therefore socially mixed, including men, women and children of all ages and different social groups. People from neighbouring communities and parishes might have attended well-publicised performances as well. Some cathedral performances may have been open to the laity, too. The performance staged by Lord Beauchamp's players at Norwich Cathedral was presumably open to the public as the players posted playbills advertising the performance in the town.[86] The performance by the Queen's Men at Gloucester Cathedral (1589–90) may also have been open to the public and is likely to have been attended by local civic officials since it was patronised by the town authorities rather than the Dean and Chapter. The churchyard may have been chosen as the playing venue because of its capacity to accommodate a large local audience. The Booth Hall was the usual venue for civic-sponsored performances, but the churchyard afforded a more commodious theatrical arena if the weather permitted an open-air performance. The Queen's Men appear to have visited Gloucester in the summer so there was a reasonable chance of fine weather. It is also possible that the players requested an open-air playing venue because they planned to entertain the Gloucester audience with an acrobatic display of the kind they staged at Shrewsbury, as noted earlier.[87] Local civic officials may have had their own reasons for permitting a performance in the churchyard. Jurisdiction over the close was a long-running 'cause of dispute between the abbey and the town authorities'.[88] The clerics insisted that authority over the close rested in their hands while the local council sought to extend town control over the area. Patronising a play performance within the close was one way of exercising civic power within the contested area and thus promoting the town's right to govern the precinct.

How spectators were accommodated is not usually mentioned in church records. When players performed in churchyards it is likely that most people simply stood around the playing area, although we know that spectators sometimes sat on the church leads (or roof) as well for amateur churchyard performances, and players would have found ready-made spectator galleries in the 'green yard' at Norwich Cathedral.[89] When performances were staged inside churches, audiences might be accommodated in the nave while the players performed at its upper end against the chancel screen. If the screen was galleried, the area above the partition might also be used for spectators, as was the case at the student performances in King's College Chapel, Cambridge in 1564.[90] In churches where there was no screen, audience members might be accommodated in the chancel as well as the nave. It was increasingly common for parish and cathedral churches to be fitted with some form of seating by the late sixteenth century and performances inside churches are likely to have taken advantage of this fact, using available benches to accommodate at least some spectators. Seating at church performances may have been determined randomly, but in an age when rules sometimes governed the allocation of seating for church services, it is possible that audiences for certain church plays were also organised more formally. Spectators might have been arranged hierarchically, for instance, the seats or spaces nearest the performance area being reserved for important clerics and parishioners. Certainly, it would not be surprising to find that some of the best seats were reserved for ecclesiastic or corporation dignitaries when they were responsible for patronising the performance.[91]

III

The decline of church performances

Church performances by professional and amateur players became less frequent in the late sixteenth and early seventeenth centuries, as complaints about playing in church grew and diocesan authorities sought to limit performances with growing rigour. Initially, criticism and control of church playing tended to focus on the performance of plays on Sundays and was voiced by reformers who sought to restrict various 'profane' activities on the Sabbath; a project known as the 'Sabbatarian campaign'.[92] But, in the latter part of the Elizabethan period, several diocesan authorities issued orders restricting the production of plays in or outside their churches at any time and used visitation articles to supervise their observance. In the Diocese of Hereford, for instance, the 1586 articles of enquiry of Bishop Herbert Westfalling included the following question: 'Whether any Lords of Misrule, dauncers, plaiers, or any other disguised persons do daunce, or play any vnseemely parts in the church, church-yard, or chappell-yard, or whether are there any playes or common drinking kept in the church, or church-yarde, who maintaine and accompany such?'[93] Similar articles appear in visitation questions prepared in the Dioceses of Worcester and Chichester in 1576 and 1586, respectively.[94] Some civic authorities also intervened to curb playing at churches. In 1578 Boston's corporation prohibited plays in the church.[95] The accession of King James brought with it a blanket ban on church playing. Order eighty-eight of the 1604 Church Canons stated that churchwardens were 'forbidden to permit any "ludos scenicos" in their churches, chapels, or cemeteries'.[96] The order did not prevent plays being performed in and around Jacobean church buildings entirely. There is evidence of amateur church performances post-1603, but such records become rare and evidence of professional players at churches virtually disappears in the Jacobean period.

The increasingly strict regulation of church performances in the sixteenth century and the attempted exclusion of plays from churches in the seventeenth century have often been regarded as consequences of a growing anti-theatrical prejudice, fostered by some branches of the Puritan movement. Yet, neither the growing opposition to church playing or the decline in professional and amateur church performances were exclusively the result of anti-theatrical feeling. Plays were not the only activity that reformers sought to exclude from Renaissance churches. Church authorities and reformers were concerned about the use of churches for secular activities in general, and had been making efforts to move various recreational activities 'outwards'.[97] In 1572 Bishop Freke of Rochester offered a very full account of the recreations he considered unacceptable at churches, 'castigating "hopping, skipping, dancing, singing, football, playing bowls, dicing, carding, stool ball" and "any other unlawful game"'.[98] Church dancing, fairs, ales, rush-bearings and sports were subject to similar critical scrutiny and were, likewise, prohibited on church property by some diocesan authorities. Indeed, in several cases diocesan visitation articles reveal a greater concern with controlling activities such as dancing and May games at churches.[99] This was not the first time that church reformers had attempted to move secular activities away from sacred ground either. As early as the thirteenth century one finds bishops trying to 'enforce a more seemly use of consecrated buildings and land', by attacking and restricting the use of church property for secular pursuits. Archbishop Stephen Langton of Canterbury 'prohibited "inhonesti" plays in churches and churchyards' in 1213–14; and Bishop Richard Poore of Salisbury prohibited 'inhonesti ludi' at churches in 1217–19.[100] But measures controlling the use of churches and churchyards were enforced with greater success in the late Elizabethan and Jacobean periods.

The introduction of ecclesiastical prohibitions was not the only factor involved in the decline of church playing either. As English towns expanded during the late sixteenth century, new and larger buildings were often erected (such as town halls and schoolhouses) providing alternative and, in some cases, more attractive playing venues for late Elizabethan acting companies. In the early seventeenth century the world of travelling theatre generally became more circumscribed, however, with players facing stricter royal and civic regulation and growing hostility in some provincial communities. And there appears to have been a general decline in the number and activity of professional touring companies in the Jacobean period. The increasingly tight regulation of church playing and the drop in professional performances at churches from the late sixteenth century can therefore also be seen as reflecting and anticipating these broader trends in provincial theatre and touring activity.[101]

Conclusion

Professional players may not have performed as frequently at churches as they did at civic halls and noble houses when on tour, but they were one of the provincial spaces potentially available and occasionally used by troupes in the early modern provinces. Companies such as Leicester's Men may have actively elected to perform in churches in the early Elizabethan period. Even in the late sixteenth century when church playing was restricted in some regions, performances continued to be permitted at certain churches. Church play productions were to become a rare occurrence in seventeenth century, however. Growing hostility to church playing and the ban on plays in and outside churches from 1604 were obvious factors in this decline. But the decreasing number of professional performances at churches was also possibly one symptom of the more general decline in touring performances witnessed in the early seventeenth century as the number and activity of touring companies reduced in the more strictly defined and policed world of Stuart provincial theatre. The performances considered in this chapter belong to a transitional cultural and theatrical moment, in which the role and use of churches as social spaces changed and the tradition of professional touring theatre began to decline. Studying professional companies' performances at Renaissance church buildings is thus not only a way of expanding our understanding of the diversity of touring playing places and of drama's place in regional cultures, but of exploring one aspect of the decline of an important theatrical tradition.

4
At Home to the Players: Travelling Players at Country Houses

Lord.	Do you intend to stay with me to-night?
2. Players.	So please your lordship to accept our duty.
Lord.	With all my heart. [. . .]
	[. . .] There is a lord will hear you play tonight.
	(*The Taming of the Shrew*, Induction, 81, 93)[1]

As the portraits of fictional acting companies in plays such as *The Taming of the Shrew* indicate, professional touring players did not confine themselves to performing in urban, public venues. Performances were also staged in private town and country houses. Indeed, for many acting companies private house performances were an important and lucrative alternative to public, urban productions; and, after 1598 and the revision of the Act against Vagabonds, they became one of the few kinds of performance permitted lesser troupes, the right to perform publicly being confined to royal and noble companies.[2] Unsurprisingly, some lesser companies (such as the itinerant Yorkshire troupe led by Catholics Robert and Christopher Simpson) specialised in private-house performances in the Jacobean period.[3]

There are many records of metropolitan and regional acting troupes performing privately on tour and more are likely to be found. Major professional companies regularly included country house stops in their touring itineraries. There is evidence of at least ninety-five company visits to such houses between 1559 and 1625 in the published REED collections alone, with visits being paid to more than a dozen country seats.[4] The actual number of country house stops and homes visited is likely to have been much greater, as is the number of performances staged in Elizabethan and Jacobean country houses.[5] In general, there is little information about performances in small town and country houses. If such house owners kept household accounts they have rarely survived. Evidence about players' visits to greater country residences is more plentiful. This chapter focuses, therefore, on larger country house performances; but the conventions of performance in these regional households are unlikely to have differed substantially from those observed when troupes staged plays in smaller provincial houses.

I

The Renaissance country house

In order to contextualise play performances in country houses some understanding of the physical make-up of the houses and their place in contemporary culture is necessary. Thanks to the work of scholars such as Mark Girouard a considerable amount of information about Renaissance England's country houses is now available. Indeed, a detailed picture of such residences and their place in contemporary English culture emerges if one consults general texts such as Girouard's *Robert Smythson and the Elizabethan Country House*, and *Life in the English Country House*, and more specialised studies such as Alice Friedman's *House and Household in Elizabethan England: Wollaton Hall and the Willoughby Family*.[6] The following brief survey of early modern country houses is indebted to this research, and draws on the findings of Girouard in particular.

In the early modern period the number of country houses proliferated as house building became popular at all levels of society. In Yorkshire, for example, 'at least 280 manor houses were either built from the ground or substantially improved' between 1559 and 1642.[7] It was not a fashion confined to the traditional wealthy classes either; gentry families and successful businessmen were also buying and building country houses. The most spectacular new homes were the so-called 'prodigy houses', which sought to be innovative as well as grand in design. Examples include Theobalds and Audley End, the latter apparently costing up to £80,000. William Harrison drew attention to the increasingly fine quality of many noble houses in his *Description of England* (1587), describing them as 'so magnificent and statelie as the basest house of a baron dooth often match in our daies' with those 'of princes in old time'.[8] The 'ability to consume conspicuously was thought to be one of the distinct attributes of a great man or woman'.[9] Erecting a grand house was therefore a means of manifesting one's wealth and gentility. In some cases, patrons were seeking to impress a very specific audience such as the monarch. Writing of the great Elizabethan 'prodigy' houses, Stone notes that: 'Their sole justification was to demonstrate status, their sole function to entertain the sovereign on one of the summer progresses.'[10] Country houses were also, traditionally, 'power houses – the houses of a ruling class'. Consequently, 'from the Middle Ages until the nineteenth century' anyone that became wealthy, 'and was ambitious for himself and his family automatically invested in a country estate'.[11]

The buildings

Renaissance country houses varied in size and lavishness of decoration, but some common characteristics can be identified. In the early Tudor period it was fashionable to build large houses (of two or more floors) around courtyards, while house building on a compact, rectangular or square plan, without courtyards, had become more popular by the end of the sixteenth century. Gawthorpe Hall (Lancashire) is a fine example of this new style of house (see Illustration 10). Many early modern manor houses are also distinguished from their medieval predecessors by their exterior symmetry and incorporation of classical decoration.[12] Internally, most housed a series of chambers (for daily use and sleeping accommodation), kitchen facilities, and a large hall. By the turn of the century, they often incorporated a long gallery and great chamber as well. A number of spaces were therefore potentially available for performance use, but most plays appear to have been staged in halls or great chambers.

The medieval hall (from which those of the early modern period derived stylistically) was generally the heart of the household, literally and metaphorically. Often in a central location, parallel with the length of the house, halls served a number of roles in the life of the household. Traditionally, they had functioned as communal dining rooms, and were used 'for receiving guests and saying goodbye to them, and for all kinds of entertainment'.[13] By the sixteenth century the hall's role in household life had changed somewhat. It was rarely used for dining; and it became less usual to receive guests there, great chambers often being favoured as the setting for such receptions.[14] But halls were still used as places of entertainment on some occasions, particularly those organised on a large scale, such as seasonal festivities. Likewise, they remained important spaces for the display of a patron's wealth and status: 'the most splendid internal features of such houses continued to be their hall screens, topped with ornate overhanging galleries and pierced by either one or two impressive archways'.[15]

The halls of early modern country houses were much like the dining halls of Oxford and Cambridge university colleges. They were usually large, rectangular spaces, varying in size. Some country houses were built with halls approaching the size of those in the great royal palaces. The hall at Kenilworth Castle, measuring 90 feet by 45 feet, was comparable in width with the halls at Windsor and Hampton Court, measuring 108 feet by 37 feet and 108 feet by 42 feet, respectively.[16] Other houses – including those visited by travelling players – contained halls of more modest dimensions. The great hall at Stoneyhurst measured 60 feet by 27 feet in the early modern period, while that at Ingatestone Hall measured roughly 40 feet by 20 feet. The dining halls at Gawthorpe and Smithills Hall (the two Lancashire houses of the Shuttleworths) are more compact, measuring 30 feet by 20 feet 4^1/$_2$ inches and approximately 30 feet by 34 feet, respectively (see Illustration 11).[17]

At the upper end of the hall there would often be a dais, lit by an oriel window, while, at the lower end, service doors typically led to the kitchen and buttery. By the sixteenth century it was common for the lower end of the hall to be fitted with a screen before the service doors as well. Such screens were often wooden and might be ornately carved. Sometimes they were topped by a minstrels' gallery, as at Gawthorpe, a house visited by several Jacobean playing companies.[18] The furnishing in halls was usually relatively simple, as is revealed by the 1612 Household Inventory for the Cholmeley family's Brafferton home (Yorkshire). Under the entry for the 'Haule' all that is listed are '1 longe table, 2 longe formes, 1 shelfe, 1 buffet throwen, 3 foetstol, 4or doers, 2 lockes & keyes [one?] iron slott'.[19] The simplicity of hall furnishings probably added to their attractiveness as performance venues. As well as affording a reasonably large playing space, they were rooms that could be readily adapted for performance use. Some of the furniture commonly found in halls such as benches might even be used for performances, providing seated accommodation for spectators.

The phrase 'great chamber' originally only specified 'a large chamber, and was used as a distinguishing description in houses that had several chambers'; but by the end of the sixteenth century it had come to refer to the room that was 'the ceremonial pivot of the house', 'the place of state, where the lord keepeth his presence'.[20] Consequently, it was common for them to be richly furnished and lavishly decorated, as at Hardwick New Hall where the room is fitted with a magnificent plaster frieze depicting the hunter goddess, Diana in the woods. They could also be large, indeed, comparable with halls in their dimensions. This is the case at Hardwick New Hall where the High Great Chamber is roughly '66 feet long' and $32^1/4$ feet wide.[21] Their frequently large size may be one of the reasons for their use as performance spaces and for their importance as recreational and social spaces more generally.[22]

The household

Country houses not only accommodated their owners and their families. They were usually home to a body of servants as well, most of whom were men. Collectively these constituted the 'household'. The size of such households varied. While the number of 'family' members was often similar (typically being confined to the owner's close relations) the number of servants retained by country house owners could differ substantially.[23] In 1600 Sir Thomas Hoby of Hackness appears to have employed only fourteen domestic servants, while the household of the powerful Stanleys of Lancashire 'exclusive of the family, varied from 115 to 140 people [. . .] in the 1580s'.[24] Players visiting a country house could probably expect to have dealings with several members of the household. They might be welcomed by its steward (the most important officer in many houses), while their payment for playing might be presented to them by a household's treasurer or 'comptroller'.[25] Another official with whom visiting entertainers might have had to liaise, if they were to perform in the hall, was the marshal of the hall. Where such an officer existed, he was responsible for maintaining discipline and order in hall, and would probably be in charge, therefore, of the accommodation and management of whatever audience was collected for a hall performance. He might also have been the figure responsible for helping players with their preparations, as is the case in Marston's *Histrio-mastix* when Sir Oliver Owlet's Men are invited to perform in the hall at the house of Lord Mavortius.[26]

Entertainment

Country houses were not only built to provide accommodation or to be status symbols. They were places of, and for, entertainment. Those families living in a country house for most or even part of the year would often have many leisure hours to fill. 'Ennui' was thus one of the hazards of country house life for their owners and families, as Lord Pembroke suggested when he complained at Wilton in 1601 that 'I have not yet been a day in the country, and I am as weary of it, as if I had been a prisoner there seven years'.[27] If such boredom was to be alleviated diversions were necessary. Country house entertainment took many forms, from card playing and banquets, to musical exhibitions and play productions. Conspicuous expenditure on such entertainment also afforded another way of impressing others with one's wealth, while inviting guests to share recreation and refreshments in one's house was a way of demonstrating one's gentility. The 'association between house-keeping and true nobility [. . .] kept alive in the conduct literature and in popular imagery' meant that great men and women were expected to be generous hosts; and country houses provided the ideal arena in which to exercise such hospitality.[28] Large-scale entertainments or grand acts of hospitality were often organised to coincide with traditional holidays or special occasions. The Petres organised a round of celebra-tions involving the local community during the Christmas holidays of 1551–52. On Christmas Day 'many Ingatestone folk were invited to dinner'; on a later day, people from the 'villages of Puttsbury and Margetting were entertained'; and on New Year's Day 'a second lot of Ingatestone people were among the guests' at dinner.[29]

Plays might form part of such celebrations but were not always 'occa-sional' entertainments. They might be staged for the exclusive amuse-ment of family or household members, as appears to have been the case when Lord Wharton's players were paid for performing 'one play before my Lo: and the Ladies at Heslewood' in 1614–15.[30] But they were also a form of entertainment that might be shared with guests. The play per-formed at Lathom House during the New Year period in 1588–89 was given before Sir John Savage and the Earl of Derby's household council. This was a select, prestigious audience, Derby's council including 'many of the leading gentry of Lancashire' (men such as Sir Richard Shireburn and Sir Peter Legh).[31] A larger, more socially mixed audience enjoyed the entertainment offered on one occasion at Sir John Yorke's house, Gowthwaite Hall (1609–10). An audience including family, friends, neighbours and local people watched the Simpson players' performance of *St Christopher* (a morality play).[32] The crowd assembled was so large in fact (numbering over 'fowerscore or a hundreth persons') that it was necessary to turn some prospective spectators away and one local woman was said to have been injured in the press of people wishing to enter the performance.[33]

Playing at country houses

The payments to players in surviving household accounts are the main source of evidence for country house play performances. The references that occur in such accounts are generally brief. Often the only details recorded are the name of the company and the amount of money they were paid.[34] The titles of the plays performed are not usually mentioned, although there are exceptions. In 1618 Sir Richard Cholmeley of Brandsby Hall rewarded Lord Wharton's Men for 'one play, the dumb Knight', while Skipton Castle's Caroline accounts include a payment to 'a certeyne company of Roguish players whoe represented A new way to pay old debts'.[35] More detailed records occasionally mention the size of the company and the timing or place of the performance(s). In 1611 the Earl of Cumberland paid three pounds to fourteen players of Lord Derby 'whoe Plaied two Plaies heere at Londsbrough', one after dinner and one after supper; while the Stanleys' 1588–89 household records allude to a play given at night 'in the halle'.[36] Additional information about the size of companies and the length of their visits sometimes emerges from kitchen accounts. The Clifford pantry records periodically list meals provided for players at their northern houses, Londesborough and Skipton Castle. When Lord Wharton's Men visited Londesborough in 1600 the troupe, consisting of eight players, was provided with supper on 28 January, dinner and supper on 29 January, and was rewarded with thirteen shillings and four pence on 30 January. It seems they visited the house – and enjoyed the Clifford family's hospitality – for two nights, arriving on the 28 January in time for supper and leaving on 30 January, after receiving their reward.[37]

Other sources such as ecclesiastic and secular court records sometimes provide supplementary evidence for private house performances. In these cases, the records usually exist because the production proved in some way contentious. For example, we learn that the Simpson players performed in Roxby Hall (Yorkshire) in 1609 from a Star Chamber complaint of Sir Thomas Hoby against Sir Richard Cholmley:

> the sayd Staige players Cominge into his sayd fathers howse at Roxby [. . .] *Sir* Richard Cholmley being then present [. . .] in despite of the sayd *Sir* Thomas his warrante [for the players' arrest] did not only suffer but [. . .] did giue leave and lycence vnto the sayd players to play diuers stage playes [. . .] Conteyninge in them much poperie.[38]

Evidence that the same playing company performed at Gowthwaite Hall (the house of fellow Yorkshire nobleman, Sir John Yorke) is to be found in the records of another contemporary Star Chamber case. The mainly Catholic troupe's production of a religious play called *St Christopher* became one of the subjects of a Star Chamber suit pressed by local Puritan justice, Sir Stephen Procter, against Yorke. The play was not seditious in itself. The controversy arose from the alleged insertion of a blasphemous interlude in which it was said an English Minister and a 'popishe preist' were 'personated', and a 'disputacon counterfeyted betwixt' them at the end of which the Minister was 'ouercome' and carried away by the Devil.[39] It was an interlude calculated to please the Simpsons' largely recusant audience at Gowthwaite and to rile local Puritans such as Procter.

In keeping with Star Chamber proceedings, depositions were taken from numerous witnesses, including several of the actors. The depositions contain detailed information about the Gowthwaite performance, but the statement made by company 'clown', William Harrison, is additionally intriguing, alluding to the performance of two other plays at Gowthwaite: 'Perocles, prince of Tire, And [. . .] kinge Lere'.[40] To find an itinerant company, based in the north of England, staging recently-published Shakespeare plays is striking. It suggests the Simpsons made 'arrangements to procure the very latest, most popular and fashionable plays from London' and were using printed plays as prompt books.[41] It had been thought that players sometimes used printed plays in this way but the Simpson case affords direct evidence of the practice and confirms that acting companies in places far removed from London had access to, and were interested in, performing plays fashionable in the capital.[42] It also suggests that the plays of Shakespeare and his contemporaries had a role to play in provincial as well as metropolitan culture.

Contemporary letters and accounts occasionally include references to country house play performances as well. In his letter to Sir Anthony Bacon about the 1595–96 Christmas festivities at Burley-on-the-hill, Jacques Petit includes a brief description of an otherwise unknown performance of *Titus Andronicus* considered below.[43] Similarly intriguing, but less reliable, is an allusion to a performance of *As You Like It* at Wilton House in 1603. It occurs in the diary William Johnston Cary, a 'nineteenth century scholar and historian', kept while a tutor at Wilton in the summer of 1865: 'The house (Lady Herbert said) is full of interest: [. . .] we have a letter, never printed, from Lady Pembroke to her son, telling him to bring King James from Salisbury to see *As You Like It*; "we have the man Shakespeare with us".'[44] The Court did visit Wilton in December 1603 and the King's Men (Shakespeare's company) were paid for 'presenting before his majestie one playe' on 2 December; but there is no further evidence to identify the play performed as *As You Like It* and the letter mentioned by Cary has not been found.[45]

Dramatic evidence can also be revealing. A number of extant plays appear to have been written for private-house performance and contain references to their auspices, including Thomas Nashe's *Summer's Last Will and Testament* (1592), thought to have been prepared for performance before Archbishop Whitgift at his palace in Croydon.[46]

Indirect evidence of the conventions observed when players mounted productions in private-houses is also supplied dramatically. A number of contemporary plays contain representations of private-house performances including *The Book of Sir Thomas More* (1592), *A Midsummer Night's Dream* (*c*.1594–96), *The Taming of the Shrew* (*c*.1592), *Hamlet* (*c*.1600), *Histrio-mastix* (*c*.1598) and *A Mad World, My Masters* (1605–06). Although these fictional portraits cannot be assumed to reflect real practices, they are written to be recognisable depictions of private-house productions and are likely to provide an insight into at least some of the conventions observed when companies mounted such performances.

Patronising players

At a simple level, patrons are likely to have sponsored play performances in their homes because they wished to be entertained, while patronage of entertainment was a way of manifesting their wealth and nobility, as noted earlier. But plays also offered cultural stimulation, and, if London companies were sponsored, a means of keeping up to date with metropolitan fashions. Some country house owners are known to have had an enthusiastic taste for drama, collecting plays for their libraries, visiting the London playhouses, patronising dramatic companies, and occasionally practising as dramatists themselves. The Stanley family was especially renowned for its interest in theatre in the Elizabethan and Jacobean periods. They hosted players at their Lancashire residences (Knowsley and Lathom House), and the leading members of the family patronised their own playing companies.[47] The 6th Earl, William Stanley, was even reported to have written plays for professional players (none of which appears to survive).[38] It was a pastime that his wife was ready to encourage as a useful distraction from potentially more dissolute pursuits. Although estranged from him she wrote to her uncle Robert Cecil on his behalf (*c*.1599–1600), to ask that his players might not be 'bared from ther accoustomed plaing [. . .] for that my Lord taking delite in them, it will kepe him from mor prodigall courses'.[49]

House owners may have had more specific reasons for inviting or accepting the services of royal or noble players. Showing generosity to players with rich and powerful patrons was politically astute. Such troupes were their patrons' servants and representatives. How they were treated was a reflection on the image of their patron. Hence, royal companies tended to be welcomed and well rewarded whichever country houses they performed in. This was a way of hosts demonstrating their allegiance to, and respect for, royalty. But a lord or lady might reward an important noble's company richly as a means of showing respect for and/or seeking favour from a fellow peer in similar fashion.[50]

Arranging performances

In Marston's *Histrio-mastix* Sir Oliver Owlet's Men are invited to perform at the home of Lord Mavortius, his steward seeking them out to request their services twice.[51] Shakespearean troupes might be invited to perform at country houses in similar fashion. On other occasions players presented themselves unannounced in the hope that their services would be accepted, as occurs in *The Taming of the Shrew* (Induction, 77). The arrival of Sir Frances Foskew's players at Grimsthorpe (the Lincolnshire home of the Duchess of Suffolk) in 1560–61 appears to have been uninvited: 'Sir Fraunces Foskewes players [. . .] came to offer them selves to playe before my Ladies Grace', receiving three shillings and four pence as a reward.[52] Troupes' services were not always accepted, although they might receive hospitality and/or a reward. When Lord Vaux's players arrived at Londesborough in 1608–09 they were not allowed to play because it was Lent, but were given ten shillings, while in 1617 twenty shillings was paid at Skipton Castle 'to Bradshawe and his companie my Lo: darbies players in reward from my Lo: in spite he wold not heare them play'.[53]

It was customary for players to present themselves on arrival to a household official who would then announce their presence to the head of the household or another senior family member, as occurs when the players visit Elsinore in *Hamlet*.[54] A meeting with the head or senior member of the household might follow if he or she wished the players to perform, the company offering a choice of plays from which the patron could choose. When the Simpson company visited Gowthwaite Hall on one occasion in 1609–10 this involved a choice between two plays: 'the players presentinge themselues before Sir John yorke, he asked them what plaies they had, they told him the thre shirleyes, & St. Christofer, whervpon he willed them to play St. Christofer'.[55] The fictional lord in *The Taming of a Shrew* is offered rather less choice, when he commands an audience with the troupe recently arrived at his country residence:

> *Lord.*   Now sirs, what store of plaies have you?
> *Sander.* Marrie my lorde tis calde The taming of a shrew.
>   Tis a good lesson for us my lord, for us that are married
>   men.

> Lord.   The taming of a shrew, thats excellent sure,
> Go see that you make readie straight.[56]

The scene offers a comic representation of the usual negotiations between noble host and visiting players, part of the humour arising from the players' limited 'store' of works. In this scenario, the host is *not* offered a choice of plays.

Having reached agreement on the play(s) to be performed the lord might arrange for the actors to be 'well be-stow'd', and for assistance to be provided with their performance preparations, as occurs in *Hamlet* and in *The Taming of the Shrew* (Induction, 102).[57] The generous treatment companies could expect when visiting some country houses is demonstrated by the household accounts of the Cliffords. The pantry records show that visiting players were usually given 'supper the day they arrived, breakfast and frequently dinner the next day before they had to leave'. On some occasions even the stabling and feeding of their horses was paid for by the lord. In 1598 a payment to Lord Derby's players is followed by a payment 'for their horssmeayte three nyghtes and laiding'.[58] The length of companies' visits and the number of performances given varied, as indicated in Chapter 1, and country house patrons offered financial rewards of differing generosity.[59] Sometimes troupes may not have received any money. When Lord Clinton's players were at Londesborough in 1600–01 they were not paid, it seems, but were given dinner, supper and breakfast. This may mean that they did not perform or that they accepted the food and accommodation as payment in kind.[60]

Performance preparations

The location of private-house performances is rarely noted in household accounts, but what evidence there is suggests that plays were usually performed in the hall, and often in the evening.[61] Other spaces such as great chambers may have been used occasionally for performances, as well. For instance, Girouard suggests that the Queen's Men performed in the great chamber or gallery, rather than the hall when they visited Hardwick Hall in 1600.[62] At least some of the plays staged in Renaissance country houses were performed on stages, but there is too little evidence to know whether this was common practice.[63] Some performances may have been acted on the hall or chamber floor in a cleared 'place', as was apparently customary for private performances of early interludes. How spectators were accommodated is not usually mentioned in surviving records and probably varied depending on the nature and size of the audience anticipated. A small, elite audience could probably expect to be accommodated on chairs, while benches may have been provided if a larger, more diverse audience was assembled, paralleling arrangements in the metropolitan hall playhouses. In some cases there may have been standing spectators, too.

As professional travelling companies customarily carried a stock of playing gear, country house performances are likely to have been staged in costume, with props and stage furniture. Companies may even have been assisted in their preparations, being provided with access to additional playing gear such as costumes, a number of nobles apparently maintaining their own costume wardrobes. Alexander Houghton of Lea bequeathed his 'playe clothes' to Sir Thomas Hesketh in his 1581 will; and the Duke of Norfolk kept a collection of playing clothes at his Norwich palace.[64] The scene involving the players at the beginning of *The Taming of a Shrew* suggests that borrowing playing gear from hosts was customary. The troupe expect the lord's household to furnish certain props for their performance – including 'a shoulder of mutton [. . .] And a little vinegre to make our Divell rore' – and the lord calls for the actors' needs to be supplied.[65] Such on-site borrowing is also treated 'as the custom' in *A Mad World, My Masters*, the phoney acting company led by Follywit exploiting this tradition for a criminal purpose. Having extracted a number of expensive items from Sir Bounteous Progress (including his watch) the troupe flee taking their borrowed 'props' with them.[66]

II

Case study: *Titus Andronicus* at Burley-on-the-Hill, Rutland (1595–96)

To complement Part I's general survey of country house theatre, we now turn to a closer analysis of an example production, the performance of *Titus Andronicus* at Burley-on-the-Hill recorded in a letter written by a Frenchman, Jacques Petit, to his patron, Sir Anthony Bacon, in January 1596. The letter is one of several (in French) describing the Christmas celebrations at the Rutland home of Sir John Harington of Exton in 1595–96.[67] Petit had 'entered the service of Anthony Bacon in 1586' and was 'one of the several Frenchmen Bacon engaged as foreign intelligencers on behalf of the Earl of Essex' in the early 1590s.[68] However, at the beginning of 1596 Petit was serving as the French tutor for Sir John Harington's three-year-old son, having joined the household at Rutland in December 1595.[69]

Petit's account of the performance of *Titus Andronicus*, which formed part of the seasonal festivities at Burley, is short but intriguing:

> Les commediens de Londres son[t] venus icy por en auoir leur part. on les feit iouér le soir leur venus & le lendemain on les despecha On a fait icy vne mascarade de linuention de Sir Edward wingfield on a aussi ioué la tragedie de Titus Andronicus mais le monstre a plus valeu que le suiect.[70]

While Petit supplies little detailed information about the performance he does reveal that it was staged at night by a company of London – and therefore probably professional – players. He also provides some insight into the impact of the performance, indicating that, in his opinion, the staging was more impressive than the play's subject. Considered alongside the information about the Christmas celebrations provided in Petit's letter (and others written in this period), we can begin to reconstruct some aspects of the performance that Petit fleetingly describes.

The host

Sir John Harington of Exton (1540–1613) was descended from a gentry family 'that owed their wealth to office-holding among the Tudor monarchs and to a series of happy matrimonies'. In 1595 he was the senior head of the Haringtons and a wealthy man, having inherited one of the largest landed fortunes in England, when his father died in 1592. As well as owning the manors of Exton and Burley in Rutland, he held Combe Abbey (Warwickshire) 'as the marriage portion of his wife'.[71] In terms of social status and power, Sir John was one of the country's rising noblemen when he organised his grand display of seasonal hospitality; and his decision to exhibit such liberality towards his family, friends and neighbours may have been one way of demonstrating his growing status.

He held a number of government offices during the Elizabethan period but was most renowned, politically, following the accession of King James I. He was a distant relation of James and entertained him at Burley-on-the-Hill in 1603, when the King was on progress to England. He also received James's daughter, Lady Elizabeth, 'for a few days at Combe Abbey' in June 1603. At the Coronation of the King, Harington was 'created Baron Harington of Exton'; and in October that year he 'received the charge' of Lady Elizabeth. She came to live with Harington and his family at Combe Abbey and remained with them until 1608.[72]

Burley-on-the-Hill and Christmas 1595–96

The Haringtons purchased the Burley estate in 1550. Sir John acquired it in 1573, 'together with the neighbouring estate of Exton', and decided to build a large house at Burley.[73] This building (also known as the Manor House) was the location for the 1595–96 Christmas festivities and the *Titus* performance. It does not survive to the present and may have been rebuilt in the Jacobean period by George Villiers, Duke of Buckingham, when he 'bought the estate from the Haringtons', although more recent research suggests the Duke might simply have 'refurbished and extended the existing Elizabethan house'.[74] If this was the case information about the house in Buckingham's day potentially provides an insight into the make-up of the house at the end of the six-teenth century. One early plan suggests that the Harington house was an E-type stone building 'facing east but with an additional wing to the west at the back'.[75] Other nobles built similar houses: Doddington Hall in Lincolnshire (*c.*1595), is one such building and an example 'of what Sir John Harington's Burley may have looked like'.[76] Although Harington's house may not have been as grand as some of the surviving 'prodigy houses' of the Renaissance, it is likely to have been an impressive, comparatively large building. The fact that Sir John was able to host as many as nine hundred people at the house daily between Christmas Eve and Twelfth Night certainly suggests that the Manor House was spacious.[77]

The specific location for the *Titus* performance is not mentioned by Petit, but it is likely that the play was staged in the hall. This had already been a venue for some of the Christmas festivities, and was probably the largest indoor space at the Manor House. It could accommodate at least a hundred people at a time for Petit describes feasts being prepared for such numbers there:

Sir Jean disnoit a la sale por recueillir ses voisins & principaulx fermiers les festoyât avec vne chere excessive de toute sorte de mets & de tout sorte de vins Son me dhostel s'attendoit a regarder que rien ne manquast <.> aultres faisant garnir 4 or 5 longues tables de viande por quatre vints ou cent personnes a la fois. (Lambeth Palace Library MS 654, n° 167)[78]

The magnificence of the festivities of which the play performance formed one part is revealed if one examines Petit's general account of the merry-making that Christmas:

> L'ordre estoit tel por bien reigner & entretenir 8 ou 9 cens voysins qui venoint chasque iour faire leur feste icy [. . .] a disner & souper la musique allo <.> [alloit] 30 ou 40 gentilshommes seruans quand ils portoint la <.> [via*n*de?] deux ou 3 cheualiers & les Dames oultre force gente <.> & damoiselles estoint a sa table, puis apres le repas ensuiuoit la dance & ieux plaisans por donner a rire <.> seruir de recreation. (Lambeth Palace Library MS 654, n° 167)[79]

No expense was to be spared, it seems, when it came to ensuring that the Christmas celebrations at the Manor House were impressive. In this context, it is quite possible that the players' visit was specially arranged to be one of the highlights of the seasonal festivities. Organising entertainment on such a grand scale was expensive, and proved a 'great drain' on Sir John's finances at a time when he was already in some difficulties despite his landed wealth.[80] His readiness to indulge in such a lavish display of hospitality in these circumstances is intriguing: it suggests the perceived importance of conspicuous consumption and shows of generosity as tokens of social status and nobility in early modern England. From Sir John's perspective as a rising nobleman, such generous hospitality was perhaps a worthwhile (maybe even a necessary) investment.

The audience

Precise details of who and how many people watched *Titus* are not provided by Petit but, with up to nine hundred people visiting the Manor House daily, assembling an audience for the performance is unlikely to have been difficult. Indeed, the audience may have been large for a private performance. The hall where the play was staged could accommodate at least a hundred people for dinner and cleared of its long tables could possibly hold even more spectators. Those entertained at the house over Christmas included relatives, friends and neighbours. The audience for the play may have been similarly diverse. It is certainly likely to have included Sir John and his family, and evidence for the identity of some of the other possible spectators is found elsewhere in Petit's letters. Sir John had apparently invited all of his relatives to join him for Christmas. A number of them had accepted this invitation and therefore possibly attended the *Titus* performance, including Sir John's recently wed daughter and literary patron-to-be, Lucy Countess of

Bedford and her husband, and two of Sir John's sisters, Mary and Sarah and 'their respective husbands Sir Edward Wingfield and Francis Lord Hastings'.[81] The audience probably included some of the friends and neighbours feasted at the house as well, while the presence of Petit reveals that at least some household staff attended.

The performers

Petit simply describes the visiting players as 'Les commediens de Londres' (the comedians from London). However, as noted earlier, that they were from London suggests they were a professional troupe, possibly specifically invited to perform at Burley. The identity of the company is not certain, but the Lord Chamberlain's Men are the play's most likely performers, as *Titus* appears to have been their play in 1595.[82] If they were the performers there is a possibility that Shakespeare was part of the company that headed northwards for the seasonal performance as he joined the troupe in 1594. That Shakespeare's company should have travelled more than two hundred miles from the capital for an individual play performance during an already hectic round of metropolitan performances is rather remarkable. It is even more so given that such a journey is likely to have taken as much as four days each way and the fact that the company were performing at Court shortly before and after the New Year (27 December and 11 January), the period in which the Burley performance occurred.[83] The company that visited Burley may have been reduced in size, some members remaining in the capital, but we need not assume that this was the case. The whole troupe could have visited Burley for, as Knutson points out, we do not know the 'possible compensations of the invitation to travel'.[84] The grand scale of Harington's festivities suggests that they may have been great and more than attractive enough to draw Shakespeare's company from London. Sir John was evidently keen to guarantee the excellence of the entertainment offered his guests and may have been ready to offer a hefty reward in order to obtain the services of one of the leading London companies.

The play

How and why *Titus* was chosen for performance at Burley is not mentioned by Petit. When professional players visited country houses they usually appear to have offered hosts a choice from a selection of plays, and it is possible that this occurred when the Chamberlain's Men visited Burley. Alternatively, Harington might have specifically asked the troupe to come and perform *Titus*, having read or seen it or having heard the play recommended.[85] In either instance, *Titus* might seem an unusual choice for a Christmas holiday performance, with its bloody, violent revenge plot. But the play had been a great success on the public stage, its first recorded performance at the Rose Theatre in 1594 yielding 'takings' that were among the highest that season; and it enjoyed enduring popularity. In 1595 it probably remained a 'company show-piece'.[86] This might be sufficient explanation for the troupe's suggestion and/or Sir John's selection of the play for performance at Burley. It promised to be a crowd-pleaser and to offer audiences a taste of the best of metropolitan theatre. Jonathan Bate suggests the play may have appealed to Harington for another reason, as well. He notes Harington's links with the Essex circle and suggests that 'the play's exploration of the question of succession, and its possible vein of Tacitism, would have been of considerable interest to him'.[87] The play's treatment of succession was of contemporary relevance. With an ageing, childless monarch on the throne there was widespread concern about the English royal succession and how it should be decided in elite circles (including Essex's faction), fuelled by Elizabeth's refusal to nominate an heir. However, while Harington may have been particularly interested in the play's subject, there is no indication in Petit's account that the play was selected for this or any other political reason.

The performance

Like many eyewitness accounts of Renaissance play performances, Petit's account of the *Titus* production at Burley is frustratingly brief. While he reveals that the play was staged at night and offers his curt opinion that the spectacle was of more merit than the play's subject, he provides no detailed description of its staging or reception. Like many of the play's later critics it would seem Petit did not share the Elizabethan taste for bloody revenge tragedies. What is less clear is his precise opinion of the 'spectacle', for the comparison he draws between 'la monstre' and 'le suiect' is relative (Lambeth Palace Library MS 654, n° 167). Evidently, he thought the performance better than the play but this does not mean that he thought the performance good. Yet, that he was able to distinguish between the content and the presentation of the play is itself revealing, suggesting that there was a distinct performance text. The players did not simply recite the play but performed it, probably using costumes and props as was customary in touring performances. The likelihood that this was the case is increased if one accepts that the performers were the Chamberlain's Men. Shakespeare's company routinely performed with playing gear and was accustomed to performing in a variety of venues, including large private residences. As one of the two leading companies in 1595–96 it is not surprising that they should prove able performers either. Their invitation to perform at Court twice during the same Christmas season is one testimony to the high regard in which their theatrical talents were held in elite circles.

That the troupe's performance of *Titus* should be in some ways more impressive or memorable than the play's story is perhaps also less surprising when one considers the play's performance demands. Visual spectacle is vitally important in *Titus* with the play calling for sophisticated staging. In one of the most memorable scenes, Act 2 scene 3, Lavinia is called to appear with *'her hands cut off and her tongue cut out, and ravished'*, while in Act 3 scene 1, Aaron *'cuts off Titus' hand on-stage'*; and in Act 5 scene 2, Titus kills Chiron and Demetrius by cutting their throats on-stage. The play is also ambitious in its call for use of a number of playing levels. Action 'above' is required at several points, as in the opening scene which begins with *'the Tribunes and Senators aloft'*.[88] The play requires the use of a below-stage area, too, as the 'pit' in which Martius and Quintus are trapped with the body of Bassianus (Act 2 scene 2). During playhouse performances the gallery and stage-trap door could be used to provide these upper and lower playing areas. More ingenuity would have been required to give the illusion of action on different levels when performing in other venues, many of which would not afford such facilities. Compromises were no doubt necessary when performing in a private house rather than a purpose-built theatre, but in seeking to reproduce the staging of the play possible in playhouses like the Rose, such performances were still likely to be visually striking.

Indirect evidence regarding the staging of *Titus* in the Elizabethan period may provide a fuller insight into the play's Burley performance. There is a contemporary illustration of two episodes from the play. Known as the 'Peacham' drawing, it is thought to have been prepared by Henry Peacham, author of *The Complete Gentleman* (1622), some time between 1595 and 1605 (see Illustration 12).[89] It conflates two scenes from the first and last acts of the play showing Tamora pleading before Titus for her sons' lives and Aaron boasting of his wickedness. Below the drawing are extracts from the play. The illustration may not be based on an actual performance but is possibly informed by Peacham's knowledge of Elizabethan theatrical conventions and could preserve valuable information about costuming for the play.[90] What is particularly intriguing about the illustration in this regard is the fact that it shows characters in period and contemporary attire. Titus is dressed in Roman style with a toga and laurels and Tamora wears a loose patterned gown in keeping with English Renaissance conceptions of Gothic female clothing; but the two soldiers that stand behind Titus wear Elizabethan dress and carry contemporary halberds. This suggests the costuming for Elizabethan productions was historically and stylistically eclectic, with companies concentrating on attiring the main characters in what was perceived to be historically accurate fashion. Hence, when the Chamberlain's Men performed at Burley it is quite possible that only the major Roman and Gothic characters wore historic costumes, while minor characters wore contemporary dress. This combination of ancient and modern styles would have been curiously appropriate for a play that 'addresses issues in contemporary history via a Roman setting'.[91] Peacham's illustration also suggests that Aaron's actor would have worn black make-up to give the illusion of having authentically black skin.

Evidence regarding the Elizabethan staging of some of the play's key scenes is afforded by another contemporary source as well. In 1620 Frederick Menius published a volume in Leipzig called *Englische Comedien und Tragedien*, 'described as "the plays acted by the English in Germany"'. The eighth play included was the 'most lamentable tragedy of Titus Andronicus and the haughty empress'. As Bate reports, the text is 'a translation of Shakespeare's play into plain German prose, with heavy cutting and a reduction of the cast to twelve parts'. The structure of the scenes is essentially the same, however.[92] What is especially interesting about the German *Titus* is the fact that its text implicitly preserves evidence of performances of the play by English players 'within or shortly after Shakespeare's own lifetime'. Thus, even if it is not a precise record of the play's performance in Elizabethan theatres it is probably 'that of a company as close to [Shakespeare]' as we can get.[93]

The German *Titus* includes detailed stage directions, including a fascinating description of the performance of the Andronici's pledge to avenge their wrongs at the end of the play's central scene, Act 3 scene 1:

> *Now* Titus Andronicus *falls upon his knees and begins to chant a dirge, all the others sitting down by the heads. Titus takes up his hand, holds it up and looks to heaven, sobs and repeats the oath softly; he beats his breast and at the conclusion of the oath sets the hand aside. Then he takes up one head and then the other, swearing by each one in turn. Finally, he goes to [his daughter], who is kneeling, and swears by her also, as he did with the others, whereupon they all rise again.*[94]

The same elaborate ritual may have been used at this point in Elizabethan productions (including that at Burley), creating a memorable tableaux.

An evocative description is likewise provided for the staging of the 'bloody banquet' in the play's final scene. Menius describes how Titus, wearing a bloodied apron and carrying a knife, 'Goes to the pasties, cuts and places portions of them before the Emperor and the Empress' and then 'walks mournfully up and down before the table'.[95] Again, the directions suggest that the play's early performers were concerned with the creation of emblematic visual tableaux, with this scene being used to represent the grim and mournful character of Titus as revenger. It is possible that the scene was staged in similarly formal, stylised manner at Burley and might have been rendered even more shocking and memorable if also staged at one of the long tables previously used for the banqueting of Sir John's guests.

Whether or not the Burley production of *Titus* was performed in as spectacular a fashion as those staged by touring English actors in Germany or mounted in the playhouses of Elizabethan London, it is evident that it was not without theatrical sophistication. Indeed, it is possible that the troupe's staging of the play was ambitious, incorporating special effects (such as realistic bloody displays) and the creation of arresting visual tableaux of the kind described by Menius. This may be one of the reasons why Petit thought the spectacle noteworthy. The audience's reaction to the production is unrecorded, but whatever the general reception there was to be no encore. By the following day the players were on their travels again. Back in London, their theatrical fortunes continued to prosper and in 1603 they became the King's players and the leading company in the country. The troupe continued to tour and to perform in private houses such as Burley after 1596, but there is no evidence of them making a return trip to the Harington residence. Similarly, whether or not Sir John watched and enjoyed the *Titus* production, he does not appear to have hosted any other professional play performances, although he did entertain King James with *A Panegyricke Congratulatory* poem commissioned from Samuel Daniel, when the new monarch visited Burley in 1603.[96]

The performance of *Titus* and the round of Christmas entertainments in 1595–96 were part of a lavish and costly display of Sir John's generosity and wealth. From the viewpoint of a lord concerned to promote his social standing and living in an era in which generosity was a marker of one's nobility, the Christmas festivities at Burley were perhaps a worthwhile expense, as suggested earlier. They may also have seemed an appropriate contribution to the local community and its cultural life for a man wishing to be recognised as one of its leading nobles. It was, however, a display of largesse that Sir John does not appear to have repeated on the same scale again. This may have been a decision resulting from his growing financial problems in the early seventeenth century; but it is a choice he might also have made because he had proved his point socially. He had established his nobility and power. In the Jacobean period his status was arguably confirmed and enhanced with his elevation to the title of Baron Harington of Exton and his appointment as guardian for the royal princess.[97]

Conclusions

Noble patrons and their country houses could play a significant role in provincial dramatic culture. Indeed, in counties such as Rutland, where the population was small and dispersed, country houses like Burley afforded cultural centres, where people could occasionally converge and enjoy shared recreation and cultural stimulation, promoting and fostering community solidarity. At the same time, the play and masque performed at Harington's country house show that there was interest in drama in such regions and that provincial communities were not necessarily unaware of, or unfamiliar with metropolitan theatrical culture. Regionally-based acting companies were not necessarily ignorant of London theatrical fashions either, as the example of the Simpson players in Yorkshire (with their repertory of religious plays and popular Shakespearean texts) demonstrates. In fact, in some parts of the country people were possibly introduced to the plays of dramatists such as Shakespeare by touring London players (as occurred at Burley in 1595) *and* by local performers such as the Simpson players. If a fuller understanding of English Renaissance theatrical culture, and of the place of particular dramatists such as Shakespeare within that culture, is to be gained, regional productions by metropolitan and provincially based companies in private as well as public venues therefore need to be examined and taken into account.

5
Drama at Drinking Houses: Inn Performances

'playars of commedies Tragedies or other stage playes [. . .] may playe in their Innes yf yt so please them'
(Bridgnorth Council, 1601–02)[1]

Playing at inns in London

Before the opening and proliferation of purpose-built playhouses in Elizabethan London, acting companies were accustomed to performing in various places in the capital, but particularly favoured playing in inns. Certain drinking houses became famous as theatrical venues in the metropolis (such as the Bell, the Bull and the Bel Savage). Even when the first playhouses opened in London, inns continued to be popular playing places, especially during winter. When Queen Elizabeth's newly-formed company returned to London after touring the provinces in the summer of 1583, they were licensed to perform on Wednesdays and Saturdays at the Bull and Bell inns, rather than at one of the available playhouses.[2] The Lord Chamberlain's Men may have been performing at the Cross Keys Inn as late as the winter of 1594 (although they had the use of The Theatre and performed at the open-air playhouse in the summer), suggesting that the inn was the players' preferred winter venue. It is a preference that may have been based on the inn's provision of an indoor playing space.[3] The conversion of a number of London drinking houses (including the Red Bull and the Boar's Head) into theatres in the Elizabethan and Jacobean periods formalised what had become one customary use of certain metropolitan inns.

The series of corporate and government regulations which attempted to restrict inn performances within the city during the late sixteenth century are another testimony to the popularity of London inns as playing places throughout the Elizabethan period. In 1565 plays were prohibited in any tavern or inn 'wher any money shalbe demaunded or payd for the syght or hyrynge of the same players'; and an injunction of January 1569 ordered that 'inns, and brewhouses used for common plays must not be used for such a purpose after the hour of five'. A month later a further injunction limited the playing hours to between three and five in the afternoon.[4] These orders were supplemented in 1574 by a Common Council Act which sought to control inn playing in another respect:

> hearetofore sondrye great disorders and inconvenyences have beene found to ensewe to this cittie by the inordynate hauntinge of greate multitudes of people, speciallye youthes to playes, enterludes, and shewes, namelye occasyon of ffrayes and quarrelles, eavell practizes of incontinencye in greate Innes, havinge Chambers and secrete places adioyninge to their open staiges and gallyries.

Consequently, it was ordered that no inn or tavern keeper (or any other person) in London should 'causse or suffer to be openlye shewed or played, within the hows, yarde or anie other place within the Liberties of this Cyttie anie playe, enterlude, commodye, Tragidie, matter, or shewe, which shall not be firste perused and Allowed'.[5] The Act affords a vivid insight into corporate anxiety about plays at inns and the potential social dangers and disorder attendant upon them. Yet it does not prohibit inn performances but rather seeks to monitor them more carefully. Notably, the city council's main motive for introducing the legislation appears to have been their desire to control what happened off-stage – in 'secret places' – perhaps under the influence or cover of performances. In this respect the Act resembles a number of the regulatory orders passed by Elizabethan and Jacobean provincial corporations controlling the theatrical use of urban venues such as town halls (see Chapter 2). At the same time, the Act indicates that inn playing was common at this date and suggests such performances were expected to continue. The custom of playing at London inns only appears to have declined significantly in the late 1590s, after the Privy Council joined with the Common Council in closing inns to players entirely in 1594, a prohibition reiterated by the Privy Council in 1600. But inn performances in the capital and its suburbs were not entirely unknown even after this date.[6] John Taylor, the Water-poet, alluded to an after-supper performance of 'the Life and Death of Guy of Warwick' by the Earl of Derby's players at the Maidenhead Inn, Islington in 1618.[7]

I

Performing at provincial drinking houses

Purpose-built or converted playhouses were rare in the Elizabethan and Jacobean provinces.[8] As in London, drinking houses were one of the spaces usually available for use as temporary theatres by professional and amateur players. Indeed, a growing number and variety of drinking houses was to be found in most late sixteenth century towns. A 1577 government survey 'listed well over 17,000 drinking houses [. . .] in 30 counties'; and individual towns might include as many as twenty-two licensed alehouses alone, as was the case at Canterbury in the year of the survey. In most early modern towns, players would have found three kinds of drinking house: inns, taverns and alehouses.[9] Inns were generally 'large, fashionable establishments offering wine, ale and beer, together with quite elaborate food and lodging to well-heeled travellers', while taverns sold 'wine to the more prosperous, but without the extensive accommodation of inns'; and alehouses were 'normally smaller premises serving ale or beer (and later spirits)' and offering fairly 'basic food and accommodation for the lower orders'.[10]

Potentially, players could seek permission to perform in any available drinking house, and there is some evidence of plays and other kinds of performance occurring in provincial taverns and alehouses, but usually the performers were amateurs. The impromptu theatrical 'skit' in which local men 'dissembled a consistorie' court at Turner's alehouse in Langport, Somerset in 1611 is a fascinating example of the pseudo-dramatic activity hosted in some provincial alehouses. The performance (reminiscent of Falstaff's 'play extempore' in *Henry IV, Part 1*) included one man placing a cushion '3: corner wise' on his head as a mock bishop's mitre.[11] A play of *Henry VIII* performed at a Warrington alehouse as late as 1632 was also acted by local amateurs.[12] Evidence of major metropolitan companies performing in regional alehouses and taverns in similar fashion is scarce; most professional performances in provincial drinking houses are likely to have been staged at inns, as was the case in London.

Professional players at provincial drinking houses

Acting troupes were sometimes entertained at inns and taverns. When the Queen's Men visited Gloucester in 1559–60 corporate money was spent on a banquet for them 'at the taverne', while at Shrewsbury in 1560–61, 'iiijs xjd' was spent on Lord Willoughby's players at 'the Gullet', a public house, 'now the Hole in the Wall in Gullet Shut'.[13]

Various contemporary sources reveal that travelling players also stayed at inns when touring. When Norwich's Corporation paid Lady Elizabeth's Men forty shillings not to perform in the town, the gift was sent to them at 'the whight horse in Tombeland', suggesting the troupe was residing at the inn.[14] Similarly, we know from a case recorded in the Woodstock Portmoot Court Book in 1608–09 that Lord Chandos's players stayed at 'ye bell' inn in 'Buck Towne', Thomas Bradford admitting that he stole money from one of the players during their stay.[15]

There is also literary evidence of companies staying at inns. The *Merrie Conceited Jests of George Peele* (1606–07) includes a story about Peele staying at the same Bristol inn as a company of players, and borrowing the players' apparel to facilitate a mischievous trick:

> There was not past three of the company come with the cariage, the rest were behinde, by reason of a long iourney they had, so that night they could not inact, which George hearing had presently a stratagem in his head, to get his Horse free out of the Stable: and money in his purse to beare his charges vp to Londone.[16]

Peele proceeded to organise a phoney play performance, persuading the local mayor to reward him and the players to gather money at the door. When the time of the performance came, Peele went on stage and read a prologue that finished with the request that the audience, 'Sit still a while, Ile send the Actors to ye'. Having exited throwing fireworks, he fled the performance leaving the players to answer for him.[17] The anecdote may not be true. Indeed, it is difficult to imagine Peele being able to gull the typically shrewd actors described in provincial records. Nonetheless, the tale offers confirmation that it was usual for players to stay at inns, and to travel with their playing gear in a carriage.[18]

In London there is information about players acting at a number of inns. Players performed in provincial inns too, but records of individual performances in regional drinking houses are comparatively rare. Research thus far has identified less than twenty references to specific drinking house performances in the Elizabethan and Jacobean English provinces. That there are few clear records of drinking house performances does not necessarily mean that playing in public houses was unusual in the early modern provinces, although there may have been variations with inn playing being less common in some regions.[19] The paucity of evidence may reveal more about early modern record keeping and the limits of surviving forms of documentation. Much of the evidence for provincial performances in the period derives from records of payments for, or relating to, performances. The chances of finding such financial documentation in relation to drinking house productions are slimmer, since performances were less likely to be sponsored by a local body or private individual. Players at drinking houses were more likely to be paying to perform, offering their host a share of their 'takings' in return for the use of his or her house as a temporary theatre. The further evidence of drinking house drama which publicans' accounts might afford is unavailable to us. Financial documents from humbler early modern individuals, such as inn, tavern or alehouse keepers, are rarely preserved (if they were kept in any detail at the time).

The majority of the known drinking house productions appear to have been inn performances, and several of them are only recorded because they proved controversial.[20] For instance, we learn of a performance by Lord Chandos's Men at the Angel in Coventry in 1600 because the players played 'contrary to M*aiste*r maiors pleasure' and were consequently arrested and imprisoned.[21] Similarly, we discover that Lady Elizabeth's players staged an evening performance at the Blue Boar Inn in Maldon in 1619 because the players reportedly had a run-in with a local bailiff and were presented at the Maldon Court Sessions (see Illustration 13):

> The Jury presented – Moore gentleman and others of the company of Princess Elizabeth's players, because when they prolonged 'ther playes untill xi of the clock in the Blue-Boore in Maldon, Mr. Baylyff coming and requesting them to breake off ther play so that the companye might departe' they called Bayliff Frauncis 'foole' 'to the great disparagement of the government' of the borough.[22]

The comparatively serious manner in which the incident was treated may have been a reflection of the civic body's concern to assert its authority over the local community and those who dared to insult its representative. But it may also have been informed by local tensions regarding recreations such as theatre; tensions that had been acute in the late sixteenth and early seventeenth centuries when the acceptability of traditional pastimes had become a point of contention between the town's increasingly large, powerful Puritan community (led by minister, George Gifford) and its non-Puritans. While local Puritans were keen to enforce observation of the Sabbath and stricter control of secular pastimes, other locals championed their right to enjoy customary forms of entertainment such as plays.[23] When Moore and his peers chose to dispute with Bailiff Francis they were perhaps deliberately offering another 'performance' calculated to entertain and appeal to the sympathies of the latter (including their possible distaste for 'precise' corporate men concerned to regulate local entertainment).

The evidence relating to most of the known performances is less detailed. The plays performed are generally unnamed and in one of the few instances where a play is identified the performance does not appear to have taken place. In 1624 Lady Elizabeth's players advertised their intention of performing a comedy called *The Spanish Contract* at the White Horse in Norwich (a lost play probably capitalising on contemporary anti-Spanish feeling).[24] The troupe had not received permission to perform, however, and the production appears to have been prevented.[25] Often all that is preserved in surviving records is the name of the inn and the year of the performance. In other cases, the playing troupe is named but the inn is not identified, as in Leicester's 1599 civic accounts, where a payment is recorded to a joint acting troupe: 'The Erle of Derbyes players and The Erle of Dudleys players, ioyned (at this present) togeyther as one company it is agreed to pay them 20s to playe at their Inn this night.'[26]

Additional evidence of drinking house performances and indirect proof that playing at inns was customary in at least some parts of provincial England is found in regional civic orders, a number of corporations issuing theatrical regulations relating or alluding to inn playing. In Norwich the corporation prohibited play performances at the White Horse Inn in 1601, suggesting that it was a recognised playing venue,[27] while in Chester, the town authorities complained about servants and apprentices resorting 'to Innehowses to behold [. . .] Plaies and there manie times wastfullie spende thar M*aste*rs goodes' in the preface to their 1616 civic order restricting plays at the Town Hall and at night in the city.[28] Other regional corporations actively encouraged the use of inns for plays. At Bridgnorth in 1601–02 civic officials prohibited players from using the Council House or Town Hall, but agreed that they might 'playe in their Innes, yf yt so please them'. In 1620 Southampton's Corporation passed a similar order prohibiting plays at the Town Hall, but allowing players to 'provide their places for their representacions in their Innes or else where they can best provide'.[29] In 1624 the civic authorities in Salisbury were more specific, passing an order which stated that 'players from hencefourthe shall make theire playes at the George in high streate'. The George possibly lent itself to performance use, having several spaces adaptable for playing, including a large chamber that survives in the inn's west range, and a galleried inn-yard (see Illustration 14).[30]

Orders restricting players' use of civic buildings were passed in a number of early modern communities but few specify an alternative venue for plays as do the orders issued by the Bridgnorth, Southampton and Salisbury authorities. However, as one of the spaces usually still available to players in Jacobean towns it is possible that inns were one of the alternative venues to which companies turned in other communities, too. Gurr suggests that inns may even have become the most common playing venue in the Stuart period, as players' access to other urban spaces was restricted and touring troupes no longer found themselves obliged to seek permission to perform from local authorities. He suggests that this shift in practice could also account for the decline in records of companies performing in regional communities in the Stuart period: troupes 'were now regularly visiting towns and playing at inns as a matter of routine without first regularly securing leave from the mayor, or at least without receiving any payment, so that the accounts take no note of them'.[31]

Positive evidence that inns became travelling players' usual playing venue in Jacobean urban communities is lacking, however, as scholars such as James Gibson have noted; and there may be other explanations for the declining number of dramatic records in some regions in the Stuart period. In East Kent, for example, the growing strength of Sabbatarianism and Puritanism led to the introduction of steadily more prohibitive legislation regarding entertainment, making it more difficult for players to tour profitably and legally in the region. 'Whether plays and popular entertainments were suppressed outright, as in Canterbury and Maidstone, or tolerated with strict controls, as in Hythe, the Stuart years must have been bleak for travelling players in Kent.'[32] In this context, Gibson argues that the apparent decline in the number of players visiting and performing in Jacobean Kent probably reflects a genuine reduction in touring and not simply a decline in records as a result of troupes performing at inns and eluding official notice. Indeed, in the cultural climate of Stuart Kent, he thinks it unlikely that playing at inns could or did flourish: 'Stage players may have been making routine unofficial performances in the local inns elsewhere in the country during the Stuart years but not, I think, in Kent.'[33] Without more evidence we cannot know definitively whether inn playing did or did not become more common in the Stuart period or whether this is one reason for the decrease in official records of players' touring. But it remains possible that inn playing became more frequent in some Jacobean cities and towns (if not in Kent) as players' access to other urban buildings was restricted.

The attractions of drinking houses

Inns lent themselves to use as playing venues in a number of ways. Major inns were often among 'the largest public buildings in a town or village' and might afford a number of spaces suitable for theatrical use, including public and private indoor chambers and open-air yards, as at the George in Salisbury.[34] William Harrison indicated how extensive some Elizabethan inns were when he described them as 'able to lodge 200 or 300 persons and their horses at ease'. At the same time, touring players could enjoy the convenience of staying at their place of performance, inns affording good accommodation and refreshments, and inn-yards usually providing a secure, spacious place for the storage of players' carts.

Staying at an inn could be expensive, however, and was usually more costly than lodging at alehouses or taverns. According to Ingram, a bed for the night would cost at least sixpence and an average meal might cost a further sixpence. Charges would also be made for the board and stabling of any horses a company travelled with. In the 1590s 'a normative charge for a night at a country inn would have been about four pence for hay and litter, and eight pence to a shilling for a bushel of oats'.[35] For a company of six players travelling with one horse and having one inn meal a day, this could amount to a daily charge of twelve shillings. Even if a company managed to make some economies and reduce its daily expenditure to ten shillings, the players would need to be performing every other day and collecting 'twenty shillings at each performance just to break even'. This was a sizeable amount of money to have to earn regularly.[36] That players sometimes found the costs of residing at inns beyond their means, finds indirect confirmation in Marston's portrait of Sir Oliver Owlet's troupe in *Histrio-mastix* (c.1598). In Act 6, scene 1, the hostess of the inn where the players have been staying complains to a local constable that they have not paid for their board and lodging, prompting the troupe's playwright to offer her 'some-what out o'th stocke' of their playing gear in lieu of payment.[37] Their real counterparts may have been occasionally obliged to resort to similar shifts while touring. In 'dire enough straits', troupes may even have agreed to play at an inn 'in exchange for room and board, with the innkeeper taking all the profits'.[38]

Inns were increasingly important in early modern England as 'social centres', particularly for the wealthy. They 'not only performed important victualling services', but 'acted as the centre point of a galaxy of commercial, governmental and leisure activities'.[39] To play at inns was to perform therefore in one of the spaces at 'the heart of the social world'; and local and visiting inn customers provided a ready, potentially generous audience, most inn customers being drawn 'from the landed, mercantile and professional classes'.[40] Hosting players and play performances had its benefits for innkeepers, too. He or she could expect to profit from the increased trade provided by the audiences drawn to performances, while hosting entertainment was a means of publicising one's inn and attracting increased trade in the longer term.

Alehouses and taverns were more numerous than inns and cheaper to stay at, but were typically smaller and less readily adaptable for performance. Some urban alehouses might include a parlour and hall which 'served as drinking rooms, with the kitchen providing extra space' when necessary, but many were 'rudimentary with little more than a hall and a loft above', both of which might be small.[41] Alehouses and taverns were not necessarily provided with a yard and did not usually afford stabling facilities either, which was a potential problem for a troupe travelling with a horse-drawn wagon. Room for performing, storing playing gear and for audiences was generally likely to be limited. Performances at taverns and alehouses were likely to be less profitable than inn productions as well, because their customers were generally poorer. This was particularly true of alehouses as the majority of alehouse customers 'were recruited from the bottom half of the social order'.[42] As playing venues, alehouses were further disadvantaged because they and their customers were subject to tighter, more prohibitive regulation than other drinking houses. Unlike inns, alehouses were required to have a licence from local justices of the peace and many corporations issued orders controlling their closing hours and the time customers were allowed to spend in such establishments.[43] However, like inns, taverns and alehouses were important social spaces and places of communal recreation, catering for the less affluent members of society, as inns catered for its wealthier members. For lower-class entertainers, alehouses and taverns were places where they could more easily gain admission and entertain their social peers; and players drawn from the lower social orders are known to have stayed and performed occasionally at alehouses.[44] Some alehouse keepers actively promoted entertainment at their houses as a way of attracting custom, too. 'John Johnson of Litherland in Lancashire "did keepe and mayteyne att his house there beare beatinge and fidlinge" in 1617, and George Burrell of Morton Tower, Essex, procured "a boye with a Hobby horse and two other men that shewed tricks and drew much companie to his house"'.[45]

II

Performances

After finding a publican ready to host dramatic entertainment, it is likely that troupes and their hosts decided between them when and where performance(s) were to be staged and agreed upon the sharing of 'takings', although not all play performances at provincial drinking houses were necessarily intended to be public or commercial. Permission to use drinking houses for playing was not always sought either. Highwayman Gamaliel Ratsey is reported to have rewarded a troupe for performing 'a private play' before him at a provincial inn in the anonymous pamphlet about his life, *Ratsey's Ghost*; while alehouse keeper, Gregory Harrison, denied knowing that a group of young men intended to perform a play at his Warrington alehouse in 1632.[46]

Direct evidence regarding the staging of professional drinking house performances is limited but some general points can be made. For instance, we know that performances were staged in the daytime and evening as in London. At Norwich in 1583 the Queen's Men played at the Red Lion in the afternoon, while Lord Chandos's Men performed at the Angel in Coventry at night in 1600.[47] Similarly, we know that plays were performed in a variety of spaces at drinking houses, including indoor chambers and open-air yards.[48] Inn-yards varied in size and shape but could be large and potentially well suited to use for entertainments involving large audiences. (For instance, the yard at the Boar's Head Inn in London appears to have measured 121 feet 52 inches at its longest point and 54 feet 6 inches at its widest point.)[49] At least one inn-yard performance is recorded in the early modern provinces, the Queen's Men performing in the yard of the Red Lion, Norwich (1583).[50] Inn chambers were used as well, and may have been the more common venue for Elizabethan and Jacobean touring performances since Shakespearean troupes generally seem to have favoured indoor venues when travelling.[51]

When Lord Berkeley's players visited Dorchester (Dorset) in 1608 and were denied permission to perform in the local town hall, they performed instead in a private inn chamber, as one local man explained: 'Sir Adryan Scroope Knight beynge at [. . .] mr Chubbes howse at supper offered that the sayd players should playe in his chamber in an Inne after supper'.[52] Similarly, the night-time performance by Lady Elizabeth's players at the Blue Boar in Maldon (1619) is likely to have taken place indoors, possibly in the spacious first floor hall apparently to be found

at the inn in the early seventeenth century.[53] Information about the size
of inn chambers is limited but suggests that they – like yards – varied in
size and shape. Some inns afforded spacious chambers. In Cambridge,
the Bear (later known as the Black Bear) was 'used for political assemblies' in 1643, 1644, and 1662, and as a concert hall 'by the Music Club'
from 1773 to 1809; uses that suggest that the inn 'had a capacious hall,
which would have been suitable for plays' of the kind staged there in
1599–1600.[54] Other inn rooms are likely to have been much smaller. The
size of the room in which Lord Berkeley's players performed at Dorchester (1608) is unknown, but it is unlikely to have been especially large
as it was a private room probably intended for accommodation rather
than entertainment.

Players performing indoors could generally expect inn chambers to
be well furnished with tables, chairs, benches and soft furnishings.
Alehouse and tavern rooms were less likely to be richly furnished but
were not necessarily barely equipped. Clark reports how, in 'the main
drinking rooms of larger premises one sees an array of chairs, joined
tables, plus the usual stools, perhaps with a mirror in the hall or a Bible
on a lectern'.[55] Such furnishings were potentially available for players'
use and for the accommodation of spectators. In some instances, players
would have been performing against a painted backdrop as well, many
drinking houses containing chambers decorated with wall paintings.
Popular subjects for such paintings included stories 'drawn from classical mythology but more frequently from the Bible'.[56] At the White Swan
Inn in Stratford-upon-Avon the ground floor room is painted with
'scenes from the story of Tobias and the Angel, divided by feigned
pilasters and flanked by panels of foliage and flowers'; while in the 1630s
Donald Lupton described how in London alehouses you might see 'the
history of Judith, Daniel in the lion's den, or Dives and Lazarus painted
upon the wall'.[57] Such painted backdrops could have occasionally
proved curiously appropriate or added to the resonance of a play's
subject (for instance, in *Henry IV Part 1* Falstaff's line about his soldiers
being as 'ragged as Lazarus in the painted cloth' might have gained
comic point and poignancy if performed in a room painted with the
story of Lazarus).[58] In other cases there might have been an interesting
tension between the subject of the play and its painted inn-chamber
backdrop.

Preparing the spaces

No evidence has been found thus far to suggest that any Elizabethan or
Jacobean provincial inns were fitted with purpose-built stages or tiring

houses of the kind erected in the yard at the Boar's Head Inn in London, but at least some inn productions were performed on stages.[59] The nature of these stages is usually unknown and may have varied from improvised platforms built on-site to demountable wooden stages brought by the players. It may not always have been practical or possible to set up a stage, however, especially if players were performing in a low-ceilinged inn chamber, and it is therefore likely that some drinking house productions were performed without any platform. How the spectators at public drinking house performances were accommodated is generally unrecorded, too. When playing indoors it is likely that the spectators were placed before the playing area and may have been seated (using available benches, stools and chairs), while during yard performances most spectators probably stood in the yard around the stage or playing area. At inns with galleried yards it may have been possible to accommodate some spectators in the galleries as well, as occurred at the open-air playhouses and converted inn theatres of the capital.

Audiences

In the early Elizabethan period players at inns may have raised money from their performances by making an audience collection at the end, as sometimes occurred when troupes played at town halls. But this practice gradually appears to have been replaced with a more formal system of entry charges of the kind used at the Elizabethan playhouses. Typically, a company member would be placed at the entry to the playing space with a collection box. Those people wishing to see performances were required to pay a fee before entering. That at least some troupes were using this system as early as the 1580s is revealed by the Queen's Men's infamous Red Lion performance at Norwich that ended in a fracas after one spectator resisted paying the gatekeeper an entry fee.[60]

Direct information about the spectators at inn performances is rare, and there is virtually no evidence in relation to alehouse or tavern audiences. However, if the audiences for inn performances were drawn at least partly from the body of usual inn customers, one would expect the spectators to be mainly male and to include people belonging to society's higher or wealthier groups (such as gentlemen and wealthy merchants). One might also expect to find some local tradesmen, craftsmen and yeomen. Although such people were less frequent inn customers a play performance may have been the kind of special occasion which would attract their custom. People from lower social groups and children were probably less likely to attend inn performances, but may not have been unknown in play audiences. Certainly, the authorities in Jacobean Chester suggested that young apprentices and servants attended inn performances in their town.[61]

III

Case study: the Queen's Men at the Red Lion, Norwich (1583)

In 1583 Edmund Tilney, Queen Elizabeth's Master of the Revels, hand-picked twelve actors from the leading troupes of the period to form a new company of Queen's Men.[62] During the summer of 1583 the players were engaged in their first provincial tour. Their travels included a visit to Norwich, the second largest city in the country and a regular 'stopping-place' for touring players. The troupe received forty shillings from the local corporation and performed at the Red Lion Inn. By November they were back in London and were licensed to perform at the Bull and Bell inns.[63] Evidence of the company's performance at the Norwich inn on 15 June 1583 is afforded indirectly. While the play was in progress an affray occurred at the gate in which at least three of the Queen's Men and a spectator became involved. The incident culminated in the killing of a local man. The references to the inn performance are to be found in a number of the depositions collected during the subsequent judicial investigation; several of the people questioned had been spectators at the play.[64]

In outline the affray appears to have unfolded as follows. While the troupe was playing at the inn, a local man named Winsdon attempted to gain entry without paying first. When the gatekeeper (possibly John Singer) refused him entry an argument ensued. Word of this disturbance reached the players and audience inside, prompting Henry Brown (a servant of Sir William Paston) and a number of the players to go to the gate (including John Bentley, Richard Tarlton, and John Singer, if he was not already at the gate as its keeper).[65] Bentley, at least, was on stage when he exited the performance to assist his fellow Queen's Man at the gate. Tarlton tried to eject Winsdon, while Bentley hit him on the head with the hilt of a sword he had carried from the stage. Winsdon fled from the gate and joined 'George', the victim, nearby. (The latter was apparently Winsdon's servant.) Bentley pursued them both. Winsdon managed to escape, leaving Bentley to chase the other man, followed by Singer and Brown. Bentley appears to have struck the man who then cast stones at Bentley's head, prompting Singer and Brown to pursue him further. Both struck 'George' with their swords, but Brown hit him first and was believed to have dealt the fatal blow.

The incident at the Red Lion is intriguing in several respects. As well as affording a startling example of the disorder that could erupt at early modern play performances, it provides an insight into the performance that was being staged at the Red Lion Inn. From Henry Brown's testimony alone we learn that the Queen's Men were playing in the inn's yard on a stage on a Saturday afternoon, and that spectators had to pay to see the performance, delivering their payment to a gatekeeper. The documentation of the incident is also revealing in the information that it affords about three of the leading actors of the newly-formed Queen's company and provincial attitudes to players.

Analysing the affray

The disturbance outside the Red Lion began when one would-be spectator 'would have intred at the gate but woold not haue payed vntyll he had been within'.[66] It was possibly 'one of the last instances of customer suspicion over plays' or a sign of declining respect for players and the system of elite patronage in regional communities such as Norwich.[67] The dispute that erupted between the gatekeeper and Winsdon became physical, Winsdon reportedly knocking the money out of the keeper's hand as he tried to force his way in to the play.[68] The dramatic intervention of a local man and two of the other players at this point (one of whom left his on-stage performance to do so) was to have serious consequences but it also raises a number of questions about the players and locals involved.

In the actions of the three players we arguably find further evidence that touring companies could be fiercely protective of their business interests. We possibly also glimpse something of the importance of mutual loyalty and protection in preserving the safety and ensuring the survival of early modern travelling companies. As the company's leading tragedian, Bentley was presumably accustomed to making grand, heroic gestures and it is possible that his acrobatic exit from the stage to go to the aid of his fellow Queen's Man was consciously theatrical and partly designed to thrill the audience. However, the belligerent behaviour of the players is open to less flattering interpretations, too. For some commentators (and their contemporary critics), the players' apparently swift and ready recourse to violence and their (apparently unfulfilled) promise to protect Brown might simply be proof of the aggressive arrogance of some of the period's leading players and acting troupes.[69]

Brown's reasons for coming to the players' assistance are equally intriguing. His own account of the incident indicates that he intervened on their behalf out of respect and honour for their patron:

> word was brought into the play that one of her ma*i*esties ser*u*ant*es* was abused at the gate wherevpon this exanynate with others went owt and one in a blew cote Cast Stones at Bentley and brocke his heade beinge one of her ma*i*esties seruant*es* wherevpon this examynate sayed [. . .] wilt thowe murder the quenes man and the fellowe called this examynate villan agayne and therevpon this examynate stroke hym with his Sworde and hyt hym on the legg.[70]

Whether Brown was genuinely 'trying to stand up for the Queen's servants is not easy to determine'.[71] He may simply have been seeking to veil his violent behaviour with a palatable justification. Yet it is evident from other evidence that the Queen's livery did command respect amongst some of her subjects in the English provinces; and, as a servant of a local nobleman, Brown may have been accustomed to respecting the authority of elite patrons. Whether his protective intentions were serious or not, Brown was to receive little recompense for his active defence of the Queen's servants. He was also to discover how little power the players had to protect others, even if they were the Queen's Men. Although Singer reportedly sought to cheer Brown after the affray with the promise that 'thowe shalt haue what ffrendshipe we can procure thee', this friendship did not materialise or proved of limited value, as shall be seen.

'George' (the only name given for the murdered man) appears to have been another, even more unfortunate victim of circumstances. He, too, suffered in defence of another, in this case Winsdon. George does not seem to have been involved in the initial dispute at the inn gate but intervened on behalf of the man he claimed as his master when Winsdon fled the inn pursued by the players. Again, however, it is difficult to determine how genuinely George was acting in defence of Winsdon, for while he referred to him as his master, Winsdon's own statement was more ambiguous. According to Elizabeth Davy, Winsdon said that George 'was not his seruante but he had been hym aboute three or iiijor dayes'.[72] The meaning of this comment is unclear. It could mean that George had been Winsdon's servant until three or four days previously or that George had been with him for that period of time only. In either instance, one wonders whether George's intervention on Winsdon's part was intended to ingratiate him with Winsdon or to encourage the man to retain or re-employ him as his servant. At any rate, his action, like Brown's, proved ill-fated and our last record of him is that of his burial in a local parish, as 'one George, slayne'.[73]

Drama in Norwich in 1583

The Queen's Men were not the only players to adopt an assertive – even aggressive – stance when touring and performing in towns such as Norwich. In 1583 the Norwich Corporation had already encountered one troublesome troupe of professional players: the Earl of Worcester's Men defied an order not to perform in the town shortly before the Queen's players' Red Lion performance, despite the fact that the corporation for 'their Lord & master his sake dyd gyve them [. . .] xxvjs viijd wherevppon they promysed to depart & not to play'.[74] Notably, the players' rebellious stance proved short-lived. When the corporation threatened that their patron 'shalbee certyfyed of their contempt', the actors were quick to apologise; and the town agreed not to contact him.[75]

The incident involving the Earl of Worcester's Men and the later affray at the Red Lion performance appear to mark the beginning of tenser relations between the Norwich Corporation and visiting players. Certainly, there is a change in the kind of dramatic records that emerge from the town after this date. Many acting companies continued to visit Norwich and to receive corporate rewards but from 1583 onwards, 'records of disputes between the civic authorities gradually increase', and Jacobean players were sometimes paid not to perform. Those players that were permitted to play faced increasingly strict regulation of their activities as well, the corporation often specifying when and where companies might perform.[76] The changing relations between players and the corporation may not have been paralleled by changes in the treatment extended to players in the town more generally. Evidently there continued to be a taste for plays in Norwich but it is possible that local attitudes to players were becoming more divided too, particularly as Puritanism thrived, with some locals continuing to accept and enjoy players' visits and others becoming opposed to theatre and actors. As one of the semi-public forums found in most early modern English communities and one of the customary playing spaces in Norwich, it is perhaps not surprising that inns should prove one of the foci for such local cultural tensions or that some of the earliest troubles with players should be associated with inn performances.

Reconstructing the performance

The inn where the Queen's Men performed is consistently named as the Red Lion in St Stephen's and the play is explicitly described as occurring in the yard in the afternoon. The performance probably began between twelve and one o'clock and may have been staged in the afternoon because the company was using the inn-yard rather than an indoor chamber. Although a number of Red Lion inns have existed in Norwich, research suggests that the inn visited by the Queen's Men was that located in Red Lion Street. Wicks described the location of the inn as early as 1925 and argued that it was that used by the Elizabethan troupe:

> Passing along the east end of Orford Place, which prior to the commencement of the tramways in 1900, was called Red Lion Street, an inn stood there known as the 'Cricketer's Arms' [. . .] But long years before that it was the old 'Red Lion', which stood partly on the site [. . .] There was a spacious yard at the side which, [. . .] was a noted place for entertainments. It was here that Richard Tarlton, the famous clown, appeared in 1583 with Bentley and Singer.[77]

More recent investigation by D. F. Rowan has lent weight to Wicks's identification of the site. Rowan's research also suggests that the yard may survive in Orford Place, although the inn does not.[78] Unfortunately, it is not clear how much the yard may have been altered since the sixteenth century as the earliest illustration of the town in which a yard is depicted in this area dates only from 1789.[79] The inn-yard may have been irregular in its shape as Joshua Manning's 1835 map of the town 'shows an enclosed roughly cruciform yard in the right location'. We do not know 'whether the plan view of 1835 bears much relation to what was there in 1583'; but, if it does, it would suggest the yard was reasonably 'spacious' as well, as Wicks indicated.[80]

Preparing the space

The stage erected in the yard may have been a temporary wooden platform owned by the Queen's Men, or an improvised platform made from barrels or forms. In either instance, it was low enough to jump from, as several players are described as coming from the stage.[81] It may have been only two or three feet in height. The precise location of the stage in the yard is not described, but it could have been placed opposite the gated entrance, possibly in the middle of the yard (if it was cruciform at this date) or parallel with the side of the inn facing the gate. This could explain how the actors became so quickly aware that there was a disturbance at the entrance. Similarly, as the performance was staged in the yard, and there are no references to the audience being seated or to the actors having to climb over seats to get from the stage to the gate, it is likely that the spectators stood around the stage. If their platform was set up in a central location, the players could have performed completely 'in the round', although it is perhaps more likely that spectators surrounded the platform on three sides at most, the space at the rear or behind the stage being reserved for a tiring area.

The audience

The size of the play's audience is not recorded, but the depositions from spectators provide some information about its social make-up. All the eyewitnesses who had been at the play were men. This does not mean that there were not any women in the audience, but they may have been fewer in number. This would not be surprising, as inn customers were predominantly male. The audience included gentlemen (such as Thomas Osborne), yeomen (such as Edmund Knee), various tradesmen and craftsmen (Edmund Brown, a draper, and William Kilby, a worsted weaver), and gentlemen's servants such as Henry Brown; a range of spectators not unlike that recorded as frequenting inns on other occasions.[82] Some information about the geographical origins of the audience is, likewise, afforded in the judicial documents, the clerk(s) occasionally noting the witnesses' place of domicile. This information reveals that the Red Lion spectators included local men (such as Thomas Holland and Edmund Brown) and people from other areas. Thomas Osborne is described as coming from 'Kyrbye Bydon', and Edmund Knee came from Yelverton.[83]

The play

The name of the play that the players had begun is not recorded in any of the depositions but a number of the witnesses observe that John Bentley played the duke.[84] With such limited information to guide us, it is not possible to identify the play performed definitively, but some of the known Queen's Men's plays can be eliminated because they do not include a 'duke' or are known to date later than 1583; and plausible suggestions can be made, based on our knowledge of the Queen's Men's repertory in the 1580s.[85] The play performed could have been *The Famous Victories of Henry V*, for example. This is one of the earlier Queen's Men's plays which includes a 'duke' (the Duke of York) and which requires a cast of twelve men, in keeping with the troupe's

size in 1583. The play also includes martial action and calls for characters equipped with swords.[86] However, there is also a possibility that the
play was one (now lost) with a duke as its leading role or authority
figure.[87]

Whichever play was performed the depositions of the witnesses reveal
that it was staged in costume and props were used. Bentley is described
as coming from the stage in his playing apparel, with 'a players berd
vppon his face'; and Edmund Knee describes how he had a 'raper in his
hand' when he left the stage to join the dispute at the gate.[88] Similarly,
Edmund Brown reports that Singer ran up 'into the stayge' and brought
an 'Armynge Sworde'. Notably, the players' swords appear to have been
genuine rather than prop arms, and the use which Bentley and Singer
made of their weapons in the affray demonstrates how readily they
could be applied to off-stage violence.[89]

The aftermath

After the killing of local man 'George' there is no indication that the
play was resumed. If this raised any outcry among spectators, their complaints are unrecorded. Brown and the two players involved in the affray
did face formal reprisal for their off-stage actions, each being imprisoned. The players were released two days later on bail (19 June 1583),
while Brown remained in prison awaiting trial for the murder. Both
Singer and Bentley received local assistance with their bail.[90] If the
players procured help for Brown as they had promised it proved of little
avail. He bore the burden of the punishment in the case. The last records
of the case date from 23 September 1583, when all three men were
charged to appear in court. The actors did not show up. Brown appeared
to face the charges of felony and homicide alone and was granted
'benefit of clergy' after confessing his guilt, thus avoiding possible
execution.[91] It seems he had discovered the limits of the players'
'ffrendshipe'.

Conclusions

Despite the dearth of specific examples, contextual evidence suggests
that playing at inns was not unusual in the early modern English
provinces. Indeed, in many parts of the country inns appear to have
been one of the quasi-public buildings traditionally used for playing by
professional travelling companies and for occasional local plays. As
privately owned but public arenas, inns also appear to have been one
of the urban spaces where companies were potentially most exposed to

local cultural tensions. The difficulty of supervising such spaces meant that they were one of the venues where locals and players theoretically had most freedom to explore and challenge official local culture as well. These combined factors may help to explain why one finds so many records of trouble as a result of or in relation to inn performances, and why some of our most vivid records of theatre outside London are examples of drinking house drama.

The appropriation of provincial drinking houses as temporary theatres parallels dramatic practices in Elizabethan London. But in a period when English drinking houses were increasingly important as social spaces, the accommodation of players and performances at early modern public houses is also arguably a further testimony to drama's popularity and perceived cultural importance in the provinces as well as the capital. Playing at inns was not a tradition confined to the metropolis or to the sixteenth century either (although there may have been regional variations). Outside London it proved a durable custom with touring players continuing to perform at inns in some regional communities throughout the Jacobean period.

6
Playing at Schools and University Colleges

Travelling players were accustomed to performing in a variety of spaces when on tour. Among the choices potentially available to them in the Renaissance were the growing number of provincial schoolhouses and the university colleges of Oxford and Cambridge. Most of the plays performed in Renaissance England's schools and colleges were classical academic dramas staged by the students; but there is some evidence of travelling companies visiting and performing in academic buildings as well.[1] Queen Elizabeth's players received rewards and may have performed at Winchester School, Trinity College, Cambridge and Christ Church, Oxford.[2] Though rare, travelling players' occasional ventures into the arena of academic drama represent a fascinating point of intersection between the professional stage and one of the most active branches of amateur theatre in Renaissance England.

I

Professional performances in schools

In 1618 the patent issued to the Children of the Revels of Bristol required that regional officials permit the troupe to play in 'all Playhowses Townehalls Schoolehouses and other places Convenient for y*at* purpose'.[3] By implication, schoolhouses were one of the public buildings that corporations occasionally allowed visiting players to use. The number of schools in Renaissance England was on the increase, with as many as 359 grammar schools in existence by 1577.[4] While some of these schools were housed in existing buildings (including guildhalls, churches and hospitals), others were established or transferred to purpose-built schoolhouses. As one of the few sizeable public (or semi-public) buildings to be found in many towns, schoolhouses lent themselves to use as performance venues. Most contained at least one room capable of accommodating a large gathering. In some cases, the school was limited to this single chamber, although it could be large. At Eton the school 'hall' used for pupils' plays measures 82 feet by 32 feet.[5] Some schools incorporated a yard potentially available for performance use as well, as at Boston (Lincolnshire) where the Elizabethan schoolhouse stood on a piece of open ground known as the Hallgarth.[6]

Some schools may have had additional recommendations as performance venues. At schools that regularly staged their own academic plays, players might have been able to look forward to assistance with performance preparations and access to school-owned playing gear.[7] At Eton players would have found a sizeable costume wardrobe in the late sixteenth century, while at Winchester College players would have found school officials accustomed to the preparation of stages and props for the plays frequently staged by pupils in the Elizabethan period.[8] Large, wealthy schools of the kind accustomed to staging lavish play productions and to hosting entertainment were potentially prestigious places in which to perform and might reward players.

Evidence

Direct evidence of professional players performing at Renaissance schools is scarce. For instance, although a number of visiting entertainers were rewarded and may have performed at Winchester College (including the Queen's players in 1568–69 and 1570–71) there is no direct record of visiting players acting in the school.[9] In the REED volumes published thus far only two professional school performances appear to be recorded and in one case the performance was not a play but a tumbling show. In 1589–90 Bristol's Corporation rewarded the Queen's players when they 'tumbled' at the Free School. The players may have performed a play as well but there is no record that they did so.[10] The record of a schoolhouse performance in Lyme Regis's archives presents a different complication. In 1606–07 the town's churchwardens reported that the Mayor had allowed 'Certaine Enterlude players to playe in a scoole howse adioyninge vnto the church being within the Compasse of the Church yerd'.[11] In this case the performance definitely occurred in the school but it is not certain the players were visiting professionals because the name of their patron is not given.

Indirect evidence of professional companies performing at schoolhouses is afforded by other sources, including players' licences and regional civic orders regulating dramatic activity. In Newark

(Nottinghamshire) in 1568 it was agreed that 'no players froom hensf[o]rth shall playe in the scole house but onelie suche as shalb<.> permitted and licenced there to playe by Thalderman for the tyme beinge at suche tyme as the same alderman and assistants shalbe [. . .] present them selves'.[12] By implication, plays had been performed in the schoolhouse in the past and were expected to be staged there in the future. The order simply regulates such performances, authorising them only if staged before the alderman and his assistants. A similar regulatory order passed by Boston's Corporation in 1578 suggests that Boston's school was likewise used as a playing venue: 'there shalbe no mo players nor interludes [. . .] in the church nor in the Chauncell nor in the hall nor scolle howse'.[13] Although the order could have been aimed at school performers its application to several venues suggests that it was intended to curb all play performances locally, while the use of the phrase 'no more' implies that each of the places listed had been used for performances in the past. As the latter example (and the case at Lyme Regis) reveals, permission to perform in schoolhouses was not necessarily easily obtained, although there is little evidence of people campaigning against professional playing at schools.

The spaces

Many of the schools that existed in Renaissance England no longer survive. Establishing precisely what facilities and kinds of space they would have afforded visiting players is therefore difficult. Fortunately, there are exceptions. The original schools survive at Winchester and Boston, as does the building that housed Newark's old grammar school. The information afforded by these buildings can be supplemented by evidence regarding those schools now lost or altered since the Renaissance. Other sources such as school records can also provide useful information about the furnishings and, in some cases, the playing gear that might have been available to visiting players at schools.

At Winchester College players would have found several sizeable spaces potentially adaptable for performances, including the Chapel (measuring 93 feet by 27 feet) and the 'school room' (46 feet by 29 feet). Any visiting performances are most likely to have taken place, however, in the school's Great Hall (the venue for at least some of the pupils' own Elizabethan play productions).[14] This first-floor hall stands above the early schoolroom and is part of the college's medieval buildings, dating back to the fourteenth century. Today, it survives 'structurally intact', measuring 62 feet by 29 feet and 40 feet in height.[15] Although smaller than the dining hall used for plays at Eton, it would have afforded a large indoor theatre.[16] The hall was easily adaptable for performances, too, being fitted in comparatively simple fashion. The main furnishings are likely to have been wooden tables and benches of the kind still to be found in the hall. One table served as 'high table' (probably standing on the upper end dais), while the others appear to have been arranged along the sides of the hall.[17] Several areas might have served as playing spaces but performances are most likely to have been staged at the upper or lower end of the hall, while spectators were accommodated in the remaining space, possibly on the available benches. If players acted at the hall's lower end, they might have entered and exited through the screens passage, behind which stand three doorways leading to the kitchen, buttery and pantry. (One of these rooms might have served as a tiring area.)[18] But evidence from the early modern universities suggests that the higher end of the hall was the more prestigious and usual location for stages in college halls, and this may have been the case in schools such as Winchester, too.[19]

The players that performed at the schoolhouse in Lyme Regis are unlikely to have found such a commodious playing venue. The school no longer exists and there is little information about the schoolhouse, although the churchwardens described it as 'adioyninge vnto the church being within the Compasse of the Church yerd' (1606–07).[20] The church in question (the surviving parish church of St Michael's) dates back to the thirteenth century and stands on 'an elevated spot in the east part of the town'.[21] The precise location of the schoolhouse within the churchyard is unclear. Although it may have been a separate building erected in the yard and now lost, Wanklyn suggests that it was a room within the church.[22] It could have been established in the old nave. This was converted into a porch in the fifteenth or early sixteenth century when the present church 'was built to the E. of the tower'. It would thus have been available for an alternative communal use and could have been described as 'adioyninge' the church. The space afforded would have been reasonably large but could have been described as a room. It measures 23 feet by 14 feet but was 'shortened by about 10 ft. in 1824'.[23]

All that remains of the Free School in Bristol where the Queen's players 'tumbled' (1589–90) is the archway leading into the old building and fragments of the walls and foundations.[24] The late sixteenth-century school (founded between 1530 and 1543) was converted from St Bartholomew's Hospital in accordance with an endowment made by Bristol merchant Robert Thorne in 1531–32.[25] The size and make-up of the schoolhouse subsequently built on the site is unknown but its use as an entertainment venue in the Elizabethan period suggests that it included at least one large schoolroom or hall, capable of accommo-dating performers and spectators. In 1577–78, for instance, the corpo-ration allowed forty shillings to 'mr Dunne Schole*master*' toward 'his char*ges* of his last playes that he had in the Barthilmews' at Christmas.[26] The school is also thought to have incorporated a yard, possibly avail-able as an open-air performance space. Again, its precise dimensions are unknown but excavations suggest it was spacious and Pilkinton specu-lates that it was used for the Queen's Men's tumbling show, noting that the 'ample courtyard/playground made a suitable place for displays of gymnastic skill'.[27]

The other two schools identified thus far as possible professional playing venues both survive comparatively unchanged, although at Newark the building no longer serves as a school. Established in 1530–31 by Archbishop Magnus, the original Newark Grammar School-house is known today as 'Tudor Hall' and is part of Millgate Museum.[28] Any performances at the school are likely to have been staged inside the large stone hall. This would have afforded a sizeable playing space interrupted only by an overhanging 'timber-framed room' at one end.[29] At Boston the grammar school founded in 1555 survives to the present and occupies the same site, although the schoolhouse erected in 1567 is now the School Library (see Illustration 15). The brick schoolhouse remained virtually unchanged until the mid-nineteenth century when additional rooms were erected at the north (1850) and south ends of the building (1856). More buildings have been added subsequently and the schoolhouse roof has been restored, but the original building is otherwise well preserved and continues to consist of one large hall (measuring approximately 20 m by 6 m).[30] Such a space would have been capable of holding large audiences and comparatively easy to adapt for performances, since it is only likely to have contained desks and benches. It is not difficult to see why players might have wished to use it. The school's yard also survives in part and might have been avail-able as an alternative performance space before and after the town pro-hibited playing within the schoolhouse (1578).[31]

Staging

Whether professional companies would have used stages when per-forming in schools is unknown. In smaller schoolrooms a stage was pos-sibly unnecessary or impractical. It is perhaps more likely that platforms were used if and when troupes performed in larger schoolrooms or halls of the kind found at the major Renaissance grammar schools such as

Winchester. In these instances players might even have been able to borrow staging material and to call upon local help, some schools having experience in setting up stages for student plays (see above).[32] Professional acting companies routinely travelled with a stock of playing gear. It is therefore probable that their schoolhouse productions were staged in costume and accompanied by stage furniture, too.

Players were also accustomed to borrowing additional items on-site when touring and this may have occurred when they visited schools. This could have included using school-owned costumes (if school authorities were willing). Some of the dramatically active Renaissance schools are also known to have made props for their academic plays that might have been available for borrowing. Perhaps most intriguing are the payments that occasionally occur for the construction of 'houses'. The 'divers expenses' relating to the student plays performed at Winchester in 1573 include money for 'little houses newly built', while at Westminster School reference is made from 1580 for 'making of the houses' for the plays staged in the school hall.[33] Similar payments sometimes occur in the records of university colleges and the Revels Accounts of the Court in this period. Some insight into the nature and role of such 'houses' is provided by a reference in the Revels Accounts of 1567–68: it alludes to a court performance of 'Orestes and a Tragedie of the kinge of Scottes to ye which belonged divers howses for the settinge forthe of the same as Stratoes howse, Gobbyns howse, Orestioes howse, Rome, the Pallace of Prosperitie, Scotland and a great Castell one thothere side'. This list suggests the 'houses' were used to designate different locations. Other payments indicate that they were typically 'wooden frameworks [. . .] covered with painted cloths of canvas', possibly finding part of their origin in the booth structures used in medieval drama.[34] The popularity of this staging device amongst at least some of the dramatically active schools probably stems from the prevailing fashion for performing classical plays in the academic world, the 'conventional classical stage-setting' being 'a street scene consisting of an open space backed by one or more "citizens" houses'.[35] Early Elizabethan court records suggest that professional players sometimes made use of stage houses as well; whether they were a customary staging device on the popular stage in the later Elizabethan and Jacobean periods is less clear.[36] There is, however, little evidence of troupes using such structures at the Shakespearean playhouses, perhaps because the tiring house provided entry and exit points and a backdrop that could represent different locations. Companies visiting schools in the late sixteenth and early seventeenth centuries may not have wished to use

1. The Old Guildhall, Barnstaple (*c.* 1823) (The North Devon Athenaeum, Barnstaple).

2. The exterior of Leicester Guildhall.

3. The Elizabethan porch at Exeter Guildhall.

4. Exterior view of the Old Guildhall, Stratford-upon-Avon.

5. Interior view of the Old Guildhall, Stratford-upon-Avon (Shakespeare Birthplace Trust Records Office, Stratford-upon-Avon).

6. The dais at the upper end of the hall, Leicester Guilhall.

7. Exterior view of All Saints Church, West Ham.

8. Sherborne church house.

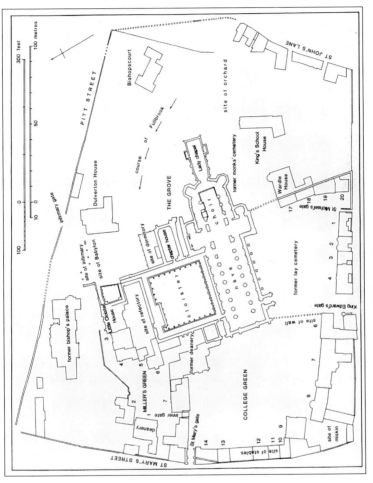

9. Plan of Gloucester Cathedral and Close, 1986.

10. Gawthorpe Hall, Lancashire (Lancashire County Museum Service, Preston).

11. The main hall at Smithills Hall, Lancashire (© Bolton Museum and Art Gallery).

12. The 'Peacham' illustration of *Titus Andronicus* (the Marquess of Bath, Longleat, Warminster, Wiltshire).

13. The Blue Boar, Maldon.

14. The inn-yard of the George Inn, Salisbury
(©Salisbury and Wiltshire Museum).

15. The original schoolhouse, Boston Grammar School (Photo. L. J. Rich).

16. The Old Hall, Trinity College, Cambridge, showing the upper end oriel window. Detail from David Loggan's *Cantabrigia Illustrata* (1690).

17. The Great Hall, Christ Church College, Oxford.

18. Interior view of the Great Hall, Christ Church College, Oxford.

19. An illustration of the apple market, Shrewsbury (Shropshire Records and Research Centre, Shrewsbury).

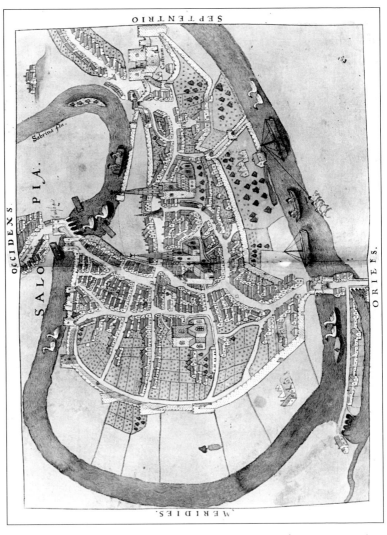

20. Burghley's 1575 Map of Shrewsbury, BL Roy.18.D.III.f89 (by permission of the British Library).

'houses', therefore, even if they were offered such stage furniture. Indeed, it is possible that the tradition of using stage houses was one increasingly confined to academic and amateur stages and that this represents one point of divergence between professional and academic staging traditions in the Renaissance.

Audiences

The nature and size of audiences at professional schoolhouse productions is likely to have depended on the kind of arrangement made between companies and schools and the size of available playing spaces. In some cases, audiences could have been small. Schools with a small schoolroom or house would not have been able to accommodate large gatherings, while the audience for school or corporate sponsored performances might have been deliberately restricted. At Winchester, for instance, the visiting players rewarded by the school may have been invited to perform privately before staff and students and/or special guests. Other schoolhouse performances might have been open to the public, as were many civic sponsored performances and some student plays.[37] In these instances, if the school hall or room was spacious a large and socially mixed audience might be assembled. Over 500 people might have been accommodated if the Queen's Men performed publicly in the Great Hall at Winchester in 1568–69.[38] Large audiences could be lively and that assembled at Winchester might have been particularly so if it included pupils as well as adults, as contemporary records suggest Winchester's boys could be boisterous. In 1566 these scholars broke the hall 'doors, locks, keys and hinges at Christmas'.[39]

II

Professional players at the universities

There were only two universities for professional players to visit in Renaissance England, Oxford and Cambridge. Both were founded in the medieval period but developed into the establishments recognisable today in the sixteenth century. During this period a number of changes occurred that led to their transformation as institutions.

At the centre of all these changes – notably, the disappearance of the religious orders, the resort to the university of increasing numbers of laymen, the vast enlargement of royal authority and the expansion of the curriculum – was the secular college, which in the Tudor period replaced the medieval hall as the typical home of the undergraduate.[40]

Colleges were generally 'endowed, quasi-independent corporations' and functioned as autonomous communities, providing their own living accommodation, dining facilities and a church/chapel for an academic population usually 'composed of a head, fellows, and scholars'.[41] The number and size of the colleges grew in both universities (as did the universities' populations) and the collegiate system came to dominate their organisation.[42] Colleges were exclusively male communities, although their members varied in numbers and age; and by the late sixteenth century they tended 'to function [. . .] as societies of privileged graduates', wealthier students outnumbering poorer ones.[43] The thriving of the universities also led to the expansion of Oxford and Cambridge and to an increase in the power of the two institutions over life in their respective communities. The latter point became a source of tension between civic and university authorities in both communities and proved a key factor in the history of professional theatre in Renaissance Oxford and Cambridge.[44]

Drama at the universities

Drama 'never had an official position' in the curriculum of early modern Oxford or Cambridge but academic play performances can be traced back as early as the fifteenth century.[45] By the mid-sixteenth century student performances were a regular phenomenon in many colleges and became increasingly frequent during the Elizabethan and Jacobean periods. Some colleges even made student performances an annual requirement.[46] The plays performed by students were typically classical or neo-classical and written in Latin, like those performed in Renaissance England's schools. This is not entirely surprising, as the primary motive for performing plays was educational at university as well as school level. Classical study remained at the heart of the curriculum and Latin was the language of learning and international scholarship. Performing classical plays was not only a way of improving students' knowledge of classical drama and their fluency in the ancient tongue but a way of training them in public speaking and oratory; skills important for those planning on careers in politics or law.

Professional players

The expanding, increasingly privileged student body afforded a potentially large audience for plays by visiting performers, too, while colleges provided ready theatres for professional as well as academic performances. University records reveal that colleges *did* occasionally play host to visiting performers from the early Tudor period. Visiting 'players and musicians' were rewarded at King's College, Cambridge from 1482, while, in Oxford, Magdalen College hosted 'travelling companies of players and musicians' from the early sixteenth century, including 'Princess Mary's players in 1530'.[47] There is some evidence of professional players visiting colleges in the Elizabethan and Jacobean periods, too, but it is rare. At Oxford there is a payment of twenty shillings 'pro Histrionibus Comitis Leicestriae' in Magdalen College's 1575–76 accounts and Christ Church paid ten shillings to the Queen's players in 1589–90. Both could be rewards for playing.[48] Similarly, at Cambridge, it is possible that the thirty shillings Trinity College paid 'to the Quenes Men at Midsomer' (1586–87) was a reward for performing.[49]

Indirect evidence of possible college performances by professional players emerges from other sources. In Ben Jonson's Epistle to *Volpone* (1607) he dedicates the play to 'The Most Noble and Equal Sisters, the Two Famous Universities For Their Love and Acceptance Shown to His Poem In The Presentation'.[50] Where *Volpone* was presented is not specified but as Jonson alludes to it being well received by the universities there is a slim possibility that it was acted within a university space in both towns. Jonson and his work were certainly known to members of the universities. He received honorary Masters degrees from 'both Oxford and Cambridge'; and Ostovich suggests he was granted the degrees as 'a result of *Volpone's* academic success'.[51] Unfortunately, there is no direct evidence to support this hypothesis. Neither can we be certain that *Volpone* was acted in Oxford or Cambridge, as there is no other evidence of its performance in either town. On the contrary, Nelson argues that in Cambridge there is strong evidence against the play's performance.[52] A similar case is presented by the claim made in the title page of the 1603 quarto of *Hamlet* that the play 'hath beene diverse times acted by his Highnesse ser/vants in the Cities of London, as also in the two/Vniversities of Cambridge and Oxford'. The allusion to performances in the universities suggests the play was performed within university colleges and/or the university towns. Again, although this may have occurred there is no firm evidence of the play being performed in the records of either community.[53]

A different problem is presented by Henry Jackson's account of the King's Men's performances of *The Alchemist* and *Othello* at Oxford in 1610. Jackson, who was a member of Corpus Christi College, Oxford, wrote briefly about the performances in a Latin letter dated September

1610. Extracts from it were 'transcribed 50 years later by another Corpus Christi man, William Fulman'.[54] As well as revealing that the company performed to 'full houses' he affords an insight into the reception of the plays. He describes the angry reaction of some theologians to *The Alchemist*'s treatment of religion, for instance, and pays particular tribute to Desdemona's performance in *Othello*: 'Moreover, that famous Desdemona killed before us by her husband, although she always acted her whole part supremely well, yet when she was killed she was even more moving, for when she fell back upon the bed she implored the pity of the spectators by her very face.'[55]

The location of the performances is less clear. Jackson describes the King's Men's use of 'pleno theatro', and 'theatro nostro' but does not identify these 'theatres' more precisely. As Tillotson notes, these phrases 'seem to imply something better than a yard and certainly state that there was more than one place recognised as available for players'. At the same time, Jackson suggests that the audience for *The Alchemist*, at least, contained university men: 'Theologi nostros, qui (pudet dicere) avidissime confluebant'.[56] The theologians who 'flocked' to *The Alchemist* might have been 'students merely or may include D.D.s'; but the tragedies 'were almost certainly attended by Jackson, and if by Jackson, then by the University at large, excepting extreme Puritans'.[57] In this context, although it remains more probable that the King's Men used local inns as their temporary theatres, it is possible that one or more of the performances was staged in a college hall.

Regulating professional theatre

That there should be few records of Shakespearean players performing at Oxford or Cambridge is unsurprising. The university authorities may have welcomed visiting players in the medieval period but from the late sixteenth century onwards acting companies faced growing hostility.[58] This aversion to players manifested itself in the regulations both universities passed restricting public theatre. Cambridge University sought to enforce a ban on public plays within five miles of their precincts as early as 1568–69; and in 1575 received a Privy Council letter granting them 'unusual powers to guarantee public order, to suppress distractions which might entice students from their studies, and to protect the whole community from the plague'.[59] In Oxford a similar strategy was followed, the University promulgating a statute prohibiting professional players from performing within its precincts in 1584.[60] The Earl of Leicester, as University Chancellor, supported the ban, saying in a letter 'that he thought "the prohibicion of common stage players very requisite"', although he did not want student plays to be suppressed.[61] In 1593 both universities received a Privy Council letter authorising a ban on professional public plays within five miles of their institutions. The Privy Council recommended that the letter be circulated to the mayor and local justices in both towns for 'better execucion' of the order.[62]

The universities also attempted to restrict students' attendance of professional plays. The 1584 Oxford statute prohibiting such performances stated that 'if it happen by extraordinarye meanes yat stage players shall gett or obtane leaue by the maior or other wayse yet it shall not be lawfull for anye master bachiler or scholler aboue the age of eighteene to repare or go to see anye such thinge vnder paine of imprisonment'.[63] In Cambridge scholars were prohibited from attending 'anye playes or games either kepte at Gogmagog hilles or els where' within five miles of Cambridge as early as 1574. In 1600 this prohibition was repeated as part of a decree restricting students' attendance of various sporting and recreational events.[64]

The passing of these prohibitions did not prevent troupes from visiting either town, as is revealed by the 'gratuity' payments not to perform and/or to leave that both universities made to players in the late sixteenth century. They did not prevent students from attending public plays either.[65] In offering players a financial inducement not to perform the universities anticipated a tactic employed by many later corporations seeking to restrict local theatrical activity (see Chapter 9). There are more than a dozen payments of this kind in the Vice-Chancellor's draft accounts at Oxford between 1587 and 1624, beginning by 'a curious irony' with a payment concerning the players of the University's Chancellor (the Earl of Leicester). A payment of twenty shillings was made to 'histrionibus comitis Lecestriae vt cum suis ludis sine maiore Academiae molestia discederent'.[66] In most cases the formula used is similar to that recorded in the payment to Leicester's troupe, indicating that the players were paid to leave the town quietly.[67] In a few cases the payments were explicitly rewards for non-performance or the prevention of performances, as in 1595–96 when the Queen's players were apparently rewarded for not acting publicly.[68]

At Cambridge there are five university payments to players between 1579 and 1597, four of which are rewards not to play and/or to leave the town. The fifth to the Queen's players (1596–97) may also be a payment for non-performance but is not explicitly described as such. The tone of some of the records betrays the distaste (and possibly the anxiety) with which players were viewed by Elizabethan university officials. In 1583–84 'Ls' was given to the Queen's players 'forbiddinge theim to playe in the towne and so to ridd theim cleane away'. The troupe was 'debarred from playinge' and sent away with a reward again in 1590–91 and 1591–92.[69] There is evidence of companies being denied permission to perform in Jacobean Cambridge as well but the custom of offering compensatory rewards appears to have been abandoned.[70]

Civic records also reveal that professional players continued to visit both university towns. Visiting players received rewards from both towns' corporations after the introduction of university prohibitions on public playing. Although the corporation in Oxford restricted players' use of the Guildhall from 1579–80, their treatment of visiting acting companies generally appears to have been generous, as is revealed by the regular rewards given to players between 1559 and 1617.[71] In Elizabethan Cambridge the town authorities also rewarded players fairly frequently, making nearly forty payments to professional troupes between 1559 and 1597.[72] At least some of these civic rewards were for performances.[73] One perhaps begins to understand why the Privy Council suggested that their 1593 letter enforcing the university ban on plays be circulated to the local mayor and civic officers in both towns. The university authorities could not count on corporate co-operation in the enforcement of the ban. Indeed, in some instances civic officials may have deliberately supported visiting players as a way of challenging the right of the respective universities to control local cultural life.[74]

The 1593 Privy Council letter renewing the ban on public playing was elicited by Cambridge University precisely because it had experienced difficulties in commanding respect for the earlier prohibition (1575). Problems had come to a head in 1592 during a visit by the Queen's players. Having been denied permission to play and rewarded to leave the town, the company proceeded to perform without license in the neighbouring village of Chesterton. This was not the first occasion that performers had turned to Chesterton as an alternative venue.[75] What was particularly galling about the 1592 incident was the fact that their playing had been unopposed by the Chesterton constables and advertised in the University's precincts, the players setting up playbills on 'Colledge gates'.[76] The actors were also supported in their unlicensed playing by local nobleman, Lord North:

> when the Players came to him for his Lordships allowaunce for theire playeinge in Chesterton, and some of vs did then tell his Lordship that wee had the Lords of the Counsells Lettres to the contrary, he openly vttered in the hearinge aswell of the Players, as of diuerse Knightes and Gentlemen of the Shier then present that the date of

those *lettres* was almost expired, And [. . .] that althoughe they should playe at Chesterton; yet the Vicechauncellor durst not commit them therefore.[77]

While the defiance of the players and the Chesterton constables was a short-term annoyance, Lord North's public, embarrassing challenge to the University's ban on players made obtaining fresh confirmation of the prohibition a political necessity and a point of honour.[78]

Opposition

The opposition of university authorities to performances by professional players was prompted by a number of concerns. In part their hostility was ethical. They were suspicious of those making their living from 'playing', and increasingly concerned about the potentially corrupting influence of players' 'lewde and euill sportes' (as the Oxford statute of 1584 put it).[79] But their concerns were also pragmatic: plays were a distraction from students' studies and an expense some could ill afford, while the large gatherings associated with public plays posed a threat to local order and public health. Notably, the Oxford order prohibiting public plays opens with an account of the town's problems with plague, resulting from 'the extraordenary concurse of poeple [. . .] to see stage playse and games', and cites the need to maintain 'health' in the town as one of the reasons for its introduction.[80] Similar concerns prompted many Elizabethan and Jacobean corporations to introduce stricter regulation of public recreations (including plays). The same general social concerns also prompted Cambridge University to act against games at the Gog Magog hills, and bear-baiting at neighbouring Chesterton.[81]

Attitudes to drama

Negative views of the public stage were not confined to the universities' governing bodies. The professional theatre had its critics amongst scholars, too, in the early modern period. The harshest critics were men who also opposed academic drama in the late sixteenth and early seventeenth centuries, but professional players did not escape the censure even of those ready to champion academic theatre.[82] Indeed, scholar playwrights such as William Gager defended academic drama by contrasting it with professional theatre.[83] Yet some university men were evidently interested in the popular stage. Such interest is occasionally manifested in academic plays. In the anonymous *Second Part of the Return From Parnassus* (the last play of a trilogy) produced at St John's College, Cambridge (1602), two characters discuss the merits of various contemporary writers, including a number of playwrights for the public theatre (such as Shakespeare and Jonson). And Richard Burbage and William Kemp, two of the period's most famous professional players, are brought on-stage to audition a pair of students for their acting company. The treatment these representatives of the public stage receive is intriguing. Both playwrights and players are satirised. While Shakespeare is criticised for his preoccupation with love, the actors are mocked for their ignorance.[84] Most famously, Kemp dismisses the skill of university playwrights and makes a classical 'gaff', mistaking *Metamorphoses* for the name of an ancient author:

> *Kempe.*   Few of the vniuersity [men] pen plaies well, they
> smell too much of that writer *Ouid*, and that writer *Meta*
> *morphoses*, and talke too much of *Proserpina & Iuppiter*.
> Why heres our fellow Shakespeare puts them all downe.[85]

That the audience is being invited to view the players critically is suggested when the student protagonists almost immediately reject a career as players and condemn the profession as 'the basest trade' (4.4.1846). However, as a satire of the popular stage the play is ambiguous in its effect. By making professional players and dramatists part of his theme the playwright immediately invests them with a degree of importance. In the audition scene one of the students even delivers a speech from Shakespeare's *Richard III*, after Burbage mischievously suggests that he would suit the part of Richard 'Humpback', allowing Shakespeare's words what may have been their only airing on an academic stage in the period:

> *Burbage.*   I like your face and the proportion of your body for
> Richard the 3., I pray [you] M. Philomusus let me see
> you
> act a little of it.
> *Philomusus.*   Now is the winter of our discontent
> Made glorious summer by the sonne of Yorke, [&c.].
> (*The Second Part of the Return From Parnassus*, 4.4.1835)

The scene is framed to invite ridicule of the players and using an example of Shakespeare's work is probably intended to be a way of satirising his abilities as a dramatist. The result is more complex. It might have proved a laughable moment in performance, but the inclusion of the speech as a recognisable piece of popular theatre only serves to confirm the fame and reputation of its author and the success the professional stage was enjoying in the late sixteenth century. At the same time it affords evidence that university academics were *au fait* with events and fashions in the world of London public theatre.

Further evidence of academic interest in, and familiarity with, the popular stage emerges if one compares the plays written by other university dramatists and professional playwrights. Although the academic plays performed at the Renaissance universities were predominantly classical or neo-classical comedies and tragedies, in the 1580s and 1590s university playwrights also began producing topical satires, Italianate romances, pastorals, and English history plays.[86] These same genres were fashionable, to varying extents, on the metropolitan public stages, suggesting there may have been some cross-fertilisation of ideas. In some cases, there is fairly clear evidence of borrowing. The anonymous *Tragedy of Caesar's Revenge* (performed *c.*1594, Trinity College, Oxford) is written in a style modelled on the revenge tragedies popular in London in 'the last decade of the sixteenth century'. It even incorporates lines from a number of successful public plays, including Marlowe's *Tamburlaine*.[87] In other cases the pattern of influence is harder to identify. For example, the university stage was, arguably, the home of the first English history play (Thomas Legge's *Richardus Tertius*), but whether this play had any direct influence on those playwrights who were to produce the famous history plays of the popular Elizabethan stage is not certain.

That the popular and academic stages should have occasionally exerted influence on each other is not as surprising as it might first appear. Although the motives and auspices for commercial and academic theatre differed there was common ground between them. A number of professional playwrights were university graduates (including Christopher Marlowe, John Marston and Thomas Heywood) and their ideas as dramatists were likely to have been informed by their experiences of academic drama. Similarly, there were opportunities for university performers and authors to learn from the public stage when touring companies visited and graduates, turned professional playwrights, were recruited to write or manage the production of college plays for special occasions. For instance, when Queen Elizabeth visited Oxford University in 1566 graduate playwright Richard Edwardes wrote and organised the performance of the two-part play, *Palamon and Arcyte*, staged before the Queen in Christ Church hall.[88] In such cases, the assistance of London-based playwrights was presumably sought because of the professional knowledge and expertise they were expected to possess. Professional and academic players sometimes had recourse to the same metropolitan theatrical resources as well, both occasionally borrowing costumes and playing gear from the Revels Office.[89]

Performing at the universities

The spaces

Academic plays were occasionally performed in college chapels and private rooms, but the most frequently recorded venue for productions was the 'hall'. College dining halls were a natural venue for entertainment and are likely to have been the venue for any professional college productions, too. Their primary function defined them as communal spaces and they were often the largest indoor space available. Like the banqueting halls of the Tudor palaces and private noble houses, most college halls were modelled on the design of the medieval great hall, generally being 'substantial rectangular rooms with distinctive upper and lower ends'.[90] The upper end was usually fitted with a dais on which the 'high table' stood and there was often a single upper end doorway through which those dining at 'high table' could enter. The main entry points to the hall were usually at its lower end. The latter was also the traditional location of the doorways to the kitchen and buttery. These lower-end doors were frequently separated from the body of the hall by a wooden screen. Such screens could be ornately carved and decorated, and might be 'roofed in and railed, forming a "minstrels' gallery" above'.[91] Tables and benches might be arranged in the main body of the hall, parallel with its length, and there was sometimes a central fireplace, too.

While sharing a common design, the size of college halls varied considerably. The old hall at Trinity College where the Queen's players might have performed (1586–87) was of comparatively modest dimensions, measuring 25 feet by 52 feet (42 feet to the screen).[92] But it conformed to the customary design of college halls. At the northern (lower) end lay the screen, buttery and kitchen, while the upper 'dais' end of the hall was fitted with an oriel window on the left, affording additional light for those dining at 'high table' in the daytime (see Illustration 16). The main entries to the hall lay at its northern end, but there was also a 'single doorway in the upper end wall' leading into 'a bay which had no other exit'.[93] There may have been a traditional central fireplace, too, as the hall roof was fitted with a central louvre. Although the fireplace might have ruled out performances in the centre of the hall, the upper and lower ends both had recommendations as playing spaces. Had the Queen's Men been allowed to perform at the upper end in 1586–87 the self-contained adjoining room might have served as a temporary tiring house, while, at the lower end, the players could have used the screen as a backdrop, and the screens passage or one of the adjoining rooms as a changing space.

Visiting players would have found larger halls but similar facilities at colleges such as Magdalen, Oxford. Magdalen's surviving fifteenth century hall (measuring 72^{1}/$_{2}$ feet by 29^{1}/$_{4}$ feet), was the venue for regular college plays and is likely to have been the space used by Leicester's players if they performed when they visited in 1575–76. The players would have found the five-bay hall much as it is today.[94] At the upper end is a dais that would have afforded an inbuilt platform for performing, while at the lower end the three original doorways 'to the buttery and pantry' lie behind the screen erected for the university visit of King James (1605). In the late sixteenth century the three doorways may not have been separated from the main body of the hall. Academic or professional players who performed at this end in the Elizabethan period might have used the doorways to the buttery and pantry as entry and exit points, while the screen would have afforded a performance backdrop for post-1605 productions.[95]

Even more capacious halls were to be found in some colleges. At Trinity College, Cambridge, the old hall was superseded in the early seventeenth century by the magnificent new hall built by Master Thomas Nevile (completed 1608). The hall – modelled upon that at Middle Temple (one of the London Inns of Court) – was nearly twice the size of the earlier hall, measuring 103 feet by 40 feet and 50 feet in height.[96] At its upper end was a new dais and at the lower end a richly decorated screen that can still be seen. Nevile set about a programme of building soon after he was appointed Master (1593). Having completed the great quadrangle, he apparently resolved to build a new hall, fearing that the 'deformity' and 'almost ruinous' state of the old hall inherited from Michaelhouse would otherwise cast 'a shade' over the magnificence of the quadrangle.[97] The building housing the old hall was not destroyed, however, but 'used for the kitchen and offices of the new hall'. The new hall at Trinity was the largest in Cambridge and became the usual location for university plays performed for visiting royalty.[98] These performances were staged at the upper end, away from the expensively decorated screen; and a room adjoining the upper end was apparently reserved as a 'tyring house' for such performances.[99]

The Great Hall at Christ Church, Oxford, where the Queen's Men might have performed (1589–90), afforded an even larger performance space. Finished in 1529 and measuring approximately 115 feet by 40 feet and 50 feet in height, the eight-bay hall is the 'largest pre-nineteenth century' hall in either university and survives 'remarkably intact' (see Illustrations 17 and 18).[100] In customary fashion, its upper end is fitted with a dais and would have been 'better illuminated than the lower end' since some of the hall's largest windows lie at its western (upper) end. The main bay is 'the second from the west on the south side of the hall with two three-light windows, three transoms and a fan vault over the alcove'. Where the design of the hall is more unusual is at its lower end. Instead of the screen found in most college halls there is 'a large anteroom', 'from which a single doorway leads into the hall'. This may have been the main entry in the early modern period, in which case it might have been more practical for the Queen's Men to perform at the upper end if they were permitted to play in the hall in 1589–90. There is another entry point in the south wall at the lower end of the present hall, and one entry point at the upper end (at the south side of the dais), but these may not be original doorways.[101] Had there been another entry at the hall's lower end, performing against the backdrop of the anteroom might have been more feasible (and the spacious adjoining room might have provided a changing area).

The hall afforded the largest, most impressive performance space in Renaissance Oxford and was the most frequently used venue for college plays. It was also the customary venue for plays staged for the entertainment of visiting royalty in the Renaissance, beginning with Queen Elizabeth in 1566. On this occasion a stage was erected at the upper end of the hall and Queen Elizabeth sat on the stage in a 'canopied chair' where she might be seen by the audience as she watched Richard Edwardes's plays.[102] With its spacious dimensions and its reputation as a venue for prestigious entertainment, Christ Church's hall 'furnished an attractive' performance space for professional as well as academic players. If the Queen's Men were given permission to perform there they probably considered themselves fortunate, but are unlikely to have been daunted by the prospect of performing in such a venue. Grand though it might be, Christ Church's hall was comparable in size with spaces used by professional troupes at Court and in some early modern towns.[103]

Staging

Professional players customarily carried a stock of playing gear on tour. If they performed in university colleges they are therefore likely to have performed in costume and to have used props, as did their academic counterparts. (Whether players were ever able to borrow additional items of playing gear from colleges with their own supply of costumes and props, such as Trinity, Cambridge, is unknown.)[104] It is also possible that players would have performed on stages, the use of platforms having become common for professional performances in and outside London from the mid-sixteenth century. Academic audiences would have been accustomed to seeing student plays acted on wooden stages, and payments for their preparation are commonplace in Renaissance college records. Indeed, 'the erection of the stage in the hall was usually the most formidable expense' when colleges mounted student plays.[105]

Although materials for academic stages were generally hired or purchased specially, some colleges built up a stock of reusable stage materials. At Trinity (Cambridge) their stage furniture in 1547–48 included ' "xij staging trystles ix long & thre short" together with "feete for the same trisles" '.[106] Queen's College (Cambridge) owned an even more complex demountable theatre 'built entirely of scaffolding materials' and erected within the college hall for its annual academic plays. It incorporated a stage and two tiring houses; and galleries for spectators were 'erected against the back wall above the stage, against the two side-walls, and against the entrance screen'.[107] Alan Nelson's research suggests that work on the stage had begun as early as 1546 and that it was 'in continuous use right through the most active decades of Elizabethan and Jacobean theatre'.[108] Such an elaborate theatre was perhaps unlikely to be constructed on behalf of visiting players at any university college. Whether professional players would have been permitted access to college-owned staging materials is also debatable, although it is intriguing to think that a troupe such as the Queen's Men might have been allowed use of the staging timber owned by Trinity (Cambridge) when they visited and possibly performed there in 1586–87.[109]

College halls would have afforded a number of possible playing areas, but most early modern evidence indicates that hall performances were staged at the upper or lower end (before the screens passage). Both ends might have recommendations for would-be performers, usually affording at least one entry and exit point, while adjoining rooms might serve as temporary changing spaces. The analogous evidence of academic performances suggests that plays were usually acted at the upper end of the hall, and this may have been the case if and when professional players performed in college halls in the Elizabethan and Jacobean periods.[110] Playing at the upper end of the hall avoided the practical problems posed by performing before the 'principal entrance to the hall' (traditionally, the lower end).[111] It also made more sense symbolically, the higher end being the area 'of the hall most associated with display' and prestigious guests.[112]

Audiences

Predicting what kind and size of audience visiting players might have encountered if and when they performed at university colleges is difficult. Audiences might have varied, as they did for academic plays. Some student plays were performed before small, select gatherings; others were performed more publicly before audiences including members of other colleges and townsmen and women.[113] If Jackson's description of the King's Men's reception at Oxford (1610) is any guide, a college performance by one of the leading professional companies had the potential to generate considerable interest within and outside the university.[114] The capacity of college halls varied but could be great. Indeed, the most capacious college halls (Christ Church, Oxford, and Trinity, Cambridge) were larger than the indoor playhouses of early seventeenth-century London and theoretically capable of accommodating greater audiences.[115] If opened to outside individuals, the audiences for any professional plays staged in large colleges could therefore have been comparable in size and social and sexual diversity with those entertained in the metropolitan indoor playhouses.

The plays performed by professional companies would not have been what university audiences were accustomed to seeing on the academic stage. As well as being written in English, they were rarely classical or neo-classical in subject or style. By the late sixteenth century, they were also less likely to involve the use of 'stage houses', whereas 'houses' continued to be used occasionally in academic plays.[116] If the satirical evidence of *The Second Part of The Return from Parnassus* is to be trusted, spectators might also have found the professional players' acting style a little different from that of academic actors. At one point 'Will Kemp' mocks the style of acting at the universities:

> *Kemp.* [. . .] 'tis good sporte in part, to
> see them neuer speak in their walke, but at the end of the
> stage, iust as though in walking with a fellow we should
> neuer speake but at a stile, a gate, or a ditch, where a man
> can go no further.
> (*The Second Part of The Return from Parnassus*, 4.3.1757)

Kemp suggests academic actors tended to deliver speeches from a stationary position, at the 'end of the stage'. This may be an exaggerated stereotype (Kemp, after all, is presented as a figure to be mocked rather than believed in the play), but if there were no truth in his characterisation of scholars' acting the scene would not be comic. In criticising academic actors for their stylised manner of performance, Kemp also implicitly suggests that professional players' use of the performance space and style of acting was generally less formal (and possibly more naturalistic) than that of their academic counterparts.

Conclusions

Records of professional troupes visiting and performing in Elizabethan and Jacobean schools and colleges are rare, the latter especially so as a consequence of university regulations preventing professional performances within five miles of their precincts. That there is any evidence of professional companies at the universities is remarkable and possibly proof that there was a taste for popular theatre in both towns despite the universities' official hostility to players. The main attraction of academic buildings as playing venues is likely to have been the large indoor spaces they often afforded. Such spaces lent themselves to playing and often served as the temporary theatres for student play productions. In some cases, professional companies may have been able to look forward to receiving rewards for their performances at schools and colleges as well. Whether they also enjoyed the assistance of officials and students when preparing to play at academic buildings is more difficult to determine. Some schools and colleges would certainly have been in a position to offer help, having experience in mounting academic plays and their own stocks of playing gear.

The fact that professional and academic performers may have shared some of the same playing spaces (if not precisely the same facilities) demonstrates that there were points of intersection between the worlds of popular and academic theatre and helps to explain the influence they occasionally exerted upon each other. Indeed, as the preceding pages have shown, there was more common ground between the two theatrical traditions than is often recognised, with professional and academic players sometimes sharing the experience and skills of similarly trained writers and craftsmen and occasionally catering for the same elite courtly audiences. Studying professional companies' visits to schools and colleges thus provides an opportunity not only to consider one of the 'theatres' shared by professional and amateur players, but to explore the relationship between the professional and academic stage and the continuing overlaps between professional and amateur drama in Renaissance England.

7
Playing in Markets and Game Places

Professional players generally appear to have favoured playing indoors when on tour in the Elizabethan and Jacobean periods but there are occasional instances of troupes performing outdoors in churchyards and inn-yards and at least one example of a patronised company performing in a market place. In 1584 the Earl of Essex's players performed in Shrewsbury's apple market. Six years later the Queen's Men performed a tumbling display in the town's neighbouring cornmarket.[1] There is also a possibility that some touring players made use of the open-air 'playing' or 'game' places found in a number of Tudor and Stuart communities. The paucity of evidence regarding professional open-air playing in the early modern provinces has meant that such productions have received comparatively little attention. Yet, if we wish to have a fuller understanding of touring companies and their practices, and of the diversity of spaces used as theatrical venues outside Shakespearean London, what evidence there is needs to be taken into account. A study of travelling players' performances in outdoor provincial spaces also affords an opportunity to explore one of the points of connection between amateur and professional theatrical culture in Renaissance England, as local amateur players also occasionally used open-air urban spaces as their temporary theatres.

I

'Playing' and 'game' places as theatrical venues

Although there were few purpose-built or converted playhouses in the Elizabethan and Jacobean provinces, there were other recreational spaces potentially available for theatrical use, such as the open-air earthen playing 'rounds' (or *plen-an-gwarry*) in Cornwall and the 'playing' or 'game' places recorded in a number of early modern English communities (including Great Yarmouth, Walsham-le-Willows and Wymondham).[2] Such open-air recreational spaces had a long tradition in many parts of the country, although few exist today. In Cornwall at least thirty-seven possible 'playing places' have been identified but only two original examples are thought to survive, at St Just (in Penwith) and Pirran; and both have been altered since the seventeenth century.[3] Like the early London playhouses, 'playing' or 'game' places were usually multi-purpose recreational venues, in keeping with the more general meanings of 'play' and 'game' in the period.[4] Hence, we find evidence of them being used for a wide variety of activities in different parts of the country including ball games, archery, wrestling matches, and dramatic performances.[5] Recreational spaces were not always known explicitly as 'game' or 'playing' places; some had other names relating to their location or origin. In early modern Shrewsbury, for instance, there is evidence of an open-air recreational space known as 'the quarry'. This amphitheatre, carved from the lands behind the town walls, derived its name from its origin as a quarry for local building materials.[6]

'Playing' or 'game' places appear to have varied in size and shape but were often open grassland areas traditionally used or reserved for local recreation. The 'playing places' found in Cornwall are generally thought to have been circular earthen amphitheatres. The most famous description of these Cornish sites is that offered by Richard Carew, High Sheriff of the County in 1586. Alluding to the Cornish Miracle Plays, he reported that for 'representing it they raise an earthen amphitheatre of enclosed playne some 40 or 50 foot'.[7] However, the two partly surviving 'playing places' are much larger than this, suggesting that Cornish playing 'rounds' may have varied considerably in size. According to Borlase, the *plen-an-gwarry* at St Just measured 126 feet in diameter and the Pirran Round 130 feet in diameter in the mid-eighteenth century, when the state of preservation of both is thought to have been better than in modern times.[8] The 'game place' recorded at Walsham-le-Willows may also have been an earthen 'round' or semi-circular amphitheatre, although the most detailed surviving description (1577) is ambiguous about the shape of the site: 'The sayd game place [. . .] is [. . .] a place compassed rownd with a fayer banke cast vp on a good height and havinge [. . .] many great trees called populers growynge about the same banke'. It may have been a sizeable space, too, like the larger Cornish 'rounds', lying on a plot of land of at least half an acre.[9] Alan Somerset's research suggests that the dry 'quarry' used for plays at

Shrewsbury was also a semi-circular amphitheatre, although it was probably larger than that found at Walsham as one contemporary estimated that it could accommodate 10,000 spectators.[10]

Other 'game places' may have been square, rectangular or even irregular in shape. The main evidence regarding the possible size of the sixteenth-century 'game place' at Great Yarmouth is found in the indenture made between town officials and Robert Coppyng for the rent of a garden and the 'game place' and 'game place house' in 1538. It suggests the plot of land that included the 'game place' may have been rectangular:

> the seid baylyffes and chamberleyns [. . .] have grunted dimissed & letten to fferme to the same Robert Coppyng and to his assign a certeyn Gardeyn lyeng on the sowth syde of the parsonage gardeyn extendyng in lenght by the same parsonage wall xxxv foote & in brede xxj foote & it abuttith vpon the town wall ageynst thest together with acertyn howse calde the game place hous with the holle profight of the grounde calde the Game place.[11]

The document only gives the dimensions of the Garden (35 feet by 21 feet), suggesting that the 'game place' was an area of the Garden, and therefore smaller. If this was the case it was evidently a recreational space of rather more modest dimensions than the 'playing places' in Cornwall and the 'quarry' at Shrewsbury.

The origins of most of the known 'game' or 'playing places' are obscure. In Cornwall some early scholars suggested that the *plen-an-gwarry* were created with theatrical use in mind, but there is no proof to confirm this hypothesis. On the contrary, there is evidence that some 'rounds' were not purpose-built as 'playing places' but, rather, were converted from earlier earthworks.[12] Similarly, there is usually no evidence that 'game' or 'playing places' were exclusively intended for dramatic use. In some cases it is possible that 'playing places' gained their name and their status as recreational sites through their customary use for various forms of 'play'. In other instances the area of land may have been specially reserved for communal recreational use, as appears to have been the case at Shrewsbury and Walsham-le-Willows.

Many 'playing places' were situated on land owned or managed by the local community. The 'game places' at Walsham-le-Willows and Great Yarmouth in the sixteenth century both appear to have been town property. In the Walsham *Field Book* (1577) it states that 'the game place in the tenure of diuers men to the vse and behofe of the towne of walsham [. . .] is customarye ground holden of the sayd manor of walsham'; while, in Great Yarmouth the bailiffs and town chamberlains leased and received rent for the 'game place' and house in the sixteenth century.[13] The property that became the Great Yarmouth 'game place' tenement had previously been part of the garden of the local Benedictine Priory.[14] Similarly, Shrewsbury's civic officers appear to have controlled much of the ex-Friary land 'behind the walls' of the city, in which the 'quarry' theatre stood.[15]

In other communities 'playing places' were located on land owned or managed by the church. In Cornwall 'a fair number of playing places' are 'situated on the glebe-land of the church'.[16] In such cases, it is possible that the creation or reservation of specific open-air 'playing' or 'game places' on church land was part of an effort to move secular events outwards from the church. Attempts to transfer various social and recreational activities from 'consecrated ground to adjacent or nearby sites' can be traced back to the medieval period; and there is evidence of alternative social venues such as guildhalls and church houses being established 'on the edges of churchyards, or within a stone's throw of them' to facilitate this process.[17]

Some 'playing places' may have included one or more buildings on their site as well. There is evidence of a 'house' at the Great Yarmouth 'game place' and there may have been a structure of some sort at the 'quarry' in Shrewsbury, although the function of the property is not clear in either instance. References to the Great Yarmouth 'game place' date back as early as 1492–93, but the 'game place house' is not mentioned until 1538–39 when five shillings was paid 'pro firma de le Game Place and domus ibidem'. In the same year the 'game place', 'game place house' and a garden were leased to Robert Coppyng.[18] The lease required that players and their audiences be allowed 'the plesure & ese of the seid house and Gameplace at all suche tyme & tymes as eny interludes or playes ther shal be ministred or played'.[19] However, while the lease makes it clear that players and spectators were to be allowed the pleasure and ease of the 'game place' *and* house, it does not specify in what way. Whether the interludes were to be performed in the 'game place' or house, or in both is also ambiguous. It is possible that plays were performed in the house and that it was, in effect, an indoor theatre, an assumption made by a number of earlier scholars.[20] However, David Galloway is probably correct when he argues that it is more likely 'that plays were performed in the game place', in keeping with the traditional use of 'game' places, while the house served as a place of hospitality, possibly affording food, drink and accommodation.[21]

There are certainly later examples of eating and drinking houses being established in affiliation with a playing venue. When John Cholmley and Philip Henslowe agreed to build the Rose Theatre in London in 1587, they decided that Henslowe would be responsible for the 'play howse now in framinge and shortly to be erekted', while Cholmley was to take charge of 'all that small tenemente or dwelling howsse scittuate and standing at the southe ende or syde of the said parcell of grownde or garden plotte to keepe victualinge in or to any other vse or vsses whatsoever'. Henslowe agreed not to allow anyone else to sell 'any breade or drinke other then such as shalbe solde to and for the behoofe' of Cholmley, suggesting that Cholmley was planning to use the property as a victualling house, catering for the audiences attracted to the playhouse.[22] Even if the Great Yarmouth 'game place house' was used for plays in the first half of the sixteenth century there is no evidence that it was being used as a theatre in the Elizabethan and Jacobean periods. There are references to the 'game place' and house in the Elizabethan civic records but there is no indication that either site was being used for plays; and the corporate order recorded in the Assembly Book on 11 March 1596 suggests that it had become usual for players to perform in the Guildhall in the late sixteenth century.[23] It alluded to 'Game players having been heretofore licensed to play in the Guildhall' and forbade future play performances at the hall.[24]

In Shrewsbury the first reference to a 'mansion' possibly constructed at the 'quarry' occurs in the records of a civic play in 1445–46 that lasted a couple of days. The town spent '7s. 6d. entertaining Lady Talbot' when 'she saw the play "in Mansione sua [in her structure] ad lusum extra muros"'. The 'quarry' apparently existed at this date and Somerset suggests that the plays took place there: 'The dry quarry was the only suitable playing-place "extra muros" [. . .] so we are safe in assuming that this structure was erected at the quarry'.[25] The nature of the mansion is unknown but it was possibly a structure in which important spectators could sit or stand to watch the plays, rather than a tavern-like place of public 'plesure & ese'. The mansion is possibly alluded to again in 1532–33 when payment was made 'for the making of one structure of two storeys for the lord president and the bailiffs at the time of the play in Whitsun week'. (Later references reveal that the two-storey structure was in the 'quarry'.)[26] The earlier mansion may simply have been 'refurbished' for the reception of the lord president, although it is possible that the two-storey structure was new.

Some open-air 'playing places' appear to have been adapted for theatrical use in more specific ways, incorporating permanent raised areas or stages for plays. In 1577 the 'game place' at Walsham-le-Willows was described as having 'in the myddest a fayre round place of earth wythe a stone wall about the same to the height of the earth made of purpose for the vse of Stage playes'.[27] The size and height of the earthen stage is unknown but its circular shape suggests that performances were staged 'in the round', while the fact that it was a permanent feature of the site could indicate that the game place was used for plays on a fairly regular basis. A number of timber stages appear to have stood in the 'game place' at Wymondham, until 1584–85 when payments were made for 'takyng downe ye stages at ye game place' and 'bringynge of ye stagyng tymber from the game place' to the church.[28] Whether these 'stages' were for players is unclear. They were perhaps wooden platforms of the kind used for medieval religious plays requiring a 'place-and-scaffold' style of staging, although it is also possible that they included (or were) spectator platforms.

The 'quarry' at Shrewsbury may have been fitted with removable timber stages, too. In 1575 the Town Assembly agreed 'that wheras the frame of timber that stood in the quarell behind the walles is taken downe that the same tymber shale presentlye be deliuered to the schalemaster' for the school's use. While this could refer to 'the two-storey structure erected for a previous play [. . .], or perhaps to some other structure erected' by local schoolmaster Thomas Ashton for the performances of his plays at the 'quarry', there is a possibility that it alludes to a stage erected in the semi-circular amphitheatre.[29] A lawsuit of 1609 in which the town bailiffs sought to assert their ownership of the land 'behind the walls' of the town provides further evidence about the 'quarry's' possible adaptation for playing. One of the questions put to the bailiffs' witnesses focused on the use of the 'quarry', asking whether it had

bene vsed and imployed by the burgesses and Inhabitants of the saide towne for bearbaytings bullbaitings makeing butts and shootinge for stage plaies and Common playes siluer games wrestling Running Leapinge, and other like actiuities and recreaions, And whether haue they as occasion serued at their will and pleasure made scaffolds erected boothes and tentes [tenements] made stayres and digged and troaden the ground & soyle aswell within the compasse of the saide drie quarell as in other parts of the close aboue the saide drie quarell for the better beholdinge and takeinge the pleasure of the said Common plaies and other exercises and disports.[30]

The precise purpose of the scaffolds, booths and tenements erected at the quarry is not made clear but the phrasing of the question suggests that they were erected for the play performances staged at the open-air theatre. Some of the structures alluded to were evidently intended for spectators (for the 'better beholdinge' of the plays) but it is possible that the scaffolds included stages set up for the players as well.

Professional performances at 'playing' places

Plays were staged in a number of open-air 'playing places' in the early modern period, but the performances were usually local amateur productions. In 1602 Richard Carew famously described the use of Cornish 'playing places' for the performance of the 'Guary miracle [. . .] a kind of Enterlude compiled in Cornish out of some Scripture history'.[31] A number of religious plays were also produced locally at the 'quarry' in Shrewsbury, including 'the playe of St Iulian the Apostate' in 1556–57.[32] In both cases the performers are likely to have been mainly amateur performers, rather than touring professionals. Professional travelling players may have had access to and performed at some 'playing places' as well, although direct evidence of such productions has been lacking thus far. Certainly, the phrasing used in some of the surviving documents relating to 'game places' suggests they could have been the venue for professional as well as amateur productions. At Great Yarmouth the 1538 lease of the 'game place' and 'game place house' to Coppyng alludes to their use by 'players', and while this could simply refer to local amateurs it might also allude to visiting professionals. Although there are few direct records of professional companies performing in the town, the 1595–96 regulatory order passed prohibiting plays in the Guildhall indicates that the town was visited by a number of travelling troupes in the sixteenth century.[33]

The description of the 'game place' at Walsham-le-Willows (1577) is similarly general in its phrasing. The earthen stage is described as being for the use of 'Stage playes'. This phrase could refer equally to plays by local and/or visiting professional players, although in this instance it is perhaps more likely that the anticipated performers were locals as there are no records of professional troupes visiting Walsham in the early modern period, while there is evidence of local dramatic activity.[34] There are records of professional companies touring in the region, however, including Leicester's Men, the company to which James Burbage belonged, builder of The Theatre, one of the first open-air playhouses in London (1576). Part of the inspiration for the permanent open-air theatres of the metropolis could lie in the open-air 'playing places' that troupes such as Leicester's Men encountered as they toured the early modern provinces. The series of references to the

Shrewsbury 'quarry' in the 1609 lawsuit mentioned above presents a similar terminological problem. The documents refer to two kinds of 'play' at the 'quarry' ('stage' plays and 'Common' plays) but the distinction between the two is unclear. 'Common' plays could be plays staged publicly (before the common people) or plays performed by 'common' players (in other words professionals). Likewise, the phrase 'stage' plays might be used to describe local religious productions performed on scaffolds or performances by professional stage players.[35] Although there are no records of professional players performing at the 'quarry', it is possible therefore that they did occasionally use the open-air venue.

II

Drama in the market place

Distinguished by their right to hold one or more weekly markets and annual fairs, the 760 market towns estimated to have existed in Tudor and Stuart England played an important role in regional social culture. 'Despite the expansion of private bargaining in the sixteenth century, the market town was still, and was destined to remain, the normal place of sale and purchase for the great majority of country people.'[36] But market towns were not only trading centres, they were social centres, where people met to 'hear the news, listen to sermons, criticise the government, or organise insurrection'.[37] One of the main forums for all these activities was the market place. In many communities it was 'the focal point' of the town.[38] Often this social and economic centrality was paralleled physically, with market places occupying a central urban location. When players staged performances in market places they were occupying a key urban space and were effectively guaranteed local attention and publicity, an obvious attraction for companies keen to draw large audiences. This was also why professional and amateur players often chose to announce forthcoming play productions at market crosses, as do Sir Oliver Owlet's players in Marston's *Histrio-mastix*.[39] Indeed, such public proclamations in a central civic location had been one of the common ways of advertising local and visiting play performances in England since the medieval period.[40] For similar reasons important public announcements (such as the proclamation of new monarchs and Acts of Parliament) were often made in the market place, the 'circuit of steps' around the standard market cross acting as a platform for their delivery.[41]

Market towns and their market places varied in size and layout in the early modern period but there were 'certain distinctive shapes or types of market place'. 'The simplest form, characteristic of small country towns, consisted of a single, long, wide street, expanding in the middle and narrowing at either end.' Other common types included 'the triangular shape, often formed at the meeting place of three roads', 'the plain rectangle', and 'the cross-shape'.[42] In larger towns there was considerable variation from these usual patterns; and in some places 'the expansion of the market obliterated the original layout or necessitated the dispersal of trade through various streets devoted to the sale of particular commodities'.[43] There is evidence of such dispersal of market activity in early modern Shrewsbury. While the cornmarket was held in the market square, the livestock market took place 'in Frankwell', hides and skins 'could be purchased on Pride Hill', and the fish market was in Fish Street.[44]

These diverse market spaces had much to recommend them as venues for public recreation. Not only were they associated with public gatherings and communal activity, but they were generally communally owned and freely available as entertainment venues. Whatever their shape, market places were also characteristically sizeable open spaces. They had the potential advantage, therefore, of being readily adaptable for playing and of being able to accommodate large audiences. Their primary function as trading spaces may have imposed restrictions on their availability for recreational uses, but most towns had only one or two weekly market days. At Shrewsbury, for instance, the main market days in the early modern period were Wednesday and Saturday.[45] On other days, market spaces were less likely to be cluttered with stalls and goods and might be available, although it may have been necessary to seek permission to use them for playing from town market officials. If permission was sought and granted, players may even have been able to look forward to some assistance with their preparations and performances from market officers. The latter's responsibilities often included 'maintaining order in the market place and surrounding streets, and keeping them clean and free of obstruction, or roaming livestock', services which players might benefit from.[46] The greatest potential drawback of market places as temporary theatres is likely to have been the fact that they were usually open-air spaces and therefore exposed to the elements, a potential shortcoming of all open-air recreational venues in England, then and now. Bad weather could be a serious obstacle to the success of open-air entertainment, as players and spectators discovered on one occasion at Chester in 1588–89. A play of King

Ebrauk was performed at the High Cross but 'such rayne fell' that the performance 'was hindered much'.[47]

Plays in market places

Given their several attractions as temporary theatres, it is perhaps not surprising to find that there is evidence of public entertainment taking place in some market places in the Renaissance and earlier. There is an intriguing early reference to a market place performance at Sandwich (Kent). In 1508–09 it was reported that the King's players showed 'sporte in the fishem[ar]ket openly'. The precise nature of the 'sporte' with which the players entertained the crowd is uncertain: they may have performed a play or staged an acrobatic show.[48] A performance of the latter kind possibly required a large playing space which may be why the troupe chose or were recommended to perform in the open-air space of the fishmarket. A troupe patronised by Elizabeth I appears to have staged a similar show of sporting activities in the cornmarket at Shrewsbury in 1590. The author of *Dr Taylor's History* of the town describes the troupe's memorable acrobatic display with a Hungarian rope-dancer on this occasion:

> there was a scaffolld put vp in the cornem*a*rket [. . .] vpon the w*h*ich an hongaria*n* and other of the queenes M*a*ies*t*ies players and tvm-blars vsid and excersisid them selves [. . .] they wold tvrne them selves twise bothe backward and forward wi*t*hout towchinge any grownde in lightinge or fallinge vpon theire feete [. . .] also a litill from the sayde stadge there was a gable roape tighted and drawen strayte vppon poales [. . .] vpon the w*h*iche roape the sayde hongaria*n* did assende and goe vppon wi*t*he his bare feete havinge a longe poale in his hanndes over his headd and wold fall stridlen*ges* vppon the sayde roap and mowntinge vp againe wold vpon the same wi*t*he hys feete verey myraculo*u*s to the beholders.[49]

As in the case of the 1508–09 Sandwich performance it is possible that the troupe chose to perform in the open-air theatre of the cornmarket because it afforded them more room in which to stage their acrobatic feats than an indoor venue. The players performed with the rope-dancer at a number of other towns they visited while travelling in 1590, and may have performed in the open-air on several occasions, possibly because they were touring a tumbling show as well as plays.[50]

Play performances are also recorded in a number of medieval and early modern market places. In Dover (Kent), the town rewarded 'players that played in the markett place one Ester mudaye' in 1550–51; and in Louth (Lincolnshire) a play was staged 'in the markit sted on corpus christi Day' in 1556–57.[51] In such cases it is not certain, however, whether the performers were local amateurs or visiting professionals. Direct evidence of professional market place performances in Elizabethan and Jacobean England is scarce. In the REED volumes published thus far there is only one clear record of a market place play performance by professional actors between 1559 and 1625 (as noted earlier), the Earl of Essex's players performing in Shrewsbury's apple market in 1584.[52] Some records of market performances may have been lost and others may be discovered as research continues, but it is likely that professional market place productions were comparatively rare in Renaissance England. Surviving evidence indicates that professional companies generally chose to play indoors at this time, where they were not only protected from some of the vagaries of the British climate, but where audience entry could be more easily regulated. The latter factor probably became increasingly important as it became customary for players to charge entry fees to their performances in and outside London. The market place performance by Essex's Men at Shrewsbury is a rare example of professional open-air playing in Shakespearean England and its closer study affords an insight into one of the more unusual branches of professional touring theatre in early modern England.

III

Case study: the Earl of Essex's Men in the apple market, Shrewsbury

Record of the players' performance in Shrewsbury's apple market is preserved in *Dr Taylor's History* of the town. The author describes how on 17 July 1584 there was 'a notable stadge playe played in the heye [high] streete in shreusbery in the aple market place there by the Earle of Essexe men openly and freely'.[53] Confirmation that the troupe was in the town at this date occurs in an equally intriguing allusion to the players in the Bailiffs' records. A payment was made 'to my Lord of essex men beinge players [. . .] and spent on them in especte of helping at ye fyer'. The 'fire' in question appears to have occurred on St John's Hill in the town on 18 July 1584. The players acted, it seems, as volunteer 'fire fighters'.[54] No further details of the performance are provided in *Dr Taylor's History* or in other contemporary sources. However, drawing upon other evidence regarding the troupe, Shrewsbury and the apple market, we can begin to reconstruct some aspects of the market play performance.

Reconstructing the performance

The troupe

The troupe that visited Shrewsbury in 1584 was patronised by Robert Devereux, the Elizabethan 2nd Earl of Essex, and records of it touring begin appearing in 1581.[55] The troupe was not one of the major playing companies in 1584. It had not acquired 'the status to warrant regular appearances at court, although Essex's was the company that went with the Queen's to play in Dublin in 1589 on what was probably at least a semi-official visit'; and there is evidence of Essex's Men performing at some of the same places and perhaps in collaboration with the Queen's players on several occasions in 1589–90.[56] The Earl may have been using his theatrical patronage politically, encouraging his players to tour and perform with the Queen's players as a way of publicising his friendship with the monarch and of promoting his reputation. At this date the Earl was the Queen's recognised court 'favourite', but was keen to be entrusted with greater military and political offices.[57] Detailed evidence of the company's touring itinerary in 1583–84 does not survive, although there are records of the troupe visiting and receiving rewards from a number of towns during this time, including Coventry, York, Gloucester, Ipswich and Leicester. In the summer and autumn of 1584 the players appear to have been touring in the Marches and the southwest: as well as being rewarded by the Shrewsbury Corporation, there are payments to the troupe in the Bath and Bristol records in this period.[58]

Early modern Shrewsbury

Shrewsbury was a 'natural stop for entertainers' touring in the Marcher counties. Not only was it the 'chief borough of the county', but it was one of the principal English market towns and lay at the junction of two major roads, 'Watling Street and the major western road north from Ludlow to Chester'.[59] It was a town where entertainers could look forward to good accommodation and where they could expect to find large audiences, including residents and visiting traders and travellers. The town authorities generally welcomed players, too, providing a further incentive for touring companies like Essex's Men to visit.[60] One finds numerous records of visiting entertainers being rewarded by the town during the early modern period. Between 1559 and 1617 the town made more than thirty payments to visiting players alone, rewarding at least one troupe (and sometimes more) almost every year in the 1580s and 1590s.[61]

Early modern Shrewsbury afforded a number of possible playing places for visiting players, including indoor venues (such as the Booth Hall) and outdoor spaces (such as the 'quarry' and the market places). Unfortunately, the location of most of the performances by visiting players is unknown, although there is at least one record of professional actors performing in the Booth Hall: Lady Elizabeth's players staged an evening performance there on 27 November 1613.[62] But, in 1584, Essex's players chose or were invited to perform outdoors in the apple market. The fact that the performance's location is recorded could be one sign that it was an unusual choice of venue for a visiting troupe. The timing of the company's trip to Shrewsbury might explain their choice of an open-air venue. The players visited in mid-July when the region could have been enjoying warm, fine weather.[63] In such conditions an open-air playing venue may have been preferable to an indoor one. Playing outdoors could also have been a way of catering for the large audiences that it might be possible to gather on a pre-market day in Shrewsbury.[64] As the corporation rewarded them it is possible that the players were encouraged to perform outdoors, as well, as it would allow more local people to enjoy the civic-sponsored entertainment.[65] While the players might have used the town's open-air amphitheatre (the 'quarry') for such a performance, the apple market was possibly deemed a more attractive venue because it was more central and well situated for the players and their audience.

In the late sixteenth century the main market place in Shrewsbury was the cornmarket, but there were other recognised market places, including the apple market (or 'green market'), where Essex's men performed.[66] In the early modern period the latter was the open space 'in front of the Booth Hall (including a length of the High Street)' (see Illustration 19).[67] The Booth Hall (built in 1451–52) stood across the town's main market area abutting on to the High Street at the northern end of the market place, and separating the cornmarket from the apple market. The main market place, shaped like a bent rectangle, survives today but is now called the Square and incorporates the old cornmarket and apple market areas, the two spaces having been merged when the Booth Hall was pulled down in 1784.[68] Situated at the top of the town's main street and before the Booth Hall, the apple market may not have been the town's main market but in 1584 it lay at the heart of the civic space in

Shrewsbury. As such it was a potentially prestigious as well as a convenient place in which to perform. A performance in such a key public space and in the town's main street was guaranteed to attract local interest. The apple market may have lent itself to performance use physically, too. The 1575 Burghley Map of Shrewsbury shows that it was a comparatively large open space (see Illustration 20) (The apple market can be seen to the left of the central church, divided from the cornmarket by the long Booth Hall.) As such it afforded plenty of room for performing and for spectators. The Burghley Map shows a sizeable open area in the cornmarket as well, but here the players would have found the open space partly obstructed by a five-bay timber structure for sheltering corn, built in the 1560s and replaced in 1596 by a Market Hall.[69] The more open space of the apple market and its High Street location may have made it the more appealing market place for the 1584 performance.

Playing in the apple market

On arriving, it is likely that Essex's players presented themselves to the local corporation to seek permission to perform in the town. At this point, it is possible that they requested or were invited to perform in the apple market. The open-air performance may have been sponsored by the corporation, as noted above, for the author of *Dr Taylor's History* describes the company as performing 'openly and freely', and the Bailiffs' accounts record that the town gave the players fifteen shillings.[70] The corporation may have dictated that the play be staged on a non-market day and the players were possibly only authorised to use the market space for the individual performance recorded. It would not have been practical to permit a recreation that might lead to the blocking of the town's main thoroughfare on several days.

Any performance preparations and adaptations of the space were probably kept to a minimum. The play is described as a stage play so it is possible that a stage was erected, having been brought or assembled on site by the players. We know that the Queen's players used a stage when they performed six years later in the cornmarket; and in a town full of traders it probably would not have been difficult to obtain barrels and boards for the construction of a temporary scaffold. Such a platform could have been set up against the backdrop of the Booth Hall, and would have made the production visible to a larger audience. Seating was probably unnecessary, the spectators simply standing to watch the performance, as they would to hear important local announcements. As the play was being staged in the open air and by natural light it is likely that it was performed in the afternoon or early evening. This would have allowed time for the company to remove their playing gear and stage ready for the following market day as well. (The play was staged on Friday 17 July and Saturday was one of the weekly market days.)[71]

The title of the play performed by Essex's Men is unknown and no information survives about the troupe's repertory in this period. However, the fact they were to perform before a possibly large audience and in the open air, may have prompted the troupe to perform a play full of visual spectacle and stage action. Such a play's narrative would hopefully be comprehensible even if spectators were not able to hear every speech (as might be the case when performing outdoors). A play of thrilling exploits and theatrical feats might well have suited the abilities and tastes of the players who showed themselves ready to spring into heroic action on behalf of the town the following day as voluntary fire-fighters, too. Whatever the name and genre of the play performed, it is likely to have been staged in costume and accompanied with props. The sight of the players in their finery performing against the civic splendour of the medieval Booth Hall was a potentially striking spectacle and may have helped to make the open-air performance notable in the eyes of the author of *Dr Taylor's History* of the town.

How many spectators enjoyed the performance offered freely by Essex's Men is unknown, but their audience could have been large. With a population in the region of 5000 people and a steady stream of visitors from neighbouring towns and counties (and occasionally, from Wales), it might have been possible to assemble an audience of several hundred people.[72] Large audiences for plays were evidently not unknown in the town, if Churchyard's description of spectator numbers for the local religious plays performed in the 'quarry' are even partially accurate. He suggested that the plays written by Thomas Ashton in the late sixteenth century drew audiences in the region of 'twenty thousand people', and estimated that the 'quarry' could hold 'ten thousand men at ease'.[73] Whether the spectators were happy with the entertainment offered is unrecorded, but the fact that the author of *Dr Taylor's History* thought the performance worth mentioning suggests that it was an occasion that proved locally memorable. The troupe's return to Shrewsbury in 1586–87 could be indirect evidence that the open-air production was popular, as it suggests the players anticipated being welcomed again. Once more, they received a civic reward but there is no indication that they performed outdoors on this occasion.[74]

Conclusion

Most of the open-air play performances recorded outside early modern London were local amateur productions. Records of professional touring companies performing outdoors in the provinces are rare, but not unknown. Travelling companies, like local amateurs, occasionally played in open-air venues such as inn-yards, churchyards and market places. Professional troupes may have performed occasionally in the open-air 'playing places' to be found in some early modern communities, too, although direct evidence of such productions has yet to be found. Open-air venues had their attractions for professional as well as amateur players. Market places, for instance, often afforded a large open theatre in a central urban location and events within them were guaranteed publicity and attention.

In the rare professional open-air productions we find an intriguing point of intersection between amateur and professional drama in early modern England, and further evidence that the two kinds of theatre were not sharply divided at this date. In the provinces at least, professional and amateur players still, occasionally, shared the same performance spaces and theatrical traditions. At the same time, in their preference for indoor venues when touring Elizabethan and Jacobean professional players anticipated the direction in which the professional theatre world and theatre design were moving. After a brief period of fashion and popularity the open-air playhouses of the Elizabethan capital – theatres that perpetuated the medieval tradition of open-air drama – were eventually displaced in number and importance by indoor theatres. By the mid-seventeenth century hall theatres were the norm in the professional theatre world and became the prototype for the playhouses built in the seventeenth century provinces. The tradition of open-air theatre and playing venues was not entirely displaced but it was largely eclipsed in importance in and outside London. The few professional open-air performances in the Shakespearean provinces represent some of the last vestiges of a theatrical tradition increasingly left behind by the developing world of professional English theatre.

8
Provincial Playhouses in Renaissance England, 1559–1625

Purpose-built or converted playhouses were 'largely' a 'metropolitan phenomenon' in Renaissance England.[1] Research thus far has identified explicit records of only three Elizabethan and Jacobean provincial theatres: the Wine Street playhouse in Bristol, the Prescot playhouse in Lancashire, and a theatre in York in 1609.[2] Indirect evidence suggests that two further regional playhouses could also have existed between 1559 and 1625.[3] The 'game place house' in Great Yarmouth, mentioned as early as 1538, may have been used by Elizabethan and Jacobean players, as discussed in Chapter 7; and the 1637 will of Sarah Barker alludes to a playhouse on the outskirts of Bristol which might have operated prior to 1625.[4]

The relative scarcity of provincial English playhouses between 1559 and 1625 is not surprising. The population and wealth of even the largest regional towns was much smaller than that of the capital. While London's inhabitants totalled around 200,000 at the end of the six-teenth century, there were only a few provincial towns with a popula-tion larger than 10,000: most 'lay within the 800–1500 range'.[5] A playhouse in any of England's provincial towns was likely to be a less lucrative enterprise than a theatre in the capital. Regional towns and their surrounding populations were not great enough to provide the kind of large, regular, and profitable audiences afforded by the metro-politan community.[6] Raising money to build a playhouse or to convert an existing building into a theatre was also potentially more difficult in a provincial town. There were generally fewer wealthy people who could be approached to act as investors in such a venture. It is probably no coincidence that two of the three provincial towns recorded as being home to a Renaissance playhouse were among England's largest and wealthiest regional towns. Robert Tittler highlights the regional importance of Bristol and York, when he describes them with Norwich as 'the three "miniature Londons" of the north, west, and east respectively'.[7]

There was perhaps not the same impetus to provide buildings exclusively for theatrical use in most regional communities either. While increasing restrictions upon where and when playing companies could perform in London encouraged players and theatrical entrepreneurs to provide alternative playing venues, beyond the immediate control of the corporation, urban play performances continued to be permitted in a number of spaces in most regional towns. Even those communities which paralleled the metropolitan corporation in introducing tighter theatrical regulations did not usually prevent the use of venues such as inns, as occurred in late Elizabethan London.

I

The playhouses: individual case studies

Records of more Elizabethan and Jacobean provincial theatres may be found as research continues. In the meantime a closer study of those regional playhouses already identified affords an insight into the beginnings of a new era in provincial theatrical culture, an era which saw the establishment of the first purpose-built or converted playhouses outside the early modern capital. In the following section the theatrical history of the three clearly identified provincial Renaissance playhouses is surveyed. As an epilogue, Part II looks at the second Bristol playhouse which may also have existed and operated as a theatre in the Jacobean period.

1. The Wine Street playhouse, Bristol

As early as 1906, Alfred Harvey noted the existence of a Renaissance playhouse in Wine Street, Bristol.[8] Scholars such as Kathleen M. D. Barker and Mark C. Pilkinton have provided fuller documentation of the playhouse more recently.[9] References to the playhouse have been found in a number of contemporary sources, including the Mayor's Audits, and the accounts of Queen Elizabeth's Hospital and St John the Baptist's Almshouse. The Mayor's Audits 'refer directly to the playhouse in Wine Street', the first allusion occurring in 1626. In this year the Audits record a payment to the corporation of a quit rent from 'a tenement sometimes a play house' in Wine Street.[10] Similar payments occur in the corporate records for a further five years (1626–31). The accounts of Queen Elizabeth's Hospital and St John the Baptist's Almshouse afford earlier evidence of the playhouse's existence, both including a series of annual payments from the playhouse after the death of its owner, Nicholas Woolfe (1614), in accordance with bequests made in his will. Those included in the hospital accounts end 'on Michaelmas (September 29) 1619', while the playhouse annuity is recorded regularly in the almshouse accounts until 1621.[11]

More detailed evidence relating to the playhouse is to be found in Richard Cooke's 1606 replication against Nicholas Woolfe. The replication restates charges Cooke made against Woolfe and his wife.[12] Woolfe apparently leased the Wine Street building which housed the playhouse to Cooke for a six-month period (*c.*1604) for five pounds. At a later date Cooke decided to move himself and his family from the house and therefore informed Woolfe that he planned to 'lett or assigne his said Interest & terme' in the property 'vnto some other'. Rather than have this happen, Woolfe apparently asked that he might have the house 'and terme soe lett by him vnto this Complainant againe to his owne vse to lett & bestowe of'. In return he promised to refund Cooke's payment for the property.[13] Cooke accepted his offer but Woolfe did not return the five pounds, eventually prompting Cooke to lodge a legal complaint against his former landlord. But what is intriguing about Cooke's statement is the insight that it provides into the building's use by players. The following passage is especially revealing, providing clear evidence of play performances at Woolfe's Wine Street property as early as 1604–05: 'the said defendantes [. . .] lodged sundrie persons of all sortes many tymes during the Complainantes terme besides certaine comedyantes whome he suffered to act and playe within the said Roomes for which the said defendantes tooke moneye'.[14] Whether Woolfe and his wife received part of the 'takings' collected from spectators or a payment from the players is unclear; but the record is interesting in either instance, suggesting that the property was functioning as a commercial playing venue from which Woolfe profited like any metropolitan playhouse owner.

Woolfe's will (2 June 1614) alludes directly to his ownership of a playhouse and to its use for plays, too, including a number of charitable bequests to be payable yearly 'out of my Play house in wynestreete' as long 'as the same house shall continewe a playe house at that such players as doe resorte to the said Cittie or inhabite within the same doe vsually playe there'. Woolfe evidently anticipated the continued functioning of the playhouse after his death, although his final proviso made allowance for its closure at some point in the future.[15] The answers which Margaret Woolfe (Nicholas's widow) and Henry Yate (one of the overseers of Nicholas Woolfe's will) gave to a suit made against Mrs Woolfe by Nicholas's son, Miles (1618–19), allude to the playhouse more briefly but provide further clues about its builder and its history. Margaret Woolfe testified that Woolfe possessed only two Bristol properties at his death: one tenement in which he lived, and 'one house with thapp*urtenau*nces in wynestreete [. . .] commonlie called the play house'; while Yate's answer includes an allusion to 'the stage in the said playho<. . .>'.[16] Although the body of evidence described above is small, it contains various pieces of information about the playhouse which can be supplemented with evidence drawn from wider sources of information about early modern Bristol and theatrical activity within its precincts.

Establishment of the playhouse

The date of the playhouse's establishment and closure are not explicitly recorded. Cooke's testimony suggests that it might have opened as early as 1604 and it 'probably closed in 1625'.[17] Although the playhouse may not have functioned continuously during this period, twenty years represents a comparatively lengthy career for a playhouse outside Renaissance London. Not all of the Elizabethan and Jacobean metropolitan playhouses survived for this length of time and the theatrical life of the other recorded provincial playhouses appears to have been much shorter.[18] What prompted Bristol cutler, Nicholas Woolfe, to open a playhouse is unknown. He does not appear to have had any 'theatrical connections' or special interest in drama. Founding the playhouse may have been 'a business opportunity as much as an artistic endeavour'.[19] In this respect, Woolfe would have had much in common with many metropolitan playhouse builders. A number of early theatre entrepreneurs were, like Woolfe, craftsmen or tradesmen by profession. James Burbage, who owned The Theatre, was a joiner, and John Cholmley, who funded the erection of the Rose playhouse with Philip Henslowe, was a grocer.[20] In setting up an indoor playhouse, Woolfe was also paralleling the example of impresarios such as Richard Farrant and Burbage, and anticipating the fashion for indoor theatres that was to prevail in the Jacobean metropolis.[21]

Professional acting companies regularly visited Bristol in the early modern period. Woolfe may have hoped to provide a central, readily available venue for these troupes and local players. Certainly, his will anticipates that visiting and local troupes will use the playhouse in the future, specifying that all the annuities payable from the playhouse should apply only while players that come to Bristol or 'inhabite within the same doe vsually playe there'.[22] He may also have been aware that it had become more difficult to gain permission to perform at the Guild-hall, a venue for many early Elizabethan performances. In 1585 the Common Council had passed an ordinance stating that players were only to be permitted at the hall if they played before the Mayor and his Brethren.[23] Notably, there are no references to performances in the Guildhall after 1597 and no civic payments to players between '10 September 1600' and 'Christmas 1608'.[24] It is possible that the establishment of Woolfe's playhouse contributed to the decline in productions hosted in the Guildhall and sponsored by the corporation.

The playhouse

All of the sources agree that the playhouse was in Wine Street in central Bristol. Identifying which building housed the playhouse has proved more difficult, especially as Woolfe appears to have leased or owned several properties there. Perhaps the strongest candidate for identifica-tion as the theatre is the Christ Church property (with 'an adjoining strip of land 16 feet deep') that Woolfe leased for forty-one years in 1598.[25] The lease authorised Woolfe, 'to New buylde the said Tenemente and everye parte thereof with thappurtenances within foure yeares nexte ensuinge the date hereof', and included permission for 'the rearinge up higher' of the tenement.[26] Although this property was described as a 'dwelling house' when it was leased to a tailor, Anthony Basset, in 1637 and as a 'house' in 1639 this does not preclude its earlier use as the playhouse.[27] One might expect the building to be described as a domestic habitation if it was promptly reconverted for domestic use following its closure in the 1620s and/or if it was used for habitation as well as playing during its life as a playhouse, as seems likely. Meanwhile, the rebuilding of the property between 1598 and 1602 might have included preparing part of it for theatrical use.

There are no plans or detailed descriptions of the playhouse, but Cooke reveals that the property contained a number of chambers and suggests that more than one may have been used for playing, describ-ing how during the term of his lease players were permitted to 'playe within the said *Roomes*' (own emphasis).[28] Yate's later allusion to the 'stage' in the playhouse (1619) suggests that one room *was* specifically converted into a theatre at some point, however.[29] For while it is not impossible that the 'stage' referred to was a demountable scaffold that could be moved between different rooms in the house, it is more likely to have been a platform fitted at one end of a particular room. In con-verting only one room of a larger building into a playhouse, Woolfe's project would not have been unusual. When Richard Farrant set up his indoor theatre in the Buttery of the ex-Blackfriars monastery in London (1576), he created the playhouse by knocking two smaller rooms into one, and used remaining parts of the property for other purposes.[30]

The size of the room used by players is unknown. It may have been comparatively small since the playhouse appears only to have occupied one part of a town house. The 'stage' mentioned by Yate is likely to have been a wooden platform like those in the metropolitan open-air and indoor playhouses (perhaps between one and three feet above the ground, depending on the height of the ceiling). Its size is unknown but it is unlikely to have been of large dimensions. Similarly, if it was fitted with a tiring house it was probably small, although an adjoining room might have served as a changing space instead. The space may have been fitted with benches as well, as was the case at other early indoor playhouses in London such as the first Blackfriars theatre.[31]

Performances

Cooke refers to players performing at the Wine Street property *c.*1604–05. And the payments received by St John the Baptist's Almshouse and Queen Elizabeth's Hospital from the playhouse after 1615 (in accordance with Woolfe's will) provide indirect evidence that the playhouse operated after Woolfe's death. There is, however, no record of any specific performance staged at the theatre, and no record of the name of any company which performed there. In the latter instance, other sources are potentially more revealing. There is, for example, a strong possibility that the Children of the Royal Chamber of Bristol performed at the playhouse. In 1615 the Master of the Revels wrote a letter to the Lord Chamberlain regarding the formation of a boy troupe under the Queen's patronage at Bristol.[32] The players were to be known as the Youths or Children of the Queen's Chamber of Bristol. The eventual patent authorising the troupe was given to John Daniel (brother of playwright and poet Samuel Daniel) and provided the King's license for the Children 'to vse and exercise the arte and qualitie of playinge Comedies histories Enterludes morralles Pastoralles Stage playes' in and outside Bristol 'in such vsuall houses as themselves shall provide, as in other convenient places' in any community in the country.[33]

The establishment of a provincial royal acting company was an innovation in itself, but what is especially interesting about the troupe, in the present context, is the fact that they were to be based in Bristol, although permitted to tour. A resident troupe would need a regular venue for performances and the Wine Street playhouse would have lent itself to use as a theatrical base. The playhouse was probably also the most obvious example of a 'usual' playing venue in the town, although Barker's playhouse in suburban Redcliffe Hill may have been operational at this date as well. That the provincial royal troupe did plan to play in the Wine Street playhouse (and possibly the Barker playhouse) could find further proof in a royal letter of 1618. The letter confirmed Daniel's authority to lead the Bristol company, but the phrasing relating to the places in which the players were authorised to perform was adapted. The Queen's Bristol players were now licensed to play '*in all Playhowses* Townehalls Schoolehowses and other places convenient for y*at* purpose' throughout the realm (own emphasis).[34] There were a number of play-houses in London, but there is no clear evidence of a playhouse oper-ating in any other regional town in 1618 (as far as we know). As an essentially provincial company, the clause authorising the troupe to perform at all playhouses would have been most relevant when the troupe was playing in Bristol. Indeed, it is possible that this clause was included primarily with the Wine Street playhouse in mind.[35]

In the light of this cumulative evidence, it seems likely that the royal Bristol troupe did perform at Woolfe's playhouse and may even have been based there for a time.[36] If this was the case, the Bristol troupe would provide a provincial parallel with earlier metropolitan boy com-panies such as the Children of St Paul's and the Children of the Chapel Royal that also used and based themselves at indoor playhouses. When Queen Anne chose to patronise a provincial boy company she proba-bly expected it to resemble the royal children's companies of the metropolis; and the idea of establishing the troupe at an indoor playhouse might have been suggested to Daniel by the example of the metropolitan boy troupes. John Daniel, who was nominated to lead the company, and Martin Slater, who became involved with the troupe, both had connections with London children's companies and indoor playhouses. In 1604 Daniel's brother, Samuel, had been made Master of the Children of the Queen's Revels at the second Blackfriars theatre, while Slater was 'manager and shareholder of the Children of the King's Revels at Whitefriars in 1608'.[37] None of the troupe's plays are known to survive. If they did, we might be afforded an example of a play staged at the Wine Street playhouse. However, the list of play-types which the Bristol company were authorised to perform suggests the dramatic fare offered at the playhouse by the royal troupe could have been varied, including comedies, histories, interludes, morals, and pastorals.[38]

Finances

In his will Woolfe called for several charitable annuities (totalling three pounds, six shillings and eight pence) to be paid out of his playhouse. This suggests that it was at least reasonably profitable, as Woolfe, presumably, would not have made the bequests unless the playhouse usually made profits in excess of this amount. He may have had a number of motives for making these gifts. There was a long tradition of including charitable donations in one's will as a way of securing the Lord's favour in the life to come, while the decision to make the annuities payable from the playhouse was possibly pragmatic. It might have been the only one of Woolfe's enterprises which generated sufficient funds for their payment. But he may also have been purposely channelling the profits of the playhouse into philanthropic projects as a way of lending the theatre respectability and palliating possible opposition to the playhouse.[39]

Later history

Why the playhouse closed (*c*.1625) is not explained in any of the surviving documents. Miles Woolfe, Nicholas's heir, was a minor when his father died, and may not have shared his father's interest in the enterprise. When old enough to take charge of the playhouse, he may have decided to convert the property into a dwelling house that he could sub-let. Alternatively, the playhouse might have ceased operating because the number of playing troupes wishing to use it had declined or because there was less local interest in, and possibly some hostility towards drama in the town. There was certainly less civic patronage of theatre in the 1620s.[40] Today, not even the building which housed the playhouse appears to survive. Modern buildings dominate contemporary Wine Street affording no trace of Bristol's innovative theatre.

2. The Prescot playhouse, Lancashire

The earliest of the known regional playhouses is that founded in the small Lancashire market town of Prescot. It was a modest home for an apparently novel theatrical venture outside London. The existence of the Prescot playhouse is recorded in several contemporary documents, including a memorandum written by local vicar and schoolmaster, Thomas Meade (*c*.1603), in which he refers to an annual rent from the 'play house builded vppon the wast by Mr Richard Harrington now Master Stuardes'.[41] The playhouse is also mentioned in the 1609 Prescot

Court Leet records, the court noting that Thomas Malbon had 'converted the play howse for a habitacion And receyved a tenant into yt'.[42] Malbon's conversion of the property would seem to mark the end of the playhouse's life, although it was still being referred to by its old name (c.1614) in the Prescot grammar school accounts.[43] The most detailed information about the size and location of the playhouse is provided in the Prescot Court Leet records of 9 June 1615. John Mercer of Eccleston appeared at the court to request permission

> to enter into one parcel of land in Prescot [. . .], lying at the upper end of the High Street leading to Eccleston, near to Churchley Field gate, comprising in width nine yards and two feet on its east end and five yards on its west end and comprising in length nineteen yards – of and upon the aforesaid parcel of land a building has been put up, earlier used as a certain house called 'a playhouse'.[44]

The playhouse's establishment

We know from Meade's memorandum that Richard Harrington was the founder of the Prescot playhouse. The date of its erection is not explicitly recorded, but the identification of Harrington as its builder does provide 'a terminal limit to the date of the building', Harrington apparently being buried at Huyton on 7 February 1603.[45] As Bailey records, 'disappointingly little is known' about Harrington and his life. For instance, although his signature upon his will indicates that he was an educated gentleman, there is no evidence of his having attended either university.[46] We do know that he was married (to Elizabeth) and that his older brother, Percival, was steward at Prescot from 1596 to 1605. (The latter's position may provide one explanation for Harrington's choice of Prescot for his playhouse.) The two men were apparently sons 'of John Harrington, esquire, lord of the manor of Huyton'; and Percival was roughly thirty years old in 1582, from which 'it may be deduced that Richard was under the age of fifty at his death'.[47]

Harrington probably moved to Prescot with his wife and family in 1601, when the lease on Prescot Hall was transferred to him from Michael Doughty. But he had bought a cottage in the town as early as 1595.[48] This cottage lay 'some 150 yards distant' from the later site of the playhouse, and might have been 'obtained in order to give Harrington a firmer local standing as a tenant of the manor' and to facilitate his playhouse project.[49] Although the playhouse could have been built shortly after this date, it seems more likely that Harrington built it after coming to live in Prescot. This would mean that the theatre was only briefly under his management, his death occurring in 1603. It might also mean that the playhouse only operated for a short time. Indeed, if his heirs did not take control of the theatre, it is possible that the theatrical career of the playhouse ended in 1603 even though it was not converted for another use until 1609.

Why Richard Harrington should have decided to found a playhouse in Prescot is more perplexing. Like Nicholas Woolfe, Harrington does not appear to have had a particular interest in drama or any theatrical connections, and Prescot was neither a large nor a wealthy town.[50] But it did have some recommendations for those working in the leisure industry. Although small, the town had many visitors. The market attracted some people, others passed through on their way to and from Liverpool and Warrington.[51] In 1592 it could also boast nineteen ale-houses and at least one other entertainment venue, a cockpit. The latter received visitors from Prescot's surrounding area as well as from local people, as the diary of Nicholas Assheton reveals. He did not live in Prescot but in 1617–18 reported that he and several other gentlemen went 'to Prescot to a cockfight'.[52] Harrington may also have hoped to capitalise on the visiting trade that regularly passed through Prescot.

The proximity of Knowsley Park, one of the homes of the Stanley family, famed for their enthusiasm for, and patronage of drama may have provided a more particular motive for building a playhouse at Prescot.[53] Indeed, there is a possibility that the 6th Earl suggested or encouraged its founding.[54] The Earl's enthusiasm for theatre is well attested. As well as patronising his own troupe of players, he was involved in reviving 'one of the great boy companies, the Children of Paul's'. In 1599 he was even reported to have 'put up' the boy players 'to his great paines and charge' and was said to be 'busy penning comedies for the common players'.[55] Stanley might have promoted the building of the playhouse with the intention of using it as a venue for the troupes which he was supporting at the turn of the century and/or as a showcase for his works.

The playhouse

The 1615 Court Leet record provides the clearest description of the playhouse's location and possible dimensions, describing the one-time playhouse property as lying at the upper end of the High Street on a plot measuring nine yards and two feet wide at its east end, five yards wide at its west end, and nineteen yards in length. (The latter convert into measurements of 29 feet, 15 feet and 57 feet, and an area of 1254 square feet.)[56] The playhouse was probably 'smaller than its site', but the difference was not necessarily great. Whether the Prescot building was 'an open-air or enclosed building is not recorded'.[57] Neither do we know what shape the playhouse was. It is unlikely to have been a round theatre: only an amphitheatre of small dimensions could have fitted within the plot and later references to the converted playhouse suggest that it was a conventional house-like building. According to Bailey, the building pulled down on the site in 1902 – which may have been that originally used as the playhouse – was nicknamed 'Flatiron Cottage', being narrower at one end like an iron. If this was the original playhouse, it would suggest that Harrington's building was not only a covered structure but one shaped like its site, tapering at one end.[58]

Whatever its precise dimensions and shape, the playhouse was clearly smaller than most of the metropolitan amphitheatres and several of the indoor playhouses.[59] But it could have been comparable in size with some of the smaller metropolitan playhouses, such as the first Blackfriars theatre (measuring $46^1/2$ feet by 25 feet).[60] No evidence about the interior of the playhouse survives so we do not know whether it was fitted with a stage and/or seating. Similarly, if a stock of costumes, props and plays was accumulated, no evidence of its existence is preserved. The inventory of goods attached to Harrington's will does mention an 'instrument', valued at nine pounds, but no further details are provided.[61] If it was a musical instrument it might have served some use in the playhouse. There are no records of plays being performed at the Prescot playhouse. This does not mean that it was not used, although this possibility cannot be ruled out. The Earl of Derby may have invited his troupe and other companies with whom he had theatrical connections (such as the Children of St Paul's) to visit and perform at Prescot and Knowsley Hall. They might even have mounted productions of the Earl's own plays. Other professional and semi-professional troupes touring Lancashire might have been attracted to the town as well, having heard that it possessed a playhouse.

Closure

By 1609 the playhouse had been converted into a domestic house.[62] Its conversion marks the latest point at which the Prescot playhouse could have been operating, although the theatre might have ceased functioning as early as 1603 when Harrington died, unless his wife or brother took over the management of the playhouse. (The latter may have assumed control of the property initially as steward of the manor.)[63] If the playhouse had continued to operate after 1603, under the management of Percival or Elizabeth Harrington, the remarriage of Richard's widow may have led to the theatre's closure, or to another change in management, with Thomas Malbon possibly assuming the control of the playhouse at this point.

But the playhouse's conversion for domestic living did not necessarily signal the end of contemporary interest in the playhouse. Bailey suggests that Henry Stanley's assumption of control of the property in 1614 (as steward of the manor) could 'point to an intention to restore the playhouse', while the rumoured reopening of the playhouse might account for the presence of Queen's players in the town in 1618.[64] However, when John Mercer took possession of the property (1615) it was described as 'earlier' used as a playhouse, suggesting that the house had *not* been reconverted into a theatre in 1614, even if this had been desired by the Stanleys and encouraged by their kinsman, Henry Stanley as steward. Mercer could have revived the playhouse, but there is no evidence that he did so.[65]

Later history

The intriguing history of Richard Harrington's building has continued to be remembered by later Prescot inhabitants. When a survey of the manor was taken in 1721 'one of the properties in the possession of George Bradshaw' who had married a descendant of Harrington, 'was described as "a cottage in Eccleston Street formerly called the Play House"'.[66] This property no longer survives, although it may have been the 'old cottage' that was preserved on the site until 1902 (see above).[67] 'Flatiron Cottage' (as the latter was known) was replaced with a building used as a factory and warehouse for the Lancashire Watch Company. The earlier nickname for the building on the playhouse site persisted, the watch factory building being known locally as 'Flat Iron House'. Like the cottage it replaced, the new building resembles an iron in shape. The Watch Company closed down in 1910 and, today, the building which stands at No. 72 Eccleston Street is used as a private storeroom.[68] It is a modest reminder of Harrington's pioneering provincial playhouse.

3. The York playhouse, 1609

The playhouse established in York in 1609 appears to have been the shortest-lived of the known Elizabethan and Jacobean provincial playhouses. On 22 September 1609 corporate permission to establish a playhouse in York was given, but by 11 December authorisation for the theatre was withdrawn. The playhouse may not have hosted a single performance. The two civic entries documenting these events provide the only known contemporary references to the theatre. The first entry (on 22 September) recorded that Richard Middleton and 'others' had presented a petition requesting permission to erect a theatre or playhouse in the City 'wherin such as have bene borne and brought vpp therin should imploye ther laborious expenses therof which might be A meanes to restrayne the frequent Comminge thervnto of other Stage plaiers'. The petitioners also promised to pay ten pounds a year to the corporation. The court provisionally granted their request but only on conditions to be after agreed.[69] The petitioners appear to have taken this as a 'green light' and proceeded with the erection of the play-house. They paid the price for their eagerness. On 11 December the court noted that

> forasmuch as [. . .] they have erected A Theater or playhowse in this Cittie, and have not attended this Court to have receyved dyreccions vpon what Condicions they might have bene permitted And have drawne vnto ther companyes straingers that did inhabitt in the Countrie, and likewise some of manuell occupacions in this Cittie who do intend to give over ther occupacions and fall to [. . .] an idle Course of life, It is nowe [. . .] agreed by this Court [. . .] that they shalbe discharged for kepeinge of anie playhowse in this Cittie.[70]

The suppression of the first York playhouse parallels the forced closure of metropolitan playhouses such as the Porter's Hall theatre (shut shortly after its completion in 1617, initial authorisation for the venture having been subsequently withdrawn).[71] The York playhouse is less fully documented than the Porter's Hall theatre, but the two entries in York's House Books do offer some insight into the brief life of York's first playhouse.

Establishment of the playhouse

The erection of the York theatre was apparently a collective enterprise, as was often the case when playhouses were founded in London, permission for its establishment being requested by Richard Middleton and 'others'.[72] The latter were probably townspeople and may have included players, as there is evidence of local actors in early modern York. In 1596–97 the 'Citties players' were rewarded for performing at the Common Hall; and in December 1605 the House Book minutes record that 'diuerse Cittizens sonnes of this cittye' requested permission to play in the city during the Christmas holidays.[73] As Middleton's is the only name mentioned in the civic documents, it is likely that he was the spokesperson for the playhouse collective. No further information about the petitioners involved in the theatre project is afforded in the civic documents, but wider research in contemporary records has yielded some information possibly relating to Middleton.

The name 'Richard Middleton' occurs several times in the city's early modern records, and in other contemporary documents. For example, Richard Middleton (or Myddeltoune) 'of Yorks, gentleman', matriculated at University College, Oxford on 7 June 1583, 'aged 19'.[74] (This Richard was born *c.*1563–64 and would have been approximately 46 in 1609.) In 1584 another Richard, son of George Middleton, draper, was 'baptised in the church of St Martin Coney Street' (York); and in 1588 Jane Turner, widow, left two shillings 'to her godson Richard Middleton, the son of John Middleton merchant, deceased' in York.[75] In June 1605, a mischievous Richard Middleton was 'committed for casting capstones from the stone bridge adjoining Skeldergate' (York), and in November of the same year another Richard was arrested and committed for breaking windows in the town.[76] On 6 February 1608 Richard Middleton married Isabel Losh at St Michael le Belfray Church; and Elinor, 'daughter of Richard Middleton, was baptised on 9 February 1609 in the church of Holy Trinity Goodramgate'.[77] In the same year as Elinor's baptism, 'Richard Myddleton gent[leman] of York' published two collections of poems together, *Epigrams and Satyres* and *Times Metamorphosis*.[78] Post-1609 there are several further references to a Richard Middleton in York, including two in 1613 and 1615: 'Richard Middleton, gentleman', living in All Saints Pavement parish was listed as a non-communicant and visited by the churchwardens, possibly as a suspected papist.[79]

Eileen White (apparently unaware of the record of a Richard Middleton attending Oxford University), suggests that most of the known references could allude to George Middleton's son (baptised 1584), and that he is a 'more likely candidate' for identification as the 'aspiring drama presenter in 1609 than someone of the generation of John Middleton's children'.[80] It is quite possible that George Middleton's son *was* the Richard involved in the playhouse venture. (The citizens' sons that asked to play in the city in 1605 demonstrate that there were young men with a taste for theatre in the town. George's son could even have been one of those involved in the seasonal plays staged that year.)[81] But we cannot rule out the possibility that the theatrical entrepreneur was John Middleton's son or the Richard that attended Oxford University (although the two older figures could be the same man). The Oxford matriculant is possibly more likely to have been the author of *Epigrams and Satyres* and *Times Metamorphosis*. In the Stationers' Register and in the university matriculation records the Richard Middleton referred to is described as a 'gentleman' of Yorkshire, and a similar variant spelling of Middleton is used ('Myddeltoune' in the university records, 'Myddleton' in the Stationers' Register).[82] Although George Middleton's son could have described himself as a gentleman, there is no record of his using this title.[83] The poems include university allusions, too, arguably increasing the likelihood that the older Middleton was their author. The narrator in *Times Metamorphosis* expresses sympathy for 'Ridentius', a university poet 'who employed his "Cambridge wits" on drama and failed'.[84] The author of the poetry collections could also be the Richard identified as a 'non-communicant' (and possible Catholic) living in All Saints Pavement parish in 1613 and 1615 as there is some evidence that he was sympathetic to Catholicism in his poems.[85]

The author of the 1608 poems shows some knowledge and experience of theatre, *Times Metamorphosis* incorporating several allusions to plays and acting (including two references to Christmas drama). If the Oxford graduate was their author it could point to his involvement in the playhouse venture. But the portrait of players offered in the poems is ambiguous. At one point, for instance, a lawyer, Pandulpho is told to 'get thee hence / Pigmey-attourney, actor, Christmas plaier, / I scorne to seat thee in my verses chaire', the epithets 'actor' and 'Christmas player' apparently being used derogatively.[86] These comments suggest the author could have been a theatrical snob. Such a figure would seem an unlikely contender for involvement in a project to establish a popular playhouse, unless he imagined that gaining control of a theatre was a way of introducing plays and performances of the kind he wished to see. Intriguing as it might be to imagine that a gentleman poet (and possible closet Catholic) was one of the first regional playhouse entrepreneurs, it remains more likely, therefore, that the playhouse spokesperson was another Richard Middleton, whether that Middleton was the twenty-five year old son of George Middleton, John Middleton's son (if he and the poet were not the same person), or another figure hidden in the records of Richard Middletons in early Jacobean York.

Reasons for establishing the playhouse

As the largest northern city in early modern England, York had obvious attractions as a playhouse location. Its population of 10,000 or more provided a large body of prospective spectators. The city was also among the wealthier provincial communities: more capital was potentially available, therefore, for investment in a new commercial enterprise such as a playhouse. There was clearly a taste for theatre in the town, too, as is manifested in the city's continuing sponsorship of its religious plays in the Elizabethan period (when many other towns had abandoned their traditional cycles of biblical plays), and by the regular visits paid the town by Shakespearean playing companies.[87] What specifically prompted Middleton and his colleagues to establish a playhouse in 1609 is more difficult to determine. Their motives are likely to have been at least partly entrepreneurial, and the proposed annual payment of ten pounds to the corporation suggests they expected the theatre to be profitable.[88] The collective's formal explanation for erecting the theatre was that they wished to provide a theatre within York wherein 'such as have bene borne and brought vpp therin should imploy ther laborious expenses'. This, they argued, was a way of preventing the frequent coming of players to York.[89] Interpreting the precise meaning of the initial explanation is difficult because the language used is ambiguous. It is not clear whether the petitioners were saying that the playhouse was intended to cater for people born and brought up in York and/or brought up in the theatre.

Whichever way one interprets the explanation, the suggestion that a York playhouse would lead to fewer acting troupes visiting the town represents a curious justification for its erection. In effect, the petitioners argue that the establishment of a playhouse in the town is a regulatory, restrictive measure that will reduce rather than increase dramatic activity in the community. There might be obvious politic reasons for making such a case in an era when corporations were increasingly concerned to regulate communal recreations as potential occasions of disorder. At the same time, the petitioners do perhaps provide an insight into their actual motives for building a playhouse. In arguing that the theatre could lead to a reduction in the activity of visiting players in the town, the petitioners suggest that the playhouse was intended for use by local companies (and possibly even a resident town troupe) of which they may have been members or supporters.

The playhouse

When the corporation decided to withdraw their authorisation for the York playhouse, they noted that it had already been erected 'in this Cittie', suggesting that the playhouse stood within the town walls.[90] Its more precise location is not recorded, but we know that the theatre was built some time between 22 September and 11 December 1609. Three months is a short period in which to have built a new playhouse, suggesting either that work on the theatre had begun before Middleton and his colleagues made their petition or that the playhouse was not an entirely new building.[91] It could have been a conversion of an existing property. In this instance, the playhouse collective would have been paralleling the example of London theatrical entrepreneurs such as Farrant and Burbage, and their establishment of indoor playhouses in older buildings. Even if the playhouse was a new building, it does not appear to have been an open-air amphitheatre, as there is no evidence of such a building in John Speed's 1610 map of the town. In all likelihood the playhouse was a rectangular or square, roofed building. Internally, it may have been fitted with a stage and seating, like the indoor metropolitan playhouses. Given the brevity of the time that elapsed between the petition to erect the theatre and its suppression, it is unlikely that the playhouse had been in operation for long, if at all. If any performances were staged before the council intervened local players (possibly including some of those involved in its founding) probably mounted them, although it is possible that the 'straingers' alluded to were professional or amateur actors drawn from neighbouring parts of Yorkshire, and that they also performed or participated in any productions staged at the theatre before its closure.[92]

Closure

When the council withdrew permission for the playhouse it was on the grounds that Middleton and his associates had not waited to receive their further directions. But the comments following this observation suggest this was not the council's main concern. Their complaints about the petitioners attracting strangers and people 'of manuell occupacions in this Cittie who do intend to give over ther occupacions and fall to [. . .] an idle Course of life' suggest they were primarily concerned with preserving order and local social hierarchies.[93] The presence of outsiders in the town and the prospect of people forsaking their professions and their responsibilities to fellow guildsmen both represented potential threats to the local status quo. The council may also have become less convinced that the playhouse's existence would lead to fewer touring players visiting the town. If the founders of the playhouse were already inviting outsiders to join their enterprise, there was no reason to believe that they would not also welcome other troupes to visit the town and theatre. Whatever the town's motives in retracting the theatre's licence, the fact that there are no further references to the playhouse after 1609 suggests that Middleton and his associates obeyed the civic order of 11 December. The playhouse was probably converted into an ordinary habitation, like that in Prescot. As its location is unknown, it has not been possible to determine whether the building survives to the present.

II

The Barker playhouse, Bristol: another Jacobean provincial theatre?

The existence of a second Bristol playhouse is recorded in the will of Sarah Barker (31 May 1637). Barker mentions a number of properties in her will, leaving five 'messuag*es* or ten*ementes*' on Redcliffe Hill to her son, Phillip Barker, and one described as a playhouse to another son:

> I [. . .] bequeath vnto my sonne William Barker all that howse [. . .] which my late husband built for a playhouse, for all my estate terme & interest therein except the Chamber over the well att th'end of the said playhowse, which Chamber I give & bequeath vnto my daughter Ellioner Barker.[94]

Unfortunately, Barker's will does not state whether the playhouse was used for plays or record the date of its erection, although it is likely that it was built and possibly operated by her husband in the Jacobean period. The playhouse-builder is not named in the will or in the parish record of his wife's burial at St Mary Redcliffe's Church; but Sarah Barker was a widow by 1628 as an audit in that year alludes to a rent received from 'the widdowe Barker for vj Tenementes' in Redcliffe Hill.[95] Further research in the parish records of St Mary Redcliffe has identified Richard Barker, 'a prominent merchant', as Sarah's probable husband.[96] In her will, Barker requests that she be buried 'in the p*a*rish churche of Redcliffe as neere my husband as may be' (St Mary Redcliffe), revealing the location of her dead husband's burial; and the parish records for the church allude in 1614 to the burial on 30 September of Richard Barker 'merchant'.[97]

This suggests the playhouse was built (and may have operated) prior to 1614. It could thus have been contemporary with the Wine Street playhouse.[98] Indeed, the success of Woolfe's theatre may have inspired Barker to build his suburban playhouse as a rival playing venue. Building and investing in a playhouse may have appealed to the merchant's entrepreneurial spirit, too. Richard Barker was not unaccustomed to investing in risky but potentially profitable ventures. In the late 1580s he appears to have been part owner of an overseas trading ship, called the *Hopewell,* and in 1605 is listed among the Bristol merchants who were members of the new Spanish trading company that received letters patent from James I.[99] Barker may have built the playhouse using profits from his work as a merchant trader. Sarah's will reveals that the playhouse was not his only building venture either. Her bequests to her son Richard include part of another Redcliffe Hill property apparently built by her husband.[100] In building several properties outside the city walls in suburban Redcliffe, Barker was perhaps making a shrewd investment. He perhaps suspected that the area would become more populous and property more valuable as Bristol expanded. Whether Barker was prompted to build the playhouse by other more personal motives (such as an interest in theatre) is unknown at present.

The playhouse

In her will Sarah Barker does not note the location of the playhouse explicitly. But in 1627–28 she paid rents on six Redcliffe Hill tenements and in her will she gives five houses on Redcliffe Hill to her son Phillip Barker. She bequeaths a sixth property (the playhouse) to William. By implication, the playhouse was housed in the sixth Redcliffe Hill building that she held. John Speed's 1610 map of the Jacobean town suggests that few houses had been built in this suburb of Bristol in the early seventeenth century.[101] Plenty of open ground would therefore have been available for the erection of a new property such as the playhouse, and land may have been more cheaply obtained in Redcliffe than in Bristol proper. Barker describes the Redcliffe theatre as having been built as a playhouse.[102] This suggests that the property was newly erected and purpose-built as a theatre. As such it would have been in the same tradition as the early open-air playhouses in the suburbs of Elizabethan London. However, the Redcliffe playhouse does not appear to have been an open-air amphitheatre. There is no sign of such a building in contemporary plans of Redcliffe or in later seventeenth century maps of Bristol such as James Millerd's (1673); and Sarah Barker alludes to a chamber at the end of the playhouse.[103] A circular building would not have had an 'end', strictly speaking. It is more likely therefore that the playhouse was another indoor theatre in a roughly rectangular building. Like the Wine Street playhouse, it appears to have contained a number of rooms as well as a theatre, including the chamber over the well reserved for Eleanor Barker. Its size is unknown, but if the playhouse resembled other Shakespearean indoor theatres the playing chamber would have been fitted with a stage, and possibly with permanent seating as well.

Performances

There are no records of performances at the playhouse, although it is possible that the theatre was used by local and visiting playing troupes, like the Wine Street playhouse. Neither is there any information about its operation or the date of its opening and closure. However, if the playhouse had not ceased operating before 1637, it was no doubt obliged to close in 1642, as were all metropolitan theatres, at the beginning of the Civil War. What happened to the property after 1637 is not clear. Presumably, Eleanor Barker continued to live there, perhaps accompanied by her brother, William, who had inherited the property. He may have assumed the management of the playhouse (if it was still functioning) but might have chosen to convert the property into a domestic dwelling. Had the playhouse survived to the present we might have been able to reconstruct its later history, but no traces of the theatre have been found as yet. Most of the buildings on Redcliffe Hill today are modern, although St Mary Redcliffe's Church where the Barkers were buried still stands. However long its career, the Barker playhouse was, like the Wine Street theatre, an innovative theatrical enterprise in the early modern provinces and a testimony to the 'vitality' of early modern Bristol's theatrical culture. Indeed, for a time in the early seventeenth century Bristol may have been in 'a situation unique in the provinces', having 'two playhouses in operation, possibly simultaneously'.[104]

Conclusions

Most provincial towns in early modern England had smaller, less wealthy populations than London. The audiences they potentially afforded for playhouses were, likewise, smaller and poorer, making theatres a less viable enterprise. To find any regional playhouses in early modern England is striking, and, although few in number, those which existed are a further proof of theatre's popularity in regions outside Renaissance London. They also demonstrate that theatrical innovation and dramatic entrepreneurs were not confined to the metropolis. Although there are no direct records of travelling companies performing in these pioneering provincial playhouses it is possible that they did. In Bristol, the Children of the Royal Chamber of Bristol might even have been based briefly at the Wine Street playhouse. Evidence of other provincial playhouses and professional performances within them may emerge as research continues, but mutually illuminating parallels which can enrich our understanding of theatrical development in England are already to be found between the provincial playhouses described above and the metropolitan theatres of Renaissance England. Most of the known Elizabethan and Jacobean regional theatres appear to have been indoor venues, anticipating the fact that indoor playhouses were to supersede open-air amphitheatres in number and importance in Caroline London. Similarly, that each of the provincial playhouses appears to have been established by a person (or people) with no obvious theatrical interests provides further evidence that the rise of the playhouse in England was largely a commercial innovation, instigated by business people, rather than by players. Finally, the closure and loss of each of the early provincial Elizabethan and Jacobean playhouses (and the buildings used) foreshadows the demise and physical disappearance of the more famous metropolitan playhouses of the Shakespearean capital.

9
The Decline of Professional Touring Theatre

'Paid given to the Queenes players at the parlor xxv s'
(Coventry Chamberlains' and Wardens' Accounts, 1636)[1]

'xx s. more paid to Players to ridd the Towne of them'
(Barnstaple Receivers' Accounts, 1636–37)[2]

Early modern England's surviving provincial dramatic records have yet to be fully catalogued but a large body of evidence covering the country's major early modern cities – Bristol, Norwich and York – and a number of other towns and counties is already available in the fifteen published collections of the REED project.[3] This representative sample of the period's regional dramatic records suggests that touring theatre was in decline in Jacobean and Caroline England.[4] Records of travelling companies become increasingly rare in the early 1620s and 'under Charles, the evidence of travelling fades away'.[5] Whether this reflects an actual decrease in touring and what might have caused such a decline is harder to determine. As the records from Caroline Coventry and Barnstaple suggest, attitudes to and treatment of touring players varied between communities and regions; some towns welcomed players, others turned them away. Generalising about touring theatre in the period is consequently difficult. It is a problem familiar to local historians of the period.[6]

Evidence of decline

Rewards to players
Records of monetary gifts to players in civic, ecclesiastic and private household accounts are one of our main sources of evidence for touring

in the sixteenth century. Such rewards become less frequent and numerous in the 1620s, as can be seen if one surveys the records of payments to patronised or licensed players included in the published REED collections (see Tables 9.1 and 9.2).[7] There is also a 'substantial decrease in the number of different companies on the road' in Stuart England.[8] Most of the records of and payments to professional companies outside London in the Jacobean period are to royal companies (or troupes at least claiming royal patronage). For instance, of the 348 payments recorded in the published volumes of REED from 1610 to 1639, 217 (approximately 62 per cent) are identified as rewards to royal troupes. If representative, the results in Tables 9.1 and 9.2 suggest that the majority of payments made to professional travelling players between 1560 and 1639 were concentrated in the late sixteenth century. Of 1496 pay-

Table 9.1   Payments made to patronised/licensed players decade by decade between 1560 and 1599 in the published REED collections

REED Collections	1560–69	1570–79	1580–89	1590–99	Total payments by collection 1560–99
Bristol	27	28	18	24	97
Cambridge	21	8	5	7	41
Chester	0	0	2	2	4
Coventry	0	29	58	59	146
Cumberland	1	1	0	0	2
Westmorland	0	0	2	4	6
Gloucestershire	20	27	40	21	108
Devon	40	27	32	15	114
Dorset	9	9	9	10	37
Cornwall	0	1	0	0	1
Herefordshire	0	1	2	4	7
Worcestershire	0	3	5	4	12
Lancashire	0	1	4	1	6
Newcastle	6	2	3	23	34
Norwich	17	4	41	20	82
Shropshire	7	6	15	16	44
Somerset	18	29	42	40	129
Sussex	10	9	15	13	47
York	0	5	20	24	49
Total payments by decade	**176**	**190**	**313**	**287**	**966**

Table 9.2 Payments made to patronised/licensed players decade by decade between 1600 and 1639 in the published REED collections

REED Collections	1600–09	1610–19	1620–29	1630–39	Total payments by collection 1600–39
Bristol	3	6	3	2	14
Cambridge	0	0	0	0	0
Chester	0	0	0	0	0
Coventry	81	41	22	14	158
Cumberland	4	16	17	4	41
Westmorland	2	10	8	5	25
Gloucestershire	0	0	0	1	1
Devon	9	13	4	5	31
Dorset	3	1	4	1	9
Cornwall	0	0	0	1	1
Herefordshire	5	10	0	0	15
Worcestershire	0	1	6	3	10
Lancashire	2	38	24	5	69
Newcastle	4	1	0	1	6
Norwich	22	8	13	8	51
Shropshire	14	14	2	2	32
Somerset	15	2	0	0	17
Sussex	0	5	0	0	5
York	18	7	6	14	45
Total payments by decade	182	173	109	66	530

ments counted, 966 (approximately 65 per cent) occurred between 1560 and 1599 and only 530 (approximately 35 per cent) between 1600 and 1639. The 1580s emerge as the peak period for rewards, with 313 (approximately 21 per cent) occurring in this decade, while the number of payments generally declines from the 1590s and decreases most sharply from the 1620s. There are regional variations from this pattern, although almost all communities show a decline in recorded payments to professional players in the 1630s.

In some places the peak period of rewards occurs earlier, as at Cambridge, where the highest number of payments was made in the 1560s. A system of paying players not to perform was also adopted much sooner than in many other communities, but by the authorities of the University rather than the town.[9] While Cambridge's civic authorities appear to have been ready to welcome or reward visiting players throughout the Elizabethan period (rewarding professional troupes thirty-five times between 1560 and 1597), the University was opposed to professional play performances in its precincts and sought to enforce a ban on public plays from the late sixteenth century.[10] In other towns and cities the peak time for rewards to playing companies is much later, as is the period during which payments decline most steeply. At Coventry ('the greenest pasture' for travelling players) the greatest number of rewards to professional troupes was made in the 1600s, but payments to players do not decline significantly until the 1620s (see Table 9.2).[11] Even then rewards remained comparatively high, and continued to be made right up until the eve of the Civil War, two companies being rewarded in the 1640s.[12]

In counties such as Herefordshire, Lancashire, Westmorland, Cumberland and Worcestershire the peak period for recorded payments is also late. In the first three counties the greatest number of rewards is recorded in the second decade of the seventeenth century, while the peak period for payments in the latter two is the 1620s (see Table 9.2). Although the fragmentary nature of the surviving records could account for these anomalies, part of the explanation for the apparently late flourishing of theatrical patronage in these counties could lie in the cultural climate that prevailed in certain northern and western communities. There continued to be more support for traditional festivities and revelry than in many parts of the south and east, where the growth of Puritanism had often been paralleled by a rise in campaigns for the more careful regulation of various local recreations, including plays. Notably, a large proportion of the regional theatrical regulations identified thus far between 1560 and 1625 was passed in towns in the south and East Anglia.[13] Playing companies that visited the north and west potentially faced fewer obstructions, civic orders regulating drama being less common in these regions, and they stood a greater chance of civic rewards in the seventeenth century. This may well have encouraged more troupes to tour there during the Stuart period.

As the records from these regions also reveal, the tradition of touring and patronising travelling players did not die easily or quickly in all towns or regions. In fact, roughly 'a quarter of the post-1550 performance locations across the country continued to reward players into the 1630s'.[14] Patterns of theatrical patronage and decline were not necessarily uniform even within counties, different histories of travelling theatre sometimes emerging from neighbouring seventeenth century communities. In Devon the county-wide peak period for payments to players is the 1560s (see Table 9.1), but in Exeter the largest number of rewards was made in the 1580s (in line with the overall average) while Barnstaple made its greatest number of payments to players in the 1600s.[15] Attitudes to players also appear to have varied between the county's communities. MacLean contrasts the behaviour of the civic bodies in Dartmouth and Plymouth: 'Plymouth begins a series of payments to discourage visiting players from performing from as early as 1599–1600; while Dartmouth's rewards continue until 1634–35'. Part of the explanation for this difference may lie in the 'religious and political attitudes' of the two towns.[16] While Puritanism thrived in early seventeenth-century Plymouth, Dartmouth appears to have been politically and religiously conservative, a conservatism reflected in the town's support for the Royalist cause in the Civil War. Such communities tended to be better disposed to customary recreations and towards royal and noble patrons and their representatives, as noted earlier.[17]

Payments not to perform

The payments made to players in the early seventeenth century are also more often *not* to perform and/or to leave communities. As Tables 9.3 and 9.4 show, the number and relative percentage of payments not to perform gradually increases from the 1590s, reaching a peak in the 1630s. The figures shown in brackets identify such payments made to unnamed playing companies. As the players in question are not identified we cannot be certain that they were professional players. The payments are not counted therefore in the overall figures of payments to patronised or licensed players in the period given in Tables 9.1 and 9.2. But they are included in Tables 9.3 and 9.4 as they may conceal some payments to professional players and provide further evidence that the practice of making these payments was increasing in some provincial communities in the 1620s and 1630s.[18]

The practice of rewarding companies for non-performance or departure appears to have become customary only in certain towns and regions in the early seventeenth century. The largest numbers of such records in the published REED collections derive respectively from Devon and Norwich. It is perhaps no coincidence that these were areas in which Puritan pressure to restrict playing was increasingly intense from the late sixteenth century. When Alan Somerset surveyed the records of professional touring entertainers (between 1563 and 1617) collected by REED and Malone Society editors (categorising each reference as either positive or negative) he found a similar clustering of records. 'Hostility to players' visits appears to have been concentrated

Table 9.3 Payments made to patronised/licensed players not to perform and/or to leave regional towns between 1560 and 1599 in the published REED collections

REED Collections	1560–69	1570–79	1590–89	1590–99	Total payments by collection 1560–99
Bristol	0	0	0	0	0
Cambridge	0	1	1	2	4
Chester	0	0	0	0	0
Coventry	0	0	0	0	0
Cumberland	0	0	0	0	0
Westmorland	0	0	0	0	0
Gloucestershire	0	0	0	0	0
Devon	1 (1)	0	0	1	2 (1)
Dorset	0	0	0	0	0
Cornwall	0	0	0	0	0
Herefordshire	0	0	0	0	0
Worcestershire	0	0	0	0	0
Lancashire	0	0	0	0	0
Newcastle	0	0	0	0	0
Norwich	0	0	5	0	5
Shropshire	0	0	0	0	0
Somerset	0	0	0	0	0
Sussex	0	0	0	0	0
York	0	0	0	3 (1)	3 (1)
Total payments by decade	1 (1)	1	6	6 (1)	14 (2)

in particular regions, such as East Anglia: 86% of the negative responses to entertainment, or 66% of the total, came from Norwich (45), Cambridge (26) and Norfolk/Suffolk (15)'.[19] Evidence of companies being barred from performance (with or without payment) does not appear to rise significantly until the 1620s either. Salingar *et al.* found that between '1615 and 1619 fewer than 16% of the visits of touring companies to provincial towns were met with refusal of permission to play', while 'the figure rose to 36%' between 1620 and 1624.[20] Somerset's research also suggests that it was comparatively rare for players to be refused permission to perform or to encounter negative treatment before the 1620s. Out of the 3279 records of touring entertainers that he surveyed between 1563 and 1617, 3119 (or 95.12 per cent) were suc-

Table 9.4 Payments made to patronised/licensed players not to perform and/or to leave regional towns between 1600 and 1639 in the published REED collections

REED collections	1600–09	1610–19	1620–29	1630–39	Total payments by collection 1600–39
Bristol	0	0	0 (1)	1 (4)	1 (5)
Cambridge	0	0	0	0	0
Chester	0	0	0	0	0
Coventry	0	0	0	1	1
Cumberland	0	0 (1)	0	0	0 (1)
Westmorland	0	0	0	0	0
Gloucestershire	0	0	0	1 (1)	1(1)
Devon	1 (1)	6 (5)	2 (10)	3 (10)	12 (26)
Dorset	0	1	2 (1)	0 (1)	3 (2)
Cornwall	0	0	0	0	0
Herefordshire	0	0	0	0	0
Worcestershire	0	0	0	3 (3)	3 (3)
Lancashire	0	0	0	0 (2)	0 (2)
Newcastle	0	0	0	0	0
Norwich	6	6	5	6	23
Shropshire	0	0	0	0	0
Somerset	0	0	0	0	0
Sussex	0	0	0	0	0
York	0	0	0	0	0
Total payments by decade	7 (1)	13 (6)	9 (12)	15 (21)	44 (40)

cessful visits, 'that is performing was allowed, rewarded or otherwise welcomed'.[21]

A decline in touring?

The dwindling evidence of professional travelling players in the Stuart provinces is not in itself proof that touring theatre was in decline. Changes in the licensing of travelling players and their plays in the late sixteenth and early seventeenth centuries may have increased the chances of troupes' touring performances eluding official record. In 1559 the royal proclamation 'Prohibiting Unlicensed Interludes and Plays' required that all plays performed in provincial towns be licensed by the local mayor (or leading civic officers), or two justices of the peace.[22] Obtaining such authorisation often involved performing before the local mayor and civic officials, for which players might receive a corporate reward, affording a record of their visit. However, in 1581 the Master of the Revels was granted a patent that made him responsible for licensing all plays for performance in and outside London. Local corporations were therefore no longer responsible for screening visiting troupes' plays, reducing the need to invite players to perform before them.[23] By the 1620s the need for players to obtain civic permission was also reduced, the Master of the Revels having gradually assumed responsibility for licensing players to tour. Stuart players with his licence 'may have simply gone straight to their familiar inns, put up their bills, and played', when they arrived in provincial towns and cities.[24] At the same time, many corporations were becoming less inclined to reward players. If players did not present themselves to corporations or receive rewards from them the chances of their visits being recorded were slender.

However, in the absence of concrete evidence, we cannot be certain that the decline in records of touring is simply or only the result of changing licensing practices and touring customs. In some regions there is evidence to suggest that it is not. In East Kent there is reason to believe that the decrease in dramatic records reflects a genuine reduction in theatrical activity. James Gibson notes the pervasive influence of Puritan reformers from the 1570s: 'Puritan magistrates, aldermen, and clergy increasingly banded together [. . .] to enforce the Puritan policy of Sabbatarianism and the strict control generally of popular entertainments.'[25] This included the introduction of corporate regulations restricting dramatic activity in communities such as Canterbury (1595) and Hythe (1615), while other towns stopped rewarding players or paid them not to perform from the early seventeenth century. In this religious and cultural climate, Gibson thinks that Stuart players are unlikely to have been 'making routine unofficial performances' in local inns or elsewhere, even if they were staging such performances in other parts of the country.[26]

Touring theatre in decline: possible causes

Theatrical regulation

Under Elizabeth I the theatrical licensing system in England tightened, with the right to patronise and license players confined to a small elite and the number of companies eligible to tour reduced. The Queen's 1559 proclamation prohibiting unlicensed plays had permitted playing companies of any description to perform regionally provided they had received authorisation from the mayor (or his equivalent) and/or two royal lieutenants or justices of the peace.[27] But this comparatively inclusive licensing system was superseded in 1572 with the promulgation of the Act for the Punishment of Vagabonds. Under the terms of the new Act, the right to authorise players was limited to the 'more senior nobility' and justices of the peace; players without a royal or noble patron were not authorised to perform publicly in or outside the capital.

When the Act was revised in 1598 the rank of people permitted to license players was further narrowed. Barons and 'other honourable Personage(s) of greater degree' remained able to patronise and authorise players but justices of the peace were no longer granted licensing powers.[28] In theory, only those acting companies with royal or noble patrons were eligible to perform or travel, and companies without such patronage faced prosecution as rogues and vagabonds.[29] Under the Stuarts the system became even more circumscribed, with the power to authorise players concentrated in royal hands. In 1603, soon after the new monarch's accession, patronage of the major playing companies was assumed by members of the royal family; while the Master of the Revels' licensing powers were enlarged by the introduction of a system of annual licences for touring by the middle of James's reign. Although it was not unknown for acting troupes to forge or use old patents, the theoretical necessity of procuring such annual licences for travelling increased the potential obstacles and work involved in planning to tour.[30]

Travelling companies found themselves subject to stricter regulation in a number of the regional communities they visited, too. Following the example of their metropolitan counterparts, various regional corporations passed orders controlling or limiting theatrical activity within their communities in the late sixteenth and early seventeenth centuries. I know of more than fifty orders relating to the regulation of dramatic activity in specific regional towns between 1559 and 1642, with the greatest number of orders being passed in the 1620s (there are likely to be more). Nearly half of the orders relate to and restrict players' use of town halls or other civic buildings.[31] The ecclesiastical authorities restricted players' access to another occasional venue for touring performances when they prohibited plays (and various other secular activities) in churches and churchyards in 1604.[32] Such civic and ecclesiastic regulations were not necessarily successfully enforced. Some civic bodies evidently encountered difficulties in imposing theatrical restrictions, finding themselves obliged to repeat regulations. In some cases the continuation of unauthorised performances is noted, as at Stratford-upon-

Avon. In 1602 the town prohibited 'pleys or enterlewdes' in the Guildhall. Yet ten years later the authorities were again 'seriouslie' considering 'the inconvenience of plaies' there, suggesting that the 1602 order had not been rigorously enforced in the interim. The 1612 order repeated the prohibition and introduced a higher fine for transgressing the ruling.[33]

Regional corporations did not only seek to control where players performed. Some towns regulated the time and number of performances. In York the corporation passed an order in 1582 limiting companies to two performances at the Common Hall during each visit.[34] Other towns introduced regulations prohibiting plays at night and some forbade performances on Sundays, in keeping with the wishes of Sabbatarian reformers (and anticipating King James's prohibition of playing on Sundays in 1603).[35] The town order issued in Gloucester in 1580 imposed several curbs upon visiting players. It prohibited playing 'in the nighte season', restricted the right to perform in the town to select troupes, and limited the number of performances they were to be permitted. The Queen's players were to be allowed to play only 'three interludes or playes within three dayes or vnder' during each visit to the city; and players of 'any subiecte being baron of the parliamente or of higher callinge or degree' were allowed to play two plays in two days.[36] No surprise that the players permitted to perform were those with the most powerful, prestigious patrons, with the most generous playing privileges being reserved for the monarch's players. In Gloucester, as in other towns, the treatment extended to players was politically determined, with troupes rewarded and judged according to the importance and influence of their patrons.

In Oxford and Cambridge travelling players faced a potentially greater curb upon their freedom to perform (see Chapter 6). Both universities sought to prohibit professional play performances within five miles of their precincts in this period and were armed from 1593 with Privy Council letters authorising them to enforce such a prohibition.[37] The prohibitions must have left something to be desired, however, since acting companies were not prevented from visiting or performing in either town in the early seventeenth century. At Cambridge Queen Anne's players were even offered local assistance in their preparations for a performance at the town hall licensed by the mayor in 1606, while the King's Men performed to full houses in Oxford as late as 1610.[38]

Regulating audiences

The university authorities in Oxford and Cambridge did not confine themselves to banning professional play performances. In their campaign to prevent students being 'distracted' by visiting players and their performances, both universities also passed orders prohibiting students from attending common plays.[39] Some civic bodies chose to regulate local play attendance in similar fashion in the Elizabethan period. In Norwich the corporation introduced an order preventing Freemen of the City from attending plays in 1589.[40] In this instance, restricting play attendance appears to have been part of the town's diversified approach to theatrical regulation: an approach that combined selective prohibition (of plays and play attendance) with regulated, licensing of players and their performances. No one appears to have been presented for attending plays in the years immediately following the introduction of the 1589 order, however, and in 1614 the prohibition was re-stated, the corporation agreeing that it should 'from henceforth be putt in execucyon'. The fact that reference is made to executing the earlier order suggests that the ruling had not been enforced in the interim. Local officials were perhaps a little more conscientious second time around since there are records of citizens being subsequently fined as 'Frequentors of stage playes'.[41]

Hull introduced a similar but more broadly applicable restriction on play attendance in 1599. It was agreed that anyone attending plays in the town in future would be 'fined half a crown', while anyone allowing players to use their house was to be fined a pound. The comment with which the regulation was prefaced is revealing, suggesting one reason why corporations might choose to police spectators as well as, or instead of, players: 'the players are for the most part strangers and therefore not so conveniently restrained from playing as the inhabitants from hearing such frivolous and vain exercises'.[42] As the authorities recognised, it was easier to exercise the law on one's resident population than on groups of unfamiliar visitors who might flee before it was possible to prosecute or punish them. However, while local people might be easier to control than itinerant players, the fact that the universities and towns such as Norwich and Hull introduced orders restricting play attendance suggests that there was a taste for plays in such communities.

Civic rewards

Rewards to players also became subject to regulation in some communities. In Bridgnorth the town agreed to restrict civic payments to players as early as 1570–71, ordering that they should not be 'receved vpon the Townes chardg*es*'.[43] In Chester they adopted a slightly different system in 1596–97, introducing a selective two-tier system of rewards. The mayor was allowed to give the Queen's players twenty shillings when they visited, and noblemen's players six shillings and eight pence.[44] Players with lesser patrons were presumably not entitled to any reward. Like the Gloucester order (1580), the special privileges accorded the players of royal and noble patrons suggest that Chester's patronage of players was politically rather than aesthetically determined. In continuing to patronise royal and noble players the town was not only seeking to maintain the goodwill of such patrons. Players were also to be rewarded because they did not want it alleged 'that this restraynte is for sparinge of the treasury of this Citie'.[45] They did not want their regulation of players to be interpreted as miserly: this would compromise the reputation and status of the corporation.

Given the economic depression that afflicted the country from the 1590s it is perhaps not surprising that some towns should have chosen to curb their expenditure upon players and entertainment more generally. But it was a change in practice that potentially reduced the money playing companies could expect to earn touring. Another form of regulation with implications for the profitability of touring was occasionally exercised at the point of payment of civic rewards, with some towns stipulating that players must not perform and/or leave the community in return for the payment, as noted earlier (see Tables 9.3 and 9.4). In these instances, although players obtained a civic fee, they were theoretically obliged to forgo local performances and the opportunity of earning further money. The introduction of fees for the use of some urban spaces (such as church houses and town halls) in the late sixteenth century represented another potential constraint upon players' touring incomes and possible obstacle to profitable performing outside Renaissance London.[46]

Reasons for regulating players

What prompted some corporations to regulate local theatrical activity more closely from the late sixteenth century is another thorny subject, but one with a bearing on the decline of touring. The increasingly strict control of touring activity, the overall decline in civic rewards to players, and the rising number of payments to players not to perform in the early seventeenth century are often seen as stemming from the same source (a source that is also seen as key to the demise of touring theatre): a growing hostility to players in regional communities, fuelled in some cases by local Puritan objections to theatre. This is much the perspective Andrew Gurr adopts as he considers the scarcity of provincial dramatic records from the 1620s. Pondering to what extent the decline in records resulted 'from civic disapproval' of players and 'how much from a relaxation of civic control', he concludes that it is likely that 'the Puritanical hatred of playing was stronger and showing itself earlier outside London, where the court had less sway'.[47]

In some communities hostility to players does appear to have played a part in the introduction of dramatic regulations. Similarly, this hostility could be described in certain cases as Puritan, although it would be a mistake simply to equate regional anti-theatrical feeling with Puritanism.[48] When the Chester authorities decided to restrict play performances at night and at the Town Hall in 1615, the order opened with an ethical condemnation of players and their plays:

> at the same Assemblie Consideracion was had of the Comon Brute and Scandall which this citie hath of late incurred and sustained by admittinge of Stage Plaiers to Acte their obscene and vnlawful Plaies [. . .] in the Common Hall of this citie [. . .] Consideringe likewise the many disorders which by reason of Plaies acted in the night time doe often times happen and fall out to the discredit of the government of this Citie and to the greate disturbance of quiet and well disposed People [. . .] It is ordered that from hensforth noe Stage Plaiers vpon anie pretence or color what soever shalbe admitted or licensed to set vp anye stage in the said Comon Hall or to act anie [. . .] Plaie by what name soever they shall terme hit, in the said Hall or in anie Place within this citie [. . .] in the night time.[49]

It would seem the Chester authorities were keen to curb players' activities in their community not only because of the disorder and disruption associated with visiting players' performances, but because they were hostile to actors. They condemn their plays in morally and legally loaded terms, while the final prescriptions of the order betray a distrust of players, implicitly characterising them as duplicitous individuals, ready to resort to 'pretence' off as well as on-stage in order to ensure that their show goes on.

Hostility to players was not necessarily the only or primary motive for the regulation or restriction of theatrical activity in early modern provincial communities. In many cases the impetus to regulate or prevent play performances appears to have been pragmatic rather than moral or religious. Many of the regulations passed by regional corporations in the late sixteenth and early seventeenth centuries reflect this, citing social and economic reasons for their introduction. One of the most common reasons for curbing plays was to prevent the spread of plague, the famously fatal disease that afflicted communities up and down early modern England. In Norwich the Earl of Worcester's players were denied permission to play in 1583 to avoid 'meetyng*es* of people this whote whethe*r'* and the possible spread of disease and 'also for that they came fro*m* an Infected place'.[50] As this demonstrates, towns might wish to restrict playing during regional plague outbreaks not only because the disease could be spread during large gatherings but because players might carry infection with them from other towns. In Bristol a total ban on stage plays in the city was temporarily enforced in 1613 because of plague outbreaks at 'Aburgavenney and other places in Wales, and the daunger thereof nowe greatly feared' in Bristol. In this instance, the prohibition was a preventative measure, passed in the hope of stopping the spread of plague from neighbouring towns and regions.[51]

A desire to avoid the damage and/or disorder potentially attendant on large gatherings of the kind attracted to plays also appears to have underpinned many of the dramatic regulations passed by Elizabethan and Jacobean towns. When York's Corporation finally decided to prohibit the use of the Common Hall and St Anthony's Hall for plays in 1592 they cited the damage to buildings and furniture caused by the audiences drawn to plays as their reason.[52] When Sudbury banned play performances at their Moot Hall in 1606–07 they, too, complained of the 'ruyn and decaye' caused 'by meanes of diu*ers* disordered and vnrulie pe*r*sons resortinge thither to playes of enterludes' previously allowed in the hall.[53] Concern about damage to property and civic buildings intensified in the late sixteenth and early seventeenth centuries, as town halls became increasingly lavish. As Tittler notes, the 'rough work of erecting scaffolding' and the large, boisterous crowds attracted to plays 'could only have seemed more dangerous' as town halls 'filled up with wall panelling, carved coats of arms, mayors' chairs [. . .] and the like'.[54] Notably, the civic order passed in Sudbury in 1606–07 prohibiting plays at the Moot Hall was a measure specifically intended to protect the newly 'repaired and bewtified' hall.[55]

Fear of social disorder was also common in the period and was heightened by the economic depression experienced nationally in the late sixteenth and early seventeenth centuries. Poverty and unemployment created an underclass. The persistent worry was that such people might be prompted to riot or rebel if permitted to fraternise in large groups.[56] Consequently, players were not the only entertainers or social group subject to tighter regulation. Similar concerns about disorder prompted town authorities and social reformers to seek the stricter regulation of recreations more generally, and underpinned Elizabethan and Jacobean

Sabbatarian campaigns. Indeed, the fact that Sabbatarianism was a movement partly motivated by a desire to reduce social disorder helps to explain the widespread support it received in early modern regional communities.[57] Even the eventual closure of all the London playhouses at the beginning of the Civil War can be seen as a piece of legislation partly concerned with preserving social order. Although it pleased 'the anti-theatre lobby' it was also 'an obvious security measure to prevent riotous assemblies and [. . .] possible Royalist propaganda by the court companies'.[58]

Economic considerations also played a role in the introduction of theatrical restrictions and the changing treatment extended to visiting players in some regional communities. It is no coincidence that the 1620s (the period during which payments to companies appear to drop most steeply nationally) is also the period during which many parts of the country experienced the most acute phase of an economic depression beginning in the 1590s. Wages, for instance, had been falling in the sixteenth century but reached 'perhaps the lowest level ever recorded in the 1620s; and many more were without work at all'.[59] In the early seventeenth century (and presumably for similar reasons) one finds the number of payments not to perform and the number of companies refused permission to play rising (see Table 9.4). As Heinemann notes, opposition to players outside the capital was 'demonstrably more marked in times of economic crisis' such as the 1620s and 1630s.[60] It was also greater in those communities particularly afflicted by industrial crises such as the partial collapse of the English cloth trade in the sixteenth century.[61]

As well as providing an added incentive to control large gatherings, economic distress left many Stuart corporations more reluctant, and possibly restricted in their ability to reward players. In Weymouth and Poole (towns that both experienced financial difficulties) it is telling that payments made to players at the beginning of the seventeenth century were subsequently disallowed, 'a decision suggesting that the boroughs were not opposed to drama but to spending public funds on it'.[62] In several cases civic officials evidently restricted play performances because they also wished to prevent local people (and the poor, in particular) from spending money during recession. There was concern in some communities about the economic effects of the disruption performances caused to working life and local industries, too, some of which were in a fragile condition in the early seventeenth century. Indeed, in their study of regional records, Salingar *et al.* concluded that 'the need to maintain production' was one of the two main considerations in the minds of regional civic officials when they curbed visiting play performances.[63]

In 1623 the Privy Council took the unusual step of authorising a temporary ban on performances by players and other entertainers at Norwich. Although their letter to the mayor and justices of the city betrayed a distaste for travelling entertainers – characterising them as a 'sort of Vagrant and Licentious Rabble' – their main motives for instituting the prohibition were apparently pragmatic and economic. By their own account, they wished to protect the city's multiple and important industries,

> wherein multitudes of people [. . .] are set one worke whoe beeing apt to bee drawne away from ther [. . .] labour by [. . .] [visiting performances] the sayd manufators are in the mean tyme in such sort neglected as Causeth dayly very great & aparent Losses & damage to the Cyty in particuler and by Consequence noe small hurt & preiudice to the Commonwellth in generall.[64]

More precisely, the Council were keen to protect the profits and national income generated by the city's industries, as their phrasing here reveals. The introduction of the prohibition was also claimed to be a way of protecting the 'purses' of servants, apprentices and poorer people from being 'emtied' in a time of scarcity.[65] Whether the Privy Councillors were as genuinely concerned with the 'purses' of poorer Norwich people as they were with the national 'purse' and the profits of local industrial magnates is harder to say. But the citing of such a reason as a plausible justification for the restriction of local entertainers indicates that there was concern about the expenditure of the poor in some provincial communities and that preventing performances was perceived as a way of controlling local expense on entertainment. Recognising that growing anxiety about the poor and unemployed and disruption to local industry was discouraging some seventeenth-century corporations from permitting players to perform in their communities, one canny troupe that visited Norwich in 1636 asked the mayor to appoint an officer on their behalf to see that 'poore people, servantes & idle persons' did not enter their performances.[66]

Although the pragmatic social and economic explanations given by corporations and the Privy Council could be (and may sometimes have been) 'mere excuses' justifying the imposition of ethically-motivated legislation against players, contextual evidence and the genuine nature of the cited concerns suggests that this was rarely entirely the case.[67] Indeed, even in London the 'City Fathers' main objections to' and reasons for restricting theatre were probably 'as much practical as doctrinal'.[68] Theoretical or moral reasons for opposing players may even have been formulated in some provincial communities as a result of the growing practical reasons for imposing restrictions on playing, as appears to have been partly the case in the metropolis. 'It was the City, with strong practical reasons for restricting playing, which paid Stephen Gosson and Anthony Munday to think of the theoretical arguments' for opposing theatre and to 'find the authority for them in the Bible and the Ancients'.[69]

Attitudes to royal authority and patronage

The growing strength and autonomy of local corporations made possible the closer regulation of theatrical activity in many regional communities. It also appears to have led to 'growing antagonism toward Crown interference in local affairs'.[70] Such antagonism may have contributed to an increasing reluctance to patronise and accept the services of visiting players since the power to authorise their performances was concentrated in royal hands in the Stuart period.[71] Declining respect for the system of elite patronage (and in some cases for royal authority) may also have contributed to the decrease in civic rewards to players and to the growing hostility and restrictions faced by touring companies in some Stuart communities. This certainly appears to have been the case in Gloucester, as Peter Greenfield notes: as the 'city fathers became increasingly radical in their Puritanism, the players suffered from civic hostility toward their royal patrons', with rewards to players all but disappearing in the Stuart period.[72] It is arguably no coincidence that the level of rewards to professional acting companies also appears to have been in general decline from the 1590s, the period in which Mary Blackstone suggests that 'the influence of a patron's prestige and consequently his ability to promote players, began to seriously deteriorate outside London'.[73] Even some of those towns that continued to reward patronised players in the Caroline era do not appear to have been as concerned about the identity or status of patrons. Payments became 'increasingly standardized' and 'some towns seem to have established a set reward for players regardless of their patron, skill or size'. General, collective entries relating to rewards to players become more common, too.[74]

That patrons' names commanded diminishing respect in parts of Stuart England did not escape the notice of travelling players. Several of the dramatic records from the Jacobean and Caroline provinces suggest that it was a sensitive subject. When Gilbert Reason, leader of the Prince's players, lost his temper with local Dorchester Bailiff, John Gould, and Justice, Sir Frances Ashley, in 1615 it was not simply because they refused his company permission to perform. What enraged Reason and prompted him to deem Gould 'little better then a traitour' was his refusal even 'to look on his Comission' (that is, the company's royal licence). He may have 'glimpsed the implications of Gould's refusal for the entire patronage system'.[75] If players' commissions were to be disregarded by provincial authorities, acting companies would be left without any significant form of leverage when seeking local permission to perform.

Metropolitan playing

Elizabethan players 'expected to tour as a normal requirement of their occupation'. It was not simply a 'last resort' to which they had recourse in times of plague in the capital.[76] Before the opening of the first London theatres there were no permanent purpose-built playhouses in the metropolis and companies did not have fixed performance bases. They were therefore obliged to be versatile and to perform in a variety of spaces, while travelling 'gave them an income, and also the great economy of constantly changing audiences'.[77] The emergence of the metropolitan playhouses in the 1570s did not lead to any immediate change in players' practices either. Troupes continued to perform in diverse spaces in and outside the capital and 'the readiness to plant a performance in whatever venue offered itself ' remained 'the guiding principle' of late Elizabethan acting companies.[78] Fixed playing places for individual companies and playing as 'an urban settled phenomenon' did not become established until the end of the sixteenth century.[79]

Once playing companies had begun to establish this more permanent foothold in the capital one of the incentives to travel began to diminish. In London playing companies had access to larger audiences, while the use of dedicated playing places provided an opportunity to tailor spaces for performance and to accumulate larger stocks of playing gear. Metropolitan residency was not without its pressures, of course: 'the city government was hostile to theatre, and the challenge of settling near the city and building a following among Londoners was the challenge of mounting a large repertory of plays and rotating them daily'; but the financial rewards promised to be large and sustained.[80]

In the Jacobean period the practical and economic incentive to travel diminished further. In Stuart London the leading companies enjoyed the protection and patronage of the new Court: King James and his family not only assumed the patronage of the major playing companies but acted as regular, generous patrons of performances. The early part of James's reign also witnessed the popularisation of indoor hall play-houses, with the King's Men becoming the first adult company to acquire and perform in an indoor theatre in 1608. Although Shakespeare's company continued to use the Globe as well as the second Blackfriars theatre, most of their peers came to favour indoor playhouses, and by the outbreak of the Civil War indoor theatres had superseded open-air playhouses in number and importance. As well as affording protection from the weather, the higher fees traditionally charged at indoor playhouses made them even more profitable than the early open-air playhouses. Having obtained lucrative indoor theatres in the capital the practical and economic case for touring inevitably grew weaker. In the case of the King's Men, touring was not even a necessary fall-back when the London playhouses were closed because of plague, the monarch offering his players compensation during these periods.[81]

Given the attractions (and potentially greater profits) of London playing it is perhaps surprising that the major playing companies did not abandon the practice of touring early in the Jacobean period. They did not, however. Even the most successful company (the King's Men) continued to tour in the early part of the century.[82] While there may have been some political pressure to travel – players' regional tours traditionally providing a way of promoting patrons' names and power – the continued travelling of the leading troupes is in large part a testimony to the durability of the tradition in contemporary theatrical culture and proof of their attachment to that way of life. But it was unlikely to be long before some major acting companies gave up touring.

By the middle of James's reign, evidence suggests that the leading players and acting companies were leaving London less frequently. But this was not the end of travelling for the major patronised troupes. Three of the royal companies (Queen Anne's players, Lady Elizabeth's players, and the Prince's players) appear to have adopted a system akin to that routinely employed by the famous Queen's Men (formed 1583), choosing to divide into more than one troupe, one specialising in touring and the other in metropolitan playing.[83] The latter was usually the main group, including the leading actors. Such specialisation could be seen as evidence of the maturity of professional theatrical culture in Stuart England but it also divided the worlds of provincial and metropolitan theatre in a way that may have facilitated and contributed to the gradual attrition of touring theatre and to the privileging of metropolitan theatre in contemporary and subsequent English theatrical culture. The emergence of resident metropolitan playing companies also marked the beginning of the end of the intimate association of professional theatre and travelling. Touring was no longer to be regarded as a customary part of one's occupation as a professional actor and the needs of touring would no longer be one of the principles automatically informing playing practices and plays.[84]

Conclusions

The tradition of touring was an enduring one, but records of professional playing companies performing outside London decrease in the Stuart period. The growing legal and financial obstacles facing travelling players (especially with lesser patrons) and the increasing rewards associated with metropolitan residency suggest that this reflects a genuine reduction in professional touring. The pace, nature and reasons for the decline of travelling theatre varied between communities and regions but it was ultimately general. Although some professional companies continued to travel throughout the Jacobean and Caroline periods, touring had become a marginal activity by the 1630s. The leading players concentrated on performing in London with resident troupes, while 'duplicate' royal companies appear to have catered for the provincial market. With the emergence of resident metropolitan troupes the intimate link between touring and professional playing was severed.

The marginalisation of touring theatre in Stuart England is a significant moment. It not only represented the decline of an important theatrical tradition but a more general turning point in professional English theatre. Touring and the habits of mind that went with it played a central role in shaping the Elizabethan theatre. In the late sixteenth century professional players expected to perform in a variety of venues and for diverse audiences. Hence, playing gear and staging effects had to be kept comparatively simple, while plays needed to be accessible to mixed audiences. The decline of travelling meant that professional playing practices need no longer be dictated by the requirements of touring. This was a change with potentially profound consequences for professional theatrical culture. The path was cleared for the development of more substantial and sophisticated stage furniture (such as scenery), for instance, and more specialised plays, tailored for particular theatres and audiences. Arguably, these are the kinds of changes that one begins to see in the world of Stuart theatre and that were realised more fully in the Restoration era.

Just as touring and its traditions helped shape and foster the plays and playing practices of Shakespeare and his peers, its decline is both a herald of and a contributory factor in the demise of the theatrical culture associated with the Renaissance stage. Studying the world of professional travelling theatre and its ebbing in the Stuart period is not only a means of enlarging our knowledge of English Renaissance theatre, therefore, but a way of enhancing our understanding of the process by which the playing practices and conventions of the Restoration stage emerged from and superseded those of the Shakespearean stage. The story of touring theatre and its decline may be complex and difficult to reconstruct but it is evidently one to which we must attend if we wish to gain more insight into this innovative period in English theatre, and that will merit further study as research in regional archives produces additional material about this turning point in the history of travelling players and early modern English drama.

Notes

1 Travelling Players and Performances in Shakespeare's England

1. William Shakespeare, *Hamlet* in *The Norton Shakespeare*, ed. by Stephen Greenblatt *et al*. (London and New York: Norton, 1997), 2.2.302. Hereafter references to the play will be cited in the text.
2. Tom Stoppard, *Rosencrantz and Guildenstern are Dead* (London: Faber & Faber, 1967), Act 1, p. 16.
3. See J. T. Murray, *English Dramatic Companies, 1558–1642*, 2 (London: Constable, 1910), pp. 19–21.
4. See Andrew Gurr, *The Shakespearean Stage, 1574–1642*, 3rd edn (Cambridge: Cambridge University Press, 1970; repr. 1992), p. 34.
5. London, PRO, State Papers 12/163/44 (Microfilm).
6. There are a number of records of touring playing companies in the late fifteenth century. Lord Arundel's players visited Dover, for instance, in 1478 and were rewarded at Rye in 1479–80. (See David Mann, *The Elizabethan Player* (London and New York: Routledge, 1991), p. 243 and *REED: Sussex*, ed. by Cameron Louis (Toronto: University of Toronto Press, 2000), p. 51.) Records of patronised touring players become more common in the early sixteenth century. In many towns the earliest records of visiting royal and noble players date from this era. (See, for example, *REED: Cambridge*, ed. by Alan H. Nelson, 1 (London and Toronto: University of Toronto Press, 1989), p. 99.) The practice of players touring professionally may date back earlier than the fifteenth century in some regions, but tracing early evidence of touring is complicated by the ambiguity of the Latin terminology used to describe medieval travelling entertainers. Common terms, such as 'mimis', 'histrionibus' and 'ministrallus' could be used to describe various performers, including musicians as well as actors. See Mann, p. 242.
7. PRO, SP 12/163/44.
8. See *REED: Lancashire*, ed. by David George (London and Toronto: University of Toronto Press, 1991), pp. 380–8.
9. *Tudor Royal Proclamations: The Later Tudors (1553–1587)*, ed. by Paul L. Hughes and James F. Larkin, 2 (London and New Haven, CT: Yale University Press, 1969), pp. 115–16.
10. Cited in Gurr, *The Shakespearean Stage*, p. 29.
11. Andrew Gurr, 'The Bare Island', *ShS*, 47 (1994), 29–43 (p. 31). Andrew Gurr, *The Shakespearian Playing Companies* (Oxford: Clarendon, 1996), p. 36.
12. Even Andrew Gurr's seminal work on Shakespearean theatre, *The Shakespearean Stage*, only deals with travelling theatre in passing. In the index of the revised 1992 edition there are only ten references to travelling players. Gurr, *The Shakespearean Stage*, p. 280.

186

13. In some towns records have been lost, and those preserved may not record players' visits. This does not mean that visits were not made. At Chester, 'there survive only sporadic accounting records in which occur only six payments to touring entertainers'. (Alan B. Somerset, ' "How chances it they travel?": Provincial Touring, Playing Places, and the King's Men', *ShS*, 47 (1994), 45–60 (p. 46).) Yet, the wording of a 1596 council order restricting civic sponsoring of plays reveals that dramatic activity was more regular, alluding to the town's 'daylie experience' of plays. *REED: Chester*, ed. by Lawrence M. Clopper (Toronto: University of Toronto Press; London: Manchester University Press, 1979), p. 184.

14. *REED: Leicestershire*, ed. by Alice B. Hamilton, forthcoming.

15. See E. K. Chambers, *The Elizabethan Stage*, 2 (Oxford: Clarendon, 1923; repr. 1961), p. 124.

16. *Shakespeare in Love*, screenplay by Marc Norman and Tom Stoppard, directed by John Madden (Universal Studios, 1998).

17. Somerset, ' "How chances it they travel?" ', p. 54.

18. E. K. Chambers, *The Elizabethan Stage*, 4 (Oxford: Clarendon, 1923; repr. 1945), pp. 269–70.

19. Chambers, *The Elizabethan Stage*, 4, p. 324.

20. Peter Roberts, 'Elizabethan Players and Minstrels and the legislation of 1572 against retainers and vagabonds', in *Religion, Culture and Society in Early Modern Britain: Essays in honour of Patrick Collinson*, ed. by Anthony Fletcher and Peter Roberts (Cambridge: Cambridge University Press, 1994), 29–55 (p. 49).

21. PRO, SP 12/163/44. Hereafter references to this manuscript will be cited in the text.

22. Roberts, p. 50.

23. London, PRO, State Papers 12/160/48 (Microfilm).

24. Roberts, p. 50.

25. Roberts, p. 50.

26. Roberts, p. 53. Brayne opened the Red Lion theatre (1567), while Burbage established The Theatre (1576). Gurr, *The Shakespearian Playing Companies*, pp. 4, 188.

27. Roberts, p. 53.

28. See Muriel Bradbrook, *The Rise of the Common Player* (London: Chatto & Windus, 1962), pp. 69–70, 73.

29. Cited in Roberts, pp. 47–8.

30. See Roberts, pp. 35–9.

31. See Bradbrook, p. 37.

32. See Jean Wilson, *The Archaeology of Shakespeare: The Material Legacy of Shakespeare's Theatre* (Stroud: Alan Sutton, 1995), pp. 69–71.

33. Gurr, *The Shakespearean Stage*, p. 213.

34. Gurr, *The Shakespearean Stage*, p. 32.

35. Gurr, *The Shakespearian Playing Companies*, p. 114.

36. Chambers, *The Elizabethan Stage*, 4, p. 283.

37. Scott McMillin and Sally-Beth MacLean, *The Queen's Men and their plays* (Cambridge: Cambridge University Press, 1998), p. 39.

38. Sally-Beth MacLean, 'Touring Routes: "Provincial Wanderings" or Traditional Circuits?', *MRDE*, 6 (1993), 1–14 (pp. 1–2).

39. Cited in Gurr, *The Shakespearian Playing Companies*, p. 214.
40. MacLean, 'Touring Routes', pp. 1, 9.
41. MacLean, 'Touring Routes', p. 10.
42. Cited in G. W. Boddy, 'Players of Interludes in North Yorkshire in the early seventeenth century', *North Yorkshire Record Office Publications*, Offprint from 7:3 (1976), p. 28.
43. 'Records of Plays and Players in Kent, 1450–1642', ed. by Giles Dawson, *MSC*, 7 (Oxford: Oxford University Press, 1965), p. 17. *REED: Oxfordshire*, ed. by Alexandra F. Johnston, forthcoming.
44. Cited in David George, 'Shakespeare and Pembroke's Men', *SQ*, 32 (1981), 305–23 (p. 306).
45. Cited in E. K. Chambers, *The Elizabethan Stage*, 1 (Oxford: Clarendon, 1923), p. 332.
46. W. F. Rothwell, 'Was there a typical Elizabethan Stage?', *ShS*, 12 (1959), 15–21 (p. 17).
47. See Gurr, *The Shakespearian Playing Companies*, pp. 88–9.
48. Somerset, '"How chances it they travel?"', p. 50.
49. Cited in G. E. Bentley, *The Profession of Player in Shakespeare's Time, 1590–1642* (Guildford and Princeton, NJ: Princeton University Press, 1984), p. 181.
50. See McMillin and MacLean, pp. 178–9.
51. Some early records suggest that players may have occasionally travelled exclusively on foot. See Dawson, p. xvi.
52. John M. Wasson, 'Professional Actors in the Middle Ages and Early Renaissance', *MRDE*, 3 (1984), 1–11 (p. 4).
53. Bentley, p. 185.
54. David Bradley, *From Text to Performance in the Elizabethan Theatre: Preparing the Play for the Stage* (Cambridge: Cambridge University Press, 1992), p. 56.
55. Leicester, LRO, Hall Papers 1598–1600, BR II/18/5, f628.
56. Dawson, p. 62. See Wallace MacCaffrey, *Elizabeth I* (London: Edward Arnold, 1993), pp. 394–5.
57. *REED: Nottinghamshire*, ed. by John C. Coldewey, forthcoming. *REED: Coventry*, ed. by R. W. Ingram (London: Manchester University Press; Toronto: University of Toronto Press, 1981), p. 300.
58. At this date there appear to have been two companies of Queen's players, touring the provinces separately. See McMillin and MacLean, p. 52.
59. *REED Shropshire*, ed. by J. Alan B. Somerset, 1 (London and Toronto: University of Toronto Press, 1994), p. 247.
60. *REED: Norwich*, ed. by David Galloway (London and Toronto: University of Toronto Press, 1984), p. 96. *REED: Bristol*, ed. by Mark C. Pilkinton (London and Toronto: University of Toronto Press, 1997), pp. 135–6.
61. Bentley alludes to one late account that notes the number of plays carried by a troupe, the Salisbury Court players reportedly visiting Oxford with fourteen plays in 1634 (p. 188). The satirical account of Lupton cited above suggests that some companies travelled with a more limited repertory.
62. Pilkinton, *REED: Bristol*, pp. 112, 115–17.

63. C. J. Sisson, 'Shakespeare Quartos as prompt-copies, with some account of Cholmeley's Players and a new Shakespeare allusion', *RES*, 70 (1942), 129–43 (p. 134).

64. George, 'Shakespeare and Pembroke's Men', p. 306.

65. Gurr, *The Shakespearian Playing Companies*, p. 42.

66. Cited in Sisson, pp. 132–3.

67. Sisson, p. 134.

68. Thomas Middleton, *The Mayor of Queenborough*, in *The Works of Thomas Middleton*, ed. by A. H. Bullen, 2 (London: Nimmo, MDCCCXXXV), 5.1.264, 266.

69. John M. Wasson and Barbara D. Palmer, 'Professional Players in Northern England, Parts I and II', a paper given at the Annual Conference of the Shakespeare Association of America, at Washington DC, 1997, 1–22 (p. 13).

70. For information on these individuals as patrons and/or dramatists see the following: Murray, 2, p. 293; *Annals of English Drama, 975–1700*, ed. by Alfred Harbage, 2nd edn revised by S. Schoenbaum, 3rd edn revised by Sylvia Stoler Wagonheim (London: Methuen, 1964; repr. New York: Routledge, 1989), pp. 82–3, 86–7, 88–9, 130–1; *Renaissance Drama by Women*, ed. by S. P. Cerasano and Marion Wynne Davies (London: Routledge, 1996), p. 45.

71. Murray, 2, p. 293. E. K. Chambers, *The Elizabethan Stage*, 3 (Oxford: Clarendon, 1923; repr. 1951), p. 137.

72. George, 'Shakespeare and Pembroke's Men', p. 307.

73. Galloway, *REED: Norwich*, pp. 71, 75.

74. Cited in Chambers, *The Elizabethan Stage*, 2, p. 547.

75. From 1559 troupes were theoretically obliged to seek such permission; they may not always have done so. See *REED: Cumberland, Westmorland, Gloucestershire*, ed. by Audrey Douglas and Peter Greenfield (London and Toronto: University of Toronto Press, 1986), p. 252.

76. Cited in Douglas and Greenfield, pp. 362–3.

77. See *REED: York*, ed. by Alexandra F. Johnston and Margaret Rogerson, 1 (London: Manchester University Press; Toronto: University of Toronto Press, 1979), p. 399.

78. *Documents relating to the Office of the Revels in the time of Queen Elizabeth*, ed. by Albert Feuillerat (London: David Nutt, 1908), p. 52.

79. See *REED: Shropshire*, ed. by J. Alan B. Somerset, 2 (London and Toronto: University of Toronto Press, 1994), p. 685 for an example.

80. Galloway, *REED: Norwich*, pp. 70–1.

81. Douglas and Greenfield, p. 311. *REED: Dorset/Cornwall*, ed. by Rosalind Conklin Hays and C. E. McGee, Sally L. Joyce and Evelyn S. Newlyn (Toronto: University of Toronto Press, 1999), p. 272.

82. See Chapter 8.

83. Shakespeare's *Titus Andronicus* was performed, probably by the Lord Chamberlain's Men. William Shakespeare, *Titus Andronicus*, ed. by Jonathan Bate (London and New York: Routledge, 1991), p. 43.

84. J. A. Sharpe, *Early Modern England: A Social History*, 2nd edn (London: Edward Arnold, 1987; repr. 1991), p. 169.

85. Cited in Chambers, *The Elizabethan Stage*, 2, p. 267.
86. John Marston, *Histrio-mastix* in *The Plays of John Marston*, ed. by H. Harvey Wood, 3 (London: Oliver & Boyd, 1939), 2.1, p. 258.
87. *REED: Cambridge*, ed. by Alan H. Nelson, 2 (London and Toronto: University of Toronto Press, 1989), p. 723.
88. Nelson, *REED: Cambridge*, 1, p. 342.
89. Johnston and Rogerson, 1, pp. 364–5. *REED: Newcastle-upon-tyne*, ed. by J. J. Anderson (London: Manchester University Press; Toronto: University of Toronto Press, 1982), p. 53.
90. George, *REED: Lancashire*, p. 182.
91. Clopper, p. 293.
92. Somerset, ' "How chances it they travel?" ', p. 54.
93. *REED: Devon*, ed. by John M. Wasson (London and Toronto: University of Toronto Press, 1986) p. 267.
94. Galloway, *REED: Norwich*, p. 136.
95. John C. Coldewey, 'Playing Companies at Aldeburgh, 1566–1635', *MSC*, 9 (Oxford: Oxford University Press, 1977), 16–23 (p. 16).
96. Galloway, *REED: Norwich*, p. 109.
97. George, *REED: Lancashire*, pp. 182, 181. John M. Wasson, 'Elizabethan and Jacobean Touring Companies', *TN*, 42 (1988), 51–7 (p. 53).
98. Cited in Chambers, *The Elizabethan Stage*, 1, p. 332.
99. Wasson and Palmer, p. 8. The rewards given by wealthier private patrons were not always as generous. Neither were troupes guaranteed a monetary reward. In the Cliffords' household accounts there are records of players visiting and receiving meals but not any payment (Palmer and Wasson, p. 8).
100. Hamilton, *REED: Leicestershire*, forthcoming.
101. Conklin Hays and McGee, Joyce and Newlyn, p. 217.
102. Hamilton, *REED: Leicestershire*, forthcoming. *REED: Somerset*, ed. by James Stokes (with Bath, ed. by Robert J. Alexander), 1 (London and Toronto: University of Toronto Press, 1996), p. 26.
103. Cited in Gurr, *The Shakespearean Stage*, p. 71.
104. *Henslowe's Diary*, ed. by R. A. Foakes and R. T. Rickert (Cambridge: Cambridge University Press, 1968), p. 269. William Ingram, 'The Costs of Touring', *MRDE*, 6 (1993), 57–62 (p. 59).
105. Douglas and Greenfield, p. 299. Dawson, pp. 47, 138. McMillin and MacLean, p. 183.
106. Wasson, 'Elizabethan and Jacobean Touring Companies', pp. 54, 53.
107. Ben Jonson, *Poetaster* in *The Works of Ben Jonson*, ed. by C. H. Herford and Percy Simpson, 4 (Oxford: Clarendon, 1932; repr. 1954), 3.4.169.
108. Pilkinton, *REED: Bristol*, p. 112.
109. Wasson, *REED: Devon*, p. 46. Rothwell, p. 19.
110. Douglas and Greenfield, p. 300.
111. Murray, 2, p. 373. Wasson, *REED: Devon*, p. 180.
112. Wasson, *REED: Devon*, p. 248.
113. Hamilton, *REED: Leicestershire*, forthcoming.
114. George, *REED: Lancashire*, p. 156.
115. Thomas Heywood, *An Apology for Actors* (1612), Sig. Gv-G2r (London and New York: Johnson Reprint Company, 1972).

116. See Sir Philip Sidney, *An Apologie for Poetry*, ed. by Geoffrey Shepherd (London: Nelson, 1965), p. 118.
117. Douglas and Greenfield, p. 363.

2 Playing the Town Halls

1. This announcement is made by Sir Oliver Owlet's players in John Marston's *Histrio-mastix* in *The Plays of John Marston*, ed. by H. Harvey Wood, 3 (London: Oliver & Boyd, 1939), 2.1, p. 258. No line numbers are used in Wood's edition.
2. See *REED: Newcastle-upon-Tyne*, ed. by J. J. Anderson (London: Manchester University Press; Toronto: University of Toronto Press, 1982), p. 45 for an example of a mayor's house performance. Many different terms were used to describe early modern civic buildings. Here, the terms 'town hall' and 'civic hall' are used generically to specify those buildings 'characteristically regarded by contemporaries as the seat of whatever degree of autonomous civic administration a particular town may have enjoyed'. See Robert Tittler, *Architecture and Power: The Town Hall and the English Urban Community, c.1500–1640* (Oxford: Oxford University Press, 1991), pp. 6, 9.
3. See *REED: Cambridgeshire*, ed. by Anne Brannen, forthcoming. *REED: Somerset*, ed. by James Stokes (with Bath, ed. by Robert J. Alexander), 1 (London and Toronto: University of Toronto Press, 1996), p. 26.
4. John Wasson, 'Professional Actors in the Middle Ages and Early Renaissance', *MRDE*, 3 (1984), 1–11 (p. 6).
5. See *REED: Bristol*, ed. by Mark C. Pilkinton (London and Toronto: University of Toronto Press, 1997), pp. 65–83, 85, 110–24, 128–9, 131, 133, 135–6, 140, 142, 147–8, 150–1; *REED: Cambridge*, ed. by Alan H. Nelson, 1 (London and Toronto: University of Toronto Press, 1989), p. 403; *REED: Cumberland, Westmorland, Gloucestershire*, ed. by Audrey Douglas and Peter Greenfield (London and Toronto: University of Toronto Press, 1986), pp. 298–300; *REED: Devon*, ed. by John Wasson (London and Toronto: University of Toronto Press, 1986), p. 150; *REED: Herefordshire/Worcestershire*, ed. by David N. Klausner (London and Toronto: University of Toronto Press, 1990), p. 448; Anderson, pp. 32, 45; *REED: Norwich*, ed, by David Galloway (London and Toronto: University of Toronto Press, 1984), pp. 51, 96, 145; *REED: Shropshire*, ed. by J. Alan B. Somerset, 1 (London and Toronto: University of Toronto Press, 1994), pp. 82, 89; Stokes, *REED: Somerset*, 1, pp. 26, 51–3; *REED: Sussex*, ed. by Cameron Louis (Toronto: University of Toronto Press, 2000), p. 120; *REED: York*, ed. by Alexandra F. Johnston and Margaret Rogerson, 1 (London: Manchester University Press; Toronto: University of Toronto Press, 1979), pp. 397, 409, 430, 435–6, 441–2, 471, 487–8, 491, 501, 521.
6. The *Oxford City* Collection, ed. by Alexandra F. Johnston, forthcoming in the REED series. *Oxford Council Acts, 1583–1626*, ed. by H. E. Salter (Oxford: Clarendon, 1928), p. 26.
7. London, PRO, Star Chamber, 8 94/17, mb. 17, mb. 2. In May 1603 King James issued a proclamation that prohibited Sunday playing. See Margot Heinemann, *Puritanism and Theatre* (Cambridge: Cambridge University Press, 1980), p. 33.

8. *William Whiteway of Dorchester: His Diary, 1618 to 1635*, ed. by David Under-down, Dorset Record Society, 12 (Dorchester: Dorset Record Society, 1991), p. 55.
9. Andrew Gurr, *The Shakespearean Stage, 1574–1642*, 3rd edn (Cambridge: Cambridge University Press, 1970; repr. 1992), p. 49.
10. The following survey of Renaissance civic buildings in England's provinces makes extensive use of Tittler's findings.
11. Tittler, p. 11.
12. Tittler, p. 69.
13. See Tittler, pp. 85, 93.
14. Tittler, pp. 28, 32.
15. Charles James Billson, *Medieval Leicester* (Leicester: Edward Backus, 1920), p. 67.
16. *REED: Coventry*, ed. by R. W. Ingram (London: Manchester University Press; Toronto: University of Toronto Press, 1981), p. 364.
17. Somerset, *REED: Shropshire*, 1, p. 219.
18. Tittler, pp. 152–3.
19. Billson, p. 55. Pete Bryan and Sue Cooper, *The Leicester Guildhall: A Short History and Guide* (Leicester: Leicester City Council, no date [1990s?]), p. 2.
20. The classification of early modern town halls into these two main types derives from S. E. Rigold. Cited in Tittler, p. 25.
21. Tittler, pp. 41–2.
22. Scott McMillin and Sally-Beth MacLean, *The Queen's Men and their Plays* (Cambridge: Cambridge University Press, 1998), p. 71. Galloway, *REED: Norwich*, p. lxxxiv.
23. See Galloway, *REED: Norwich*, pp. 96, 145–6. The great halls in the royal palaces were generally large (for example, Hampton Court's measured 106 feet by 40 feet and Whitehall's 100 feet by 45 feet). E. K. Chambers, *The Elizabethan Stage*, 1 (Oxford: Clarendon, 1923), p. 15.
24. McMillin and MacLean, p. 74.
25. Gurr, *The Shakespearean Stage*, p. 156.
26. Alan B. Somerset, ' "How chances it they travel?": Provincial Touring, Playing Places, and the King's Men', *ShS*, 47 (1994), 45–60 (p. 59). *VCH: A History of the County of Warwick*, ed. by Philip Styles, 3 (London: Oxford University Press, 1945), p. 228. McMillin and MacLean, p. 71.
27. In his study of Cambridge college halls, Nelson describes Queen's hall as representing the standard size, measuring approximately 27 feet wide and 44 feet 'from the upper-end wall to the screens'. Alan H. Nelson, *Early Cambridge Theatres* (Cambridge: Cambridge University Press, 1994), p. 62.
28. Elizabeth Holland, 'The Earliest Bath Guildhall', *Bath History*, 2 (1988), 163–80 (p. 170). Tittler, p. 34.
29. David George, 'Jacobean Actors and the Great Hall at Gawthorpe, Lancashire', *TN*, 37 (1983), 109–21 (p. 116).
30. Nelson, *REED: Cambridge*, 1, pp. 200, 403.
31. Pilkinton, *REED: Bristol*, p. 85.
32. Tittler, p. 45.
33. Tittler, p. 113.
34. Pilkinton, *REED: Bristol*, p. 122.

35. Pilkinton, *REED: Bristol*, p. 85.
36. See Tittler, pp. 114–15.
37. *Tudor Royal Proclamations: The Later Tudors (1553–1587)*, ed. by Paul L. Hughes and James F. Larkin, 2 (London and New Haven, CT: Yale University Press, 1969), pp. 115–16. E. K. Chambers, *The Elizabethan Stage*, 4 (Oxford: Clarendon, 1923; repr. 1945), p. 270.
38. *Documents relating to the Office of the Revels in the time of Queen Elizabeth*, ed. by Albert Feuillerat (London: David Nutt, 1908), p. 52.
39. Tittler, p. 139.
40. Andrew Gurr, *The Shakespearian Playing Companies* (Oxford: Clarendon, 1996), p. 38.
41. See Galloway, *REED: Norwich*, pp. 145, 147.
42. Galloway, *REED: Norwich*, p. 180.
43. Galloway, *REED: Norwich*, pp. 180–1.
44. Galloway, *REED: Norwich*, p. 181.
45. Galloway, *REED: Norwich*, p. 182.
46. *REED: Chester*, ed. by Lawrence M. Clopper (London: Manchester University Press; Toronto: University of Toronto Press, 1979), p. 184.
47. Douglas and Greenfield, p. 172.
48. In Kendal in 1586 the town authorities spoke despairingly of the insistent local demand for the revival of the town's Corpus Christi play. Douglas and Greenfield, p. 171.
49. Tittler, p. 132.
50. See Wasson, *REED: Devon*, p. 72; *REED: Shropshire*, ed. by J. Alan B. Somerset, 2 (London and Toronto: University of Toronto Press, 1994), p. 563.
51. Gurr, *The Shakespearian Playing Companies*, p. 38.
52. Gurr, *The Shakespearian Playing Companies*, p. 39.
53. Johnston and Rogerson, 1, p. 399.
54. Klausner, pp. 453–4.
55. 'Records of Plays and Players in Norfolk and Suffolk, 1330–1642', ed. by John M. Wasson and David Galloway, *MSC*, 11 (Oxford: Oxford University Press, 1980–1), p. 163.
56. Durham, Durham Record Office, The Order Book of the City of Durham, DU 1/4/4, f15v.
57. Stratford-upon-Avon, SBTRO, Stratford-upon-Avon Council Minutes 1593–1628, BRU2/2, p. 95.
58. SBTRO, Stratford-upon-Avon Council Minutes 1593–1628, BRU2/2, p. 226.
59. See Nelson, *REED: Cambridge*, 1, pp. 276, 349, 399.
60. See Heinemann, p. 33.
61. Heinemann, p. 22. *The Casebook of Sir Francis Ashley JP, Recorder of Dorset 1614–35*, ed. by J. H. Bettey, Dorset Record Society, 7 (Dorchester: Dorchester Record Society, 1981), p. 10.
62. Clopper, pp. 292–3.
63. Johnston and Rogerson, 1, p. 449.
64. Wasson and Galloway, p. 198.
65. Nelson, *REED: Cambridge*, 1, p. 403.
66. McMillin and MacLean, p. 71.
67. Alan H. Nelson, 'Hall Screens and Elizabethan Playhouses', in *The*

Development of Shakespeare's Theater, ed. by John H. Astington (New York: AMS Press, 1992), 57–76 (pp. 69–70). Klausner, pp. 453–4.

68. Douglas and Greenfield, p. 298.
69. *REED: Leicestershire*, ed. by Alice B. Hamilton, forthcoming.
70. Douglas and Greenfield, p. 314.
71. Douglas and Greenfield, pp. 362–3.
72. Pilkinton, *REED: Bristol*, p. 112.
73. Pilkinton, *REED: Bristol*, p. 122.
74. Somerset, *REED: Shropshire*, 1, p. 305.
75. Evidence that plays taken on tour were typically those already tried and tested in London is supplied by Henslowe's Diary. See Roslyn Lander Knutson, *The Repertory of Shakespeare's Company, 1594–1613* (Fayetteville, AR: University of Arkansas Press, 1991), p. 106.
76. Gurr, *The Shakespearian Playing Companies*, pp. 267, 271–2.
77. See David George, 'Shakespeare and Pembroke's Men', *SQ*, 32 (1981), 305–23 (p. 306).
78. Gurr, *The Shakespearian Playing Companies*, p. 269.
79. Stokes, *REED: Somerset*, 1, p. 15.
80. Tittler, p. 146.
81. The armoury lay next to the first-floor council chamber. Holland, p. 178.
82. William Shakespeare, *Titus Andronicus* in *The Riverside Shakespeare*, ed. by G. Blakemore Evans *et al.* (Boston, MA: Houghton Mifflin, 1974), p. 1042. *The True Tragedy of Richard Duke of York*, ed. by W. W. Greg (Oxford: Oxford University Press, 1958), p. 40. There are no act or scene divisions or line numbers in the original quarto.
83. William Shakespeare, *Titus Andronicus*, ed. by Jonathan Bate (London and New York: Routledge, 1991), p. 77.
84. Douglas and Greenfield, p. 362.
85. Douglas and Greenfield, pp. 362–3.
86. Douglas and Greenfield, pp. 362–3.
87. See Douglas and Greenfield, p. 253.
88. Douglas and Greenfield, p. 363.
89. *Medieval England: An Encyclopedia*, ed. by Paul E. Szarmarch, M. Teresa Tavormina and Joel T. Rosenthal (New York and London: Garland, 1998), p. 246.
90. The genre had not disappeared entirely (see Szarmarch, Tavormina, Rosenthal, p. 246). For evidence of the genre's influence on Elizabethan plays see Robert Potter, The *English Morality Play* (London: Routledge & Kegan Paul, 1975).
91. Douglas and Greenfield, p. 253.
92. The Booth Hall functioned as the main civic building up until the nineteenth century and was eventually demolished in 1957. See *VCH: A History of the County of Gloucester*, ed. by N. M. Herbert, 4 (Oxford: Oxford University Press, 1988), p. 248.
93. See Herbert, *VCH: Gloucester*, 4, p. 248.
94. Douglas and Greenfield, p. 423. Herbert, *VCH: Gloucester*, 4, p. 248.
95. Herbert, *VCH: Gloucester*, 4, p. 248.
96. Douglas and Greenfield, p. 363.
97. Douglas and Greenfield, p. 363.

98. Douglas and Greenfield, p. 363.
99. See T. W. Craik, *The Tudor Interlude: Stage, Costume and Acting*, 3rd edn (Leicester: Leicester University Press, 1958; repr. 1967), p. 52.
100. Cesare Ripa, *Baroque and Rococo Pictorial Imagery*, ed. and trans. by Edward A. Maser (New York: Dover, 1971), plate 126.
101. Craik, p. 59.
102. Craik, p. 60.
103. Craik, p. 57.
104. Douglas and Greenfield, p. 363.
105. Douglas and Greenfield, p. 363
106. Douglas and Greenfield, p. 363.
107. See Glynne Wickham, *Early English Stages, 1300–1600*, 2:i (London: Routledge & Kegan Paul, 1963), p. 317.
108. The portrait, painted by an unknown contemporary Dutch artist, is held at the Scottish National Portrait Gallery.
109. Douglas and Greenfield, p. 363.
110. Trowbridge, Wiltshire and Swindon Record Office, Salisbury City Ledger Book, SH/DB/CR 72 Misc. 7/128.
111. *REED: Dorset/Cornwall*, ed. by Rosalind Conklin Hays and C. E. McGee, Sally L. Joyce and Evelyn S. Newlyn (Toronto: University of Toronto Press, 1999), p. 127.

3   Playing to the Gods: Church as Theatre

1. Professional players may have performed in at least one vicarage too. In 1559–60 Plymouth's Corporation paid 'playars of london' that played in 'the vycarage'. Unnamed players also performed there in 1575–76. As touring metropolitan players the former could have been professionals, although their patron is unidentified. *REED: Devon*, ed. by John Wasson (London and Toronto: University of Toronto Press, 1986), pp. 234, 244.
2. John C. Coldewey, 'Playing Companies at Aldeburgh, 1566–1635', *MSC*, 9 (Oxford: Oxford University Press, 1977), 16–23 (p. 19). *REED: Norwich*, ed. by David Galloway (London and Toronto: University of Toronto Press, 1984), p. 96.
3. See *REED: Somerset*, ed. by James Stokes (with Bath, ed. by Robert J. Alexander), 1 (London and Toronto: University of Toronto Press, 1996), pp. 48, 219; and *REED: Dorset/Cornwall*, ed. by Rosalind Conklin Hays and C. E. McGee, Sally L. Joyce and Evelyn S. Newlyn (Toronto: University of Toronto Press, 1999), p. 272.
4. *REED: Cumberland, Westmorland, Gloucestershire*, ed. by Audrey Douglas and Peter Greenfield (London and Toronto: University of Toronto Press, 1986), p. 311.
5. Paul Whitfield White, '"Drama in the Church": Church Playing in Tudor England', *MRDE*, 6 (1993), 15–36 (p. 15).
6. Paul Whitfield White, *Theatre and Reformation: Protestantism, Patronage, and Playing in Tudor England* (Cambridge: Cambridge University Press, 1993), p. 16.
7. Cited in Whitfield White, *Theatre and Reformation*, p. 134.
8. Whitfield White, *Theatre and Reformation*, p. 135.

9. David Dymond, 'God's Disputed Acre', *The Journal of Ecclesiastical History*, 50:3 (1999), 464–97 (p. 484).

10. Cited in Glynne Wickham, *Early English Stages, 1300–1600*, 2:i (London: Routledge & Kegan Paul, 1963), p. 14.

11. Margot Heinemann, *Puritanism and Theatre* (Cambridge: Cambridge University Press, 1980), p. 21. Coldewey, 'Playing Companies at Aldeburgh', p. 19. John M. Wasson, 'The English Church as Theatrical Space', in *A New History of Early English Drama*, ed. by John D. Cox and David Scott Kastan (New York: Columbia University Press, 1997), 25–37 (pp. 36–7).

12. There are seven clear records of named professional troupes acting at churches in the Elizabethan and Jacobean period in the published REED and Malone Society collections. (Only records in which it is explicitly stated that the players performed in a church building or its grounds are counted.) See Wasson, *REED: Devon* (Plymouth, 1559–60) p. 234, (Dartmouth, 1569–70) p. 67; Galloway, *REED: Norwich*, (1590) p. 96; Douglas and Greenfield (Gloucester, 1589–90) p. 311; *REED: Herefordshire/Worcestershire*, ed. by David N. Klausner (London and Toronto: University of Toronto Press, 1990) (Bewdley, 1571–72) p. 361; Coldewey, 'Playing Companies at Aldeburgh' (1573–74) p. 19; Conklin Hays and McGee, Joyce and Newlyn (Lyme Regis, 1558–59) p. 212. The performances at Plymouth, Dartmouth and Aldeburgh were by Leicester's players.

13. Scott McMillin and Sally-Beth MacLean, *The Queen's Men and their plays* (Cambridge: Cambridge University Press, 1998), pp. 21, 31.

14. See Wasson, *REED: Devon*, pp. 234, 67; Douglas and Greenfield, p. 311; Klausner, p. 361; Coldewey, 'Playing Companies at Aldeburgh', p. 19; Conklin Hays and McGee, Joyce and Newlyn, p. 212.

15. Wasson, *REED: Devon*, p. 279. Galloway, *REED: Norwich*, pp. 59, 62, 64.

16. *REED: Chester*, ed. by Lawrence M. Clopper (London: Manchester University Press; Toronto: University of Toronto Press, 1979), pp. 135, 159, 162, 166. *REED: York*, ed. by Alexandra F. Johnston and Margaret Rogerson, 1 (London: Manchester University Press; Toronto: University of Toronto Press, 1979), pp. 382, 403, 413, 451, 462, 473, 494.

17. G. E. Aylmer and Reginald Cant, *A History of York Minster* (Oxford: Clarendon, 1977), p. 434.

18. E. R. Brinksworth, 'The Archdeacon's Court: Liber Actorum, 1584', *Oxfordshire Record Society*, 23 (1942), 124–5 (p. 125).

19. Brinksworth, pp. 124–5.

20. See Galloway, *REED: Norwich*, p. 96, and Ralph Houlbrooke, 'Refoundations and Reformation, 1538–1628', in *Norwich Cathedral, Church, City and Diocese, 1096–1996*, ed. by Ian Atherton *et al.* (London: Hambledon Press, 1996), 507–39 (p. 509).

21. Cited in C. H. B. Quennell, *The Cathedral Church of Norwich* (London: George Bells & Sons, 1898), p. 43.

22. Chelmsford, ERO, Archdeacon's Court Records, D/AEA 8, f283.

23. Whitfield White, '"Drama in the Church"', p. 23.

24. ERO, D/AEA 8, f283.

25. See E. K. Chambers, *The Elizabethan Stage*, 4 (Oxford: Clarendon, 1923; repr. 1945), p. 328.

26. Wasson, 'The English Church', p. 25. Charges were sometimes exacted for the use of church house rooms.
27. Rosalind Conklin Hays, 'Dorset Church Houses and the Drama', *RORD*, 31 (1992), 13–23 (p. 16).
28. Wasson, *REED: Devon*, p. 234. *The Buildings of England: S Devon*, ed. by Nikolaus Pevsner (London: Penguin, 1952), p. 229.
29. Coldewey, 'Playing Companies at Aldeburgh', p. 19. *The Collins Guide to English Parish Churches*, ed. by John Betjeman (London: Collins, 1958), p. 342. H. P. Clodd, *Aldeburgh: The History of an Ancient Borough* (Ipswich: Norman Adlard, 1959), p. 101.
30. Cited in Karl Pearson, *The Chances of Death and Other Studies in Evolution*, 2 (London: Edward Arnold, 1897), pp. 414, 421.
31. See Conklin Hays, 'Dorset Church Houses', pp. 14–15.
32. *Dramatic Texts and Records of Britain: A Chronological Topography to 1558*, ed. by Ian Lancashire (Toronto: University of Toronto Press, 1984), p. 156. *RCHM: An Inventory of Historical Monuments in Essex*, 4 (London: HMSO, 1923), p. 69. Eric Fernie, *An Architectural History of Norwich Cathedral* (Oxford: Clarendon, 1993), pp. 205, 105.
33. *RCHM: An Inventory of Historical Monuments in Essex*, 2 (London: HMSO, 1921), p. 250.
34. *The Buildings of England: Lincolnshire*, ed. by Nikolaus Pevsner and John Harris, revised by Nicholas Antram, 2nd edn (London: Penguin, 1964, repr. 1995), p. 156. 'Records of Plays and Players in Lincolnshire, 1300–1585', ed. by Stanley J. Kahrl, *MSC*, 8 (Oxford: Oxford University Press, 1969 [1974]), p. 5.
35. Screens had been common in medieval churches but some were destroyed during the Reformation when the removal of the rood (usually located above the screen) was ordered. See J. Charles Cox, *Churchwardens' Accounts from the fourteenth century to the close of the seventeenth century* (London: Methuen, 1913), p. 82.
36. Francis Bond, *Screens and Galleries in English Churches* (London: Oxford University Press, 1908), p. 36.
37. Bond, p. 111.
38. Cox, *Churchwardens' Accounts*, p. 82.
39. Although possibly amateurs or musicians, the unnamed performers that paid 'for playinge in the church lofte' could have been professional visiting players. Cox, *Churchwardens' Accounts*, p. 280.
40. Alfred Heneage Cocks, 'The Parish Church of All Saints, Great Marlow', *Records of Buckinghamshire*, 6 (1887–91), 326–40 (pp. 326–7).
41. Clopper, p. 135.
42. See Ian Atherton, 'The Close' in Atherton *et al.*, 634–64 (pp. 657, 660).
43. Cox, *Churchwardens' Accounts*, p. 287.
44. Conklin Hays, 'Dorset Church Houses', p. 15.
45. Conklin Hays, 'Dorset Church Houses', pp. 14–15. *VCH: A History of the County of Somerset*, ed. by R. W. Dunning, 3 (London: Oxford University Press, 1974), p. 149. Of the three church houses hired by named professional players in the published REED collections only one survives (at Sherborne). Bridgwater's house was rebuilt in the late eighteenth century,

and Somerton's parish house 'was demolished *c*.1840'. *VCH: A History of the County of Somerset*, ed. by R. W. Dunning, 6 (Oxford: Oxford University Press, 1992), p. 233. Dunning, *VCH: Somerset*, 3, p. 149.

46. Dunning, *VCH: Somerset*, 3, p. 149. Conklin Hays, 'Dorset Church Houses', p. 14.
47. Conklin Hays, 'Dorset Church Houses', pp. 14–15.
48. Conklin Hays, 'Dorset Church Houses', p. 14.
49. Stokes (with Alexander), 1, p. 220. Conklin Hays, 'Dorset Church Houses', p. 14.
50. The military equipment had 'disappeared' or 'been sold' by the 1580s. Conklin Hays, 'Dorset Church Houses', pp. 14–15.
51. Conklin Hays, 'Dorset Church Houses', p. 16.
52. David Welander, *The History, Art and Architecture of Gloucester Cathedral* (Stroud: Alan Sutton, 1991), p. 304.
53. Whether the college churchyard was the upper or lower yard is not clarified in contemporary documents. Today, the areas are joined and known collectively as 'College Green'.
54. See Galloway, *REED: Norwich*, p. 96 and *REED: Bristol*, ed. by Mark C. Pilkinton (London and Toronto: University of Toronto Press, 1997), pp. 135–6.
55. Somerset, *REED: Shropshire*, 1, p. 247.
56. Dymond, p. 467.
57. Dymond, pp. 467–8.
58. Dymond, pp. 467–8.
59. Quennell, p. 43.
60. See Pamela Burgess, *Churchyards* (London: SPCK, 1980), p. 3.
61. See Galloway, *REED: Norwich*, p. 73.
62. *VCH: A History of the County of Gloucester*, ed. by N. M. Herbert, 4 (Oxford: Oxford University Press, 1988), p. 275.
63. Galloway, *REED: Norwich*, p. 96. J. T. Murray, *English Dramatic Companies, 1558–1642*, 2 (London: Constable, 1910), p. 402.
64. William Le Hardy, 'Elizabethan Players in Winslow Church', *TN*, 12 (1957–58), 107.
65. ERO, D/AEA 8, f283.
66. Wasson, *REED: Devon*, pp. 234, 67. Klausner, p. 361.
67. Kahrl, p. 73.
68. Chelmsford, ERO, D/AE/A11, f56. F. G. Emmison, *Elizabethan Life: Morals and the Church Courts* (Chelmsford: Essex County Council, 1973), p. 111.
69. Religious plays were not unknown but rare in the repertories of professional Shakespearean companies (for example, Lord Strange's Men performed a 'play of Jerusalem', 1591). Lancashire, p. 220.
70. *The Annals of English Drama, 975–1700*, ed. by Alfred Harbage, 2nd edn revised by S. Schoenbaum, 3rd edn revised by Sylvia Stoler Wagonheim (London: Methuen, 1964; repr. New York: Routledge, 1989), pp. 44–5. McMillin and MacLean, p. 35.
71. See Andrew Gurr, *The Shakespearian Playing Companies* (Oxford: Clarendon, 1996), p. 210; and McMillin and MacLean, pp. 92–3.
72. Boston's civic officials prohibited plays in the church chancel in 1578, sug-

gesting that it was recognised (and had perhaps been used) as a playing space. Kahrl, p. 5.
73. Whitfield White, *Theatre and Reformation*, p. 146.
74. Whitfield White, *Theatre and Reformation*, p. 147.
75. The 'maintenance of the nave' was usually 'the responsibility of the parishioners through the churchwardens'. Emmison, *Elizabethan Life: Morals and the Church Courts*, p. 248.
76. *The Buildings of England: Devon*, ed. by Bridget Cherry and Nikolaus Pevsner, 2nd edn (London: Penguin, 1952; repr. 1991), p. 323. Wasson, *REED: Devon*, p. 67. The nave measures approximately 20 metres by 14 metres. Information kindly provided by the Reverend Simon Wright, Vicar for the Parish of Dartmouth.
77. Brinksworth, p. 125. *VCH: A History of the County of Oxford*, ed. by Alan Crossley, 11 (Oxford: Oxford University Press, 1983), p. 221.
78. Cox, *Churchwardens' Accounts*, p. 280.
79. Side chapels appear to have been used as stage houses and/or tiring houses when Cambridge students performed in King's College Chapel for Queen Elizabeth (1564). See Whitfield White, *Theatre and Reformation*, p. 143.
80. ERO, D/AEA 8, f283. *RCHM: Essex*, 2, p. 250.
81. See Alan H. Nelson, 'Hall Screens and Elizabethan Playhouses', in *The Development of Shakespeare's Theater*, ed. by John H. Astington (New York: AMS Press, 1992), 57–76 (pp. 69–70).
82. See Conklin Hays, 'Dorset Church Houses', p. 14. Dunning, *VCH: Somerset*, 3, p. 149.
83. Dymond, pp. 467–8.
84. Alexandra F. Johnston, ' "What Revels are in Hand?": Dramatic Activities sponsored by the Parishes of the Thames Valley', *English Parish Drama*, ed. by Alexandra F. Johnston and Wim Husken (Amsterdam, Atlanta: Rodopi, 1996), 95–104 (p. 98).
85. Conklin Hays and McGee, Joyce and Newlyn, p. 261. Wasson, *REED: Devon*, p. 66.
86. Galloway, *REED: Norwich*, p. 96.
87. Somerset, *REED: Shropshire*, 1, p. 247.
88. Herbert, *VCH: Gloucester*, 4, p. 275.
89. See Conklin Hays and McGee, Joyce and Newlyn, p. 269.
90. E. K. Chambers, *The Elizabethan Stage*, 1 (Oxford: Clarendon, 1923), p. 226.
91. See Cox, *Churchwardens' Accounts*, p. 68.
92. See Ronald Hutton, *The Rise and Fall of Merry England* (Oxford: Oxford University Press, 1994; repr. 1996), p. 156.
93. Klausner, p. 58.
94. Klausner, p. 312. *REED: Sussex*, ed. by Cameron Louis (Toronto: University of Toronto Press, 2000), p. 5.
95. Kahrl, p. 5.
96. Lancashire, p. 76.
97. Dymond, p. 481.
98. Dymond, p. 484.
99. See, for example, the Elizabethan injunctions and visitation articles issued in the Province of York and Diocese of Chester. Cited in *REED: Lancashire*,

ed. by David George (London and Toronto: University of Toronto Press, 1991), pp. 213–14.

100. Wasson, 'The English Church', p. 26.

101. See Chapter 9 for a fuller discussion of the decline of touring. There may have been additional reasons for the decline in amateur parish plays at churches, including the institution of new ways of raising money (such as parish rates), one of the traditional purposes of parish plays having been to raise funds for the church. See Beat Kumin, *The Shaping of a Community: The Rise and Reformation of the English Parish, c.1400–1560* (Aldershot: Scolar Press, 1996), p. 214.

4   At Home to the Players: Travelling Players at Country Houses

1. William Shakespeare, *The Taming of the Shrew* in *The Riverside Shakespeare*, ed. by G. Blakemore Evans *et al.* (Boston, MA: Houghton Mifflin, 1974). Hereafter references to the play will be cited in the text.

2. E. K. Chambers, *The Elizabethan Stage*, 4 (Oxford: Clarendon, 1923; repr. 1945), pp. 269–70.

3. See G. W. Boddy, 'Players of Interludes in North Yorkshire in the early seventeenth century', *North Yorkshire Record Office Publications*, Offprint from 7:3 (1976), p. 20.

4. These figures are based on the records found in the fifteen published REED collections. *REED: Cumberland, Westmorland and Gloucestershire*, ed. by Audrey Douglas and Peter Greenfield (London and Toronto: University of Toronto Press, 1986), pp. 128, 138–41. *REED: Lancashire*, ed. by David George (London and Toronto: University of Toronto Press, 1991), pp. 160, 164, 166–72, 175–7, 180–2, 185–95, 270. *REED: Sussex*, ed. by Cameron Louis (Toronto: University of Toronto Press, 2000), pp. 202, 205.

5. Further evidence of players visiting country houses (1559–1625) has been identified by editors working on forthcoming REED volumes and can be found in other published sources such as the Malone Society Collections. See 'Companies of Players entertained by the Earl of Cumberland and Lord Clifford, 1607–39', ed. by Lawrence Stone, *MSC*, 5 (Oxford: Oxford University Press, 1958 [1960]), 17–28 (pp. 21–6); and 'Records of Plays and Players in Norfolk and Suffolk, 1330–1642', ed. by John M. Wasson and David Galloway, *MSC*, 11 (Oxford: Oxford University Press, 1980–81), pp. 160, 165–6.

6. See Mark Girouard, *Robert Smythson and the Elizabethan Country House* (London: Country Life, 1983) and *Life in the English Country House* (London: Penguin, 1980); and Alice T. Friedman, *House and Household in Elizabethan England: Wollaton Hall and the Willoughby Family* (Chicago, IL: University of Chicago Press, 1989).

7. J. T. Cliffe, *The Yorkshire Gentry from the Reformation to the Civil War* (London: Athlone Press, 1969), pp. 102–3.

8. Cited in *How They Lived: An Anthology of Original Accounts written between 1485 and 1700*, ed. by Molly Harrison and O. M. Royston, 2 (Oxford: Basil Blackwell, 1965), p. 37.

9. J. A. Sharpe, *Early Modern England: A Social History, 1550–1760*, 2nd edn (London: Edward Arnold, 1987; repr. 1991), p. 167.

10. Lawrence Stone, *The Crisis of the Aristocracy, 1558–1641*, abridged edn (Oxford: Oxford University Press, 1967), p. 252.

11. Girouard, *Life*, p. 2.

12. See, for example, Girouard, *Robert Smythson*, p. 58.

13. Girouard, *Life*, pp. 32–3.

14. See James Chambers, *The English Houses* (London: Methuen, 1985), p. 39.

15. Timothy Mowl, *Elizabethan and Jacobean Style* (London: Phaidon, 1993), p. 146.

16. Girouard, *Life*, p. 33. E. K. Chambers, *The Elizabethan Stage*, 1 (Oxford: Clarendon Press, 1923), p. 15.

17. *VCH: A History of the County of Lancashire*, ed. by William Farrer and J. Brownbill, 7 (London: Constable, 1912; repr. Folkestone: Dawsons, 1992), p. 11. See F. G. Emmison, *Tudor Secretary: Sir William Petre at Court and at Home* (London: Longman, 1961), p. 29. David George, 'Jacobean Actors and the Great Hall at Gawthorpe, Lancashire', *TN*, 37 (1983), 109–21 (p. 116). Angela Thomas (Bolton Museum), kindly provided the information about the dimensions of the Great Hall at Smithills. Stoneyhurst, Gawthorpe and Smithills in Lancashire, and Ingatestone Hall (Essex), were all visited by players in the early modern period. See George, *REED: Lancashire*, pp. 164, 166–77 and Emmison, p. 217.

18. George, 'Jacobean Actors', p. 116.

19. 'The Memorandum Book of Richard Cholmeley of Brandsby, 1602–1623', *North Yorkshire County Record Office Publications*, 44 (1988), p. 37.

20. Girouard, *Life*, pp. 40, 88.

21. Scott McMillin and Sally-Beth MacLean, *The Queen's Men and their plays* (Cambridge: Cambridge University Press, 1998), pp. 81–2.

22. Girouard, *Life*, p. 88.

23. See Stone, *Crisis*, p. 269.

24. Cliffe, p. 385. Girouard, *Life*, p. 82.

25. Kate Mertes, *The English Noble Household, 1250–1600: Good Governance and Politic Rule* (Oxford: Basil Blackwell, 1988), p. 22.

26. See *The Plays of John Marston*, ed. by H. Harvey Wood, 3 (London: Oliver & Boyd, 1939), 2.1. (p. 264). No line numbers are given in this edition.

27. Cited in Girouard, *Life*, pp. 5–6.

28. Felicity Heal, 'The Idea of Hospitality in Early Modern England', *Past and Present*, 102 (1984), 66–93 (p. 70).

29. Emmison, p. 123.

30. Stone, 'Companies of Players', p. 22.

31. George, *REED: Lancashire*, pp. 180–1 and 354.

32. London, PRO, Star Chamber 8 19/10, mb. 6.

33. PRO, STAC 8 19/10, mb. 6, mb. 19.

34. See, for example, George, *REED: Lancashire*, p. 167.

35. 'The Memorandum Book', p. 150. Stone, 'Companies of Players', p. 26. Lewis Machin and Gervase Markham's *The Dumb Knight* was first printed in 1608. See *Annals of English Drama, 975–1700*, ed. by Alfred Harbage, 2nd edn revised by S. Schoenbaum, 3rd edn revised by Sylvia Stoler Wagonheim (London: Methuen, 1964; repr. New York: Routledge, 1989), pp. 94–5. Philip

Massinger's *A New Way to Pay Old Debts* was possibly first performed by Prince Charles' players in 1625, but not published until 1633. See Andrew Gurr, *The Shakespearean Stage, 1574–1642*, 3rd edn (Cambridge: Cambridge University Press, 1970; repr. 1992), p. 239, and David Bradley, *From Text to Performance in the Elizabethan Theatre: Preparing the Play for the Stage* (Cambridge: Cambridge University Press, 1992), p. 241.

36. Stone, 'Companies of Players', p. 21. George, *REED: Lancashire*, pp. 180–1.
37. John M. Wasson and Barbara D. Palmer, 'Professional Players in Northern England, Parts I and II', a paper given at the Annual Conference of the Shakespeare Association of America, in Washington DC in 1997, 1–22 (p. 8).
38. London, PRO, Star Chamber 8 12/11, mb. 2.
39. PRO, STAC 8/19/10, mb. 18.
40. PRO, STAC 8 19/10, mb. 30.
41. *King Lear* was printed in 1608 and *Pericles* in 1609. Boddy, p. 16.
42. See C. J. Sisson, 'Shakespeare Quartos as prompt-copies. With some account of Cholmeley's Players and a new Shakespeare allusion', *RES*, 70 (1942), 129–43 (p. 143).
43. London, Lambeth Palace Library MS 654, n° 167.
44. Roslyn Lander Knutson, *The Repertory of Shakespeare's Company, 1594–1613* (Fayetteville, AR: University of Arkansas Press, 1991), p. 109.
45. Knutson, p. 109.
46. See *The Works of Thomas Nashe*, ed. by Ronald B. McKerrow, revised by F. P. Wilson, 3 (Oxford: Basil Blackwell, 1958). There are allusions to the 'Lord' who is the honoured spectator (l. 206), to the play's hall performance (l. 974), and to local places (l. 1830, l. 1879).
47. Peter Thomson, *Shakespeare's Professional Career* (Cambridge: Cambridge University Press, 1992), p. 44.
48. J. T. Murray, *English Dramatic Companies, 1558–1642*, 1 (London: Constable, 1910), p. 293.
49. Thomson, p. 44.
50. See George, 'Jacobean Actors', p. 113.
51. Marston, *Histrio-mastix*, 2.1. (p. 260), 3.1. (p. 274).
52. *HMC: Report on the MSS of the Earl of Ancaster preserved at Grimsthorpe* (Dublin: HMSO, 1907), p. 459.
53. Wasson and Palmer, p. 8. John M. Wasson, 'Elizabethan and Jacobean Touring Companies', *TN*, 42 (1988), 51–7 (p. 53).
54. William Shakespeare, *Hamlet*, in *The Riverside Shakespeare*, ed. by G. Blakemore Evans *et al.* (Boston, MA: Houghton Mifflin, 1974), 2.2.389.
55. PRO, STAC 8 19/10, mb. 6. *The Three Shirleys* (or *The Travels of the Three English Brothers*) was apparently written by Day, Rowley, and Wilkins and published in 1607. See Gurr, *The Shakespearean Stage*, p. 242. *St Christopher* does not survive and is otherwise unknown.
56. Anonymous, *A Pleasant Conceited Historie, Called the Taming of a Shrew*, ed. by Graham Holderness and Bryan Loughrey (Hemel Hempstead: Harvester Wheatsheaf, 1992), p. 45. There are no act or scene divisions in this edition.
57. *Hamlet*, 2.2.522.
58. Wasson, 'Elizabethan and Jacobean Touring Companies', pp. 54, 53.
59. Visits between one and at least four days are recorded, with players

performing between one and as many as five plays. See Stone, 'Companies of Players', pp. 21, 24. Payments range from a few shillings to several pounds (see George, *REED: Lancashire*, p. 167; Wasson and Palmer, p. 9).
60. Wasson and Palmer, p. 8.
61. The Stanley household accounts allude to afternoon and evening performances. George, *REED: Lancashire*, pp. 181–2.
62. Mark Girouard, *Hardwick Hall* (London: National Trust, 1989), p. 33.
63. See, for example, PRO, STAC 8 19/10, mb. 6. There is no evidence of the nature or size of the stages used.
64. George, *REED: Lancashire*, p. 350. Neville Williams, *Thomas Howard, 4th Duke of Norfolk* (London: Barrie & Rockliff, 1964), pp. 45–6.
65. *The Taming of A Shrew*, p. 45.
66. Thomas Middleton, *A Mad World, My Masters*, ed. by Standish Henning (London: Edward Arnold, 1965), 5.1.119.
67. Gustav Ungerer, 'Shakespeare in Rutland', *Rutland Record*, 7 (1987), 242–8 (p. 242).
68. Bacon was one of Essex's closest advisers. See Robert Lacey, *Robert Earl of Essex: An Elizabethan Icarus* (London: Weidenfeld & Nicolson, 1971), p. 109.
69. Ungerer, 'Shakespeare in Rutland', p. 242. Petit's association with Bacon and the Earl of Essex may have been one of the reasons Harington accepted him as tutor, Harington having links with the Essex circle. Ungerer, 'Shakespeare in Rutland', pp. 247, 242.
70. London, Lambeth Palace Library MS 654, n° 167. (Hereafter references to this manuscript will appear in the text.) 'The comedians of London have come here to play their part. They were asked to perform the evening that they arrived and were dispatched the following day. A masque devised by Sir Edward Wingfield was performed here; the tragedy of *Titus Andronicus* was also played but the spectacle was of more value than the subject.' (Author's translation.)
71. Ungerer, 'Shakespeare in Rutland', p. 243.
72. *Dictionary of National Biography*, ed. by Sir Leslie Stephen and Sir Sidney Lee, 8 (London: Oxford University Press, 1949–50), p. 1272.
73. Anne Blandamer, 'The Duke of Buckingham's House at Burley on the Hill', *Rutland Record*, 18 (1998), 349–60 (p. 349).
74. The present house replaced Buckingham's. *VCH: A History of the County of Rutland*, ed. by William Page, 2 (London: St. Catherine Press, 1935), p. 113. Blandamer, p. 360.
75. Blandamer, pp. 354, 356.
76. Blandamer, p. 357.
77. Ungerer, 'Shakespeare in Rutland', p. 244.
78. 'Sir John used to dine in the hall where he received his neighbours and most important farmers, regaling them with excessive good cheer of all sorts of dishes and wines. His steward saw to it that the others lacked for nothing, having 4 or 5 long tables decked with food-stuffs for eighty or a hundred persons at a time'. Translated by Ungerer, 'Shakespeare in Rutland', p. 244.
79. 'To entertain and cater for eight or nine hundred neighbours, who every day came to feast here, the following order was observed. [. . .] There was music at lunch and dinner; thirty or forty gentlemen were in attendance

when they brought [dishes]; two or three knights and their ladies were seated at his table besides a great many gentlemen and gentlewomen. Then after the meals there was dancing and pleasant games for fun and amusement.' Translated by Ungerer, 'Shakespeare in Rutland', p. 244.

80. See Ungerer, 'Shakespeare in Rutland', p. 244.
81. Ungerer, 'Shakespeare in Rutland', p. 243.
82. William Shakespeare, *Titus Andronicus*, ed. by Jonathan Bate (London and New York: Routledge, 1991), p. 43.
83. Ungerer, 'Shakespeare in Rutland', p. 245. Knutson, p. 218.
84. Knutson, p. 218.
85. See Bate, pp. 70–1.
86. Bate, pp. 70–1.
87. Bate, p. 43.
88. G. Harold Metz, 'The Early Staging of *Titus Andronicus*', *Shakespeare Studies*, 14 (1981), 99–109 (p. 100).
89. It is known as the Peacham drawing because 'Henricus Peacham' is written at the bottom of the single folio on which it appears in the Portland Manuscript at Longleat. Bate, p. 39.
90. Bate, p. 41.
91. Bate, p. 43.
92. Bate, p. 44.
93. Bate, p. 46.
94. Cited in Bate, p. 46.
95. Cited in Bate, p. 46.
96. Ungerer, 'Shakespeare in Rutland', p. 243.
97. Stephen and Lee, p. 1272.

5 Drama at Drinking Houses: Inn Performances

1. *REED: Shropshire*, ed. by J. Alan B. Somerset, 1 (London and Toronto: University of Toronto Press, 1994), p. 21.
2. O. L. Brownstein, 'A Record of London Inn Playhouses from *c*.1565–90', *SQ*, 22 (1971), 17–24 (p. 22).
3. Glynne Wickham, *Early English Stages, 1300–1600*, 2:i (London: Routledge & Kegan Paul, 1963), p. 188. Andrew Gurr, *The Shakespearean Stage, 1575–1642*, 3rd edition (Cambridge: Cambridge University Press, 1970; repr. 1992), p. 118. The Lord Chamberlain requested that his troupe be allowed the use of the inn that winter (1594). Permission may not have been granted, as it would have breached the ban on players using London inns passed that year. (Information kindly provided by Andrew Gurr.)
4. Wickham, 2:i, p. 193. F. P. Wilson, *The English Drama, 1485–1585*, ed. by G. K. Hunter (Oxford: Clarendon, 1969), p. 169.
5. E. K. Chambers, *The Elizabethan Stage*, 4 (Oxford: Clarendon, 1923; repr. 1945), pp. 272–4.
6. Andrew Gurr, *The Shakespearian Playing Companies* (Oxford: Clarendon, 1996), p. 31. Chambers, *The Elizabethan Stage* 4, p. 300.
7. Cited in E. K. Chambers, *The Elizabethan Stage*, 2 (Oxford: Clarendon, 1923; repr. 1961), p. 127.
8. See Chapter 8 for a discussion of provincial Renaissance playhouses.

9. Peter Clark, *The English Alehouse: A Social History, 1200–1830* (London and New York: Longman, 1983), pp. 2, 49. Thanks to the pioneering research of earlier scholars such as R. F. Bretherton and contemporary historians such as Clark, there is detailed information about early modern drinking houses and their place in society. The discussion of drinking houses in this chapter is indebted to this research and Clark's work in particular.

10. P. Clark, p. 5.

11. *REED: Somerset*, ed. by James Stokes (with Bath, ed. by Robert J. Alexander), 1 (London and Toronto: University of Toronto Press, 1996), p. 155. Falstaff's improvised play involves him pretending to be the king and wearing a cushion as his crown. See William Shakespeare, *Henry IV, Part 1* in *The Norton Shakespeare*, ed. by Stephen Greenblatt *et al.* (London and New York: Norton, 1997), 2.5.342. (Andrew Gurr kindly drew this parallel to my attention.)

12. *REED: Lancashire*, ed. by David George (London and Toronto: University of Toronto Press, 1991), pp. 95–6. The play is likely to have been Shakespeare's *Henry VIII* or Samuel Rowley's *When You See Me, You Know Me*. See George, *REED: Lancashire*, p. 337.

13. *REED: Cumberland, Westmorland, Gloucestershire*, ed. by Audrey Douglas and Peter Greenfield (London and Toronto: University of Toronto Press, 1986), p. 298. Somerset, *REED: Shropshire*, 1, p. 207. *REED: Shropshire*, ed. by J. Alan B. Somerset, 2 (London and Toronto: University of Toronto Press, 1994), p. 654.

14. *REED: Norwich*, ed. by David Galloway (London and Toronto: University of Toronto Press, 1984), p. 147.

15. *REED: Oxfordshire*, ed. by Alexandra F. Johnston, forthcoming.

16. *REED: Bristol*, ed. by Mark C. Pilkinton (London and Toronto: University of Toronto Press, 1997), p. 166.

17. Pilkinton, *REED: Bristol*, p. 166.

18. Pilkinton, *REED: Bristol*, pp. 166–7.

19. See, for instance, *REED: Devon*, ed. by John M. Wasson (London and Toronto: University of Toronto Press, 1986), p. xxvi.

20. In the fifteen published REED collections there appear to be only six direct records of players performing at drinking houses. In 1600 'certayne players' performed at The Bear, Cambridge. (*REED: Cambridge*, ed. by Alan H. Nelson 1, (London and Toronto: University of Toronto Press, 1989) p. 378.) Lord Chandos's players performed at the Angel, Coventry (1600) (*REED: Coventry*, ed. by R. W. Ingram (London: Manchester University Press; Toronto: University of Toronto Press, 1981), p. 356.) Lord Berkeley's players performed at a Dorchester inn (1608) (*REED: Dorset/Cornwall*, ed. by Rosalind Conklin Hays and C. E. McGee, Sally L. Joyce and Evelyn S. Newlyn (Toronto: University of Toronto Press, 1999), p. 342.) Albert Pearson was recompensed in Kendal for money that he gave 'ye players at ye dragon' (1593–94) (Douglas and Greenfield, p. 174.) In Norwich the Queen's players performed at the Red Lion (1583); and in 1616 Queen Anne's players were authorised to play at 'Powles' house, also known as the White Horse (Galloway, *REED: Norwich*, pp. 70–1, 146, xxx.) These are not all clear records of performances by licensed travelling players, however. In the case of the Cambridge and Kendal records it is not clear whether the players were

professionals as the name of the troupe is not given; and we cannot be certain that the Kendal payment was for a performance at the Dragon. It could have been for entertaining the players at the inn.

21. R. W. Ingram, pp. 356, 355. The Angel does not survive and its original location is uncertain although it could be the inn later recorded as the Angel in Cook Street (p. 592).

22. A. Clark, 'Maldon Records and the Drama', *N&Q*, 10th series, 8 (1907), 43–4 (p. 44). I have not been able to check the original manuscript thus far. Fragments from the Maldon Court Rolls for this year are preserved in D/B3/3/197 at Essex County Record Office, but the fragility of the documents means that they are currently unavailable for consultation. There is no reference to the case or company in the 1619 civic accounts but the list of officers' fees includes a payment to 'Mr william ffrancys one of his highnes Bayliffes of the said Burrowe this yeare' (Chelmsford, ERO, Maldon Borough Records, Chamberlain's Accounts, D/B3/3/289, f6).

23. The town's treatment of visiting players fluctuated during this period of cultural tension. In the early Elizabethan period, the town rewarded noble and royal acting companies almost every year, but were rewarding few by the end of the century. (See A. Clark, 'Maldon Records and the Drama', *N&Q*, 10th series, 7 (1907), 422–3 (p. 422). A. Clark, 'Maldon Records and the Drama', 8, p. 43.) The growth of Puritanism in the town may have been paralleled by increased corporate distaste for theatre. At least one local man interpreted the change in the town's treatment of players in religious terms. In 1590 a former bailiff and chief magistrate of the borough complained that noblemen's players no longer received the hospitable treatment they once had and implied that the corporation was puritanically biased against players, accusing them of being 'A sort of precisians and Brownists'. (See W. A. Mepham, 'Visits of Professional Touring Companies to Essex, 1537–1642', *Essex Review*, 57 (1948), 205–16 (p. 208).) By the time Lady Elizabeth's players visited, the civic position appears to have shifted once more, with the town occasionally rewarding players again, but not in 1619.

24. Galloway, *REED: Norwich*, p. 181.

25. See Galloway, *REED: Norwich*, p. 180.

26. Leicester, LRO, Hall Papers 1598–1600, BR II/18/5, f628.

27. See Galloway, *REED: Norwich*, pp. 117, 146.

28. *REED: Chester*, ed. by Lawrence M. Clopper (London: Manchester University Press; Toronto: University of Toronto Press, 1979), p. 293.

29. Somerset, *REED: Shropshire*, 1, p. 21. C. E. Burch, 'Minstrels and Players in Southampton, 1428–1635', *Southampton Papers*, 7 (1969), p. 35.

30. Trowbridge, Wiltshire and Swindon Record Office, Salisbury City Ledger Book, SH/DB/CR 72 Misc. 7/128. In this instance the nominated inn may have been chosen because the corporation owned it and therefore could still exercise some control over visiting players. See *RCHM: An Inventory of Historical Monuments in the City of Salisbury*, 1 (London: HMSO, 1980), p. 97 for an account of the history of the George Inn.

31. Gurr cited in James Gibson, 'Stuart players in Kent: Fact or Fiction?', *REED: Newsletter*, 20:2 (1995), 1–12 (pp. 1–2).

32. Gibson, pp. 2–3, 11.

33. Gibson, p. 11.

34. P. Clark, p. 7.
35. William Ingram, 'The Costs of Touring', *MRDE*, 6 (1993), 57–62 (p. 58).
36. W. Ingram, p. 59.
37. John Marston, *Histrio-mastix* in *The Plays of John Marston*, ed. by H. Harvey Wood, 3 (London: Oliver & Boyd, 1939), 6. 1. No line numbers are given in Wood's edition.
38. W. Ingram, p. 58.
39. See P. Clark, pp. 9, 14.
40. P. Clark, p. 7.
41. P. Clark, p. 65.
42. P. Clark, p. 123.
43. P. Clark, p. 40.
44. See G. W. Boddy, 'Players of Interludes in North Yorkshire in the early seventeenth century', *North Yorkshire County Record Office Publications*, Offprint from 7:3 (1976), p. 24.
45. Keith Wrightson, 'Alehouses, Order and Reformation in Rural England, 1590–1660', in *Popular Culture and Class Conflict, 1590–1914: Explorations in the History of Labour and Leisure*, ed. by Eileen Yeo and Stephen Yeo (Brighton: Harvester; Atlantic Highlands, NJ: Humanities Press, 1981), 1–27 (p. 9).
46. *Ratseis Ghost*, cited in Gurr, *The Shakespearean Stage*, p. 81. George, *REED: Lancashire*, pp. 95–6.
47. Galloway, *REED: Norwich*, p. 70. R. W. Ingram, p. 356.
48. Traditionally, it was assumed that inn-yards were the usual location for inn performances. See D. F. Rowan, 'Inns, Inn-Yards, and Other Playing Places', *Elizabethan Theatre* 9, (date unknown, prob. 1982–8), 1–20.
49. Herbert Berry, *The Boar's Head Playhouse* (London and Toronto: Associated University Presses, 1986), p. 144.
50. Galloway, *REED: Norwich*, p. 70.
51. Wickham was among the first scholars to question whether most inn performances were staged in inn-yards, pointing out that such performances posed practical difficulties at inns with a single courtyard: 'the yard is virtually the only place in the inn that cannot be closed to traffic without paralysing all its services'. (Wickham, 2:i, p. 188.) Some inns had several yards, however, and were not necessarily always busy with inn traffic. (See Rowan, 'Inns, Inn-Yards', p. 19.) We must be equally cautious, therefore, about assuming that most plays were staged indoors.
52. The performance may have been staged at the George Inn, reportedly Dorchester's best inn. The original inn does not survive. Conklin Hays and McGee, Joyce and Newlyn, pp. 195, 342.
53. *RCHM: An Inventory of Historical Monuments in Essex*, 2 (London: HMSO, 1921), pp. 174–5.
54. Nelson, *REED: Cambridge*, 1, p. 378. *REED: Cambridge*, ed. by Alan H. Nelson, 2 (London and Toronto: University of Toronto Press, 1989), pp. 1231–2.
55. P. Clark, p. 67.
56. Edward Croft-Murray, *Decorative Painting in England, 1537–1837*, 1 (London: Country Life, 1911), p. 28.
57. Croft-Murray, 1, p. 186. Lupton cited in P. Clark, p. 67.

58. *Henry IV, Part 1*, 4.2.23.
59. Berry, p. 24.
60. Galloway, *REED: Norwich*, p. 73.
61. Clopper, p. 293.
62. See Scott McMillin and Sally-Beth MacLean, *The Queen's Men and their plays* (Cambridge: Cambridge University Press, 1998), pp. 194–7.
63. Galloway, *REED: Norwich*, p. xxxii. Gurr, *The Shakespearian Playing Companies*, p. 212.
64. Galloway, *REED: Norwich*, pp. 70–6.
65. Singer may have been the gatekeeper as Edmund Brown refers to the man 'in the blacke dublet wich kept the gate', and Henry Brown alludes to 'one other in a black dublyt called Synger'. Galloway, *REED: Norwich*, pp. 73, 71.
66. Galloway, *REED: Norwich*, pp. 72–3.
67. Gurr, *The Shakespearian Playing Companies*, p. 203.
68. Galloway, *REED: Norwich*, p. 73.
69. Galloway, *REED: Norwich*, p. 71.
70. Galloway, *REED: Norwich*, p. 70.
71. Gurr, *The Shakespearian Playing Companies*, p. 204.
72. Galloway, *REED: Norwich*, p. 74.
73. Galloway, *REED: Norwich*, p. 395.
74. Galloway, *REED: Norwich*, pp. 65–6.
75. Galloway, *REED: Norwich*, p. 66.
76. Galloway, *REED: Norwich*, p. xxxiv.
77. Cited in D. F. Rowan, 'The Players and Playing Places of Norwich', in *The Development of Shakespeare's Theater*, ed. by John H. Astington (New York: AMS Press, 1992), 77–94 (p. 88).
78. Rowan, 'The Players', p. 89.
79. Hochstetter's 'Plan of the City of Norwich' (1789) shows 'three yards on the east side' of Red Lion Lane. Rowan, 'The Players', pp. 88–9.
80. The yard shown in Manning's plan corresponds to 'the central one' on the Hochstetter Map and is next to the Cricketer's Arms, the inn that the Red Lion became (*c*.1843–59). Rowan, 'The Players', pp. 88–9.
81. Galloway, *REED: Norwich*, pp. 71–3.
82. Galloway, *REED: Norwich*, pp. 71–3.
83. Galloway, *REED: Norwich*, pp. 73–4.
84. Galloway, *REED: Norwich*, pp. 72–3.
85. McMillin and MacLean list nine plays known to have been in the troupe's repertory between 1583 and 1599: *Sir Clyomon and Sir Clamydes, The Famous Victories of Henry V, Friar Bacon and Friar Bungay, King Leir, Three Lords and Three Ladies of London, The Troublesome Reign of King John, The Old Wives' Tale, Selimus,* and *The True Tragedy of Richard III* (pp. 88–9). Records of their court performances in the 1580s and 1590s identify several other plays apparently in their repertory in this period, but now lost. (See McMillin and MacLean, pp. 92–3.) A number of the clearly identified Queen's Men's plays appear to post-date 1583 (including *Friar Bacon and Friar Bungay, The Troublesome Reign of King John, The Old Wives' Tale,* and *Selimus*) and therefore could not have been performed at the Red Lion. See *Annals of English Drama, 975–1700*, ed. by Alfred Harbage, 2nd edn revised by S. Schoenbaum, 3rd

edn revised by Sylvia Stoler Wagonheim (London: Methuen, 1964; repr. New York: Routledge, 1989), pp. 54–5; *The Troublesome Raigne of John, King of England*, ed. by J. W. Sider (London and New York: Garland, 1979), p. xxi; and David Bradley, *From Text to Performance in the Elizabethan Theatre: Preparing the Play for the Stage* (Cambridge: Cambridge University Press, 1992), pp. 231–2. Other plays can be eliminated as candidates for performance at the Red Lion because they do not contain a 'duke' (such as *Sir Clyomon and Sir Clamydes* and *Three Lords and Three Ladies of London*). Determining whether the troupe could have been performing one of their lost plays is more difficult. These aside, *The Famous Victories of Henry V* and *The True Tragedy of Richard III* remain as possible candidates for performance in Norwich: both include a 'duke' (the Duke of York) and there is evidence of the troupe performing *The Famous Victories* in the 1580s. See *Narrative and Dramatic Sources of Shakespeare*, ed. by Geoffrey Bullough, 4 (London: Routledge & Kegan Paul, 1962), pp. 289–90.
86. The Duke of York's part is not a major one, which could count against *The Famous Victories'* identification as the play performed at the Red Lion. As the troupe's leading tragedian, one would not expect Bentley to play a minor role.
87. I am indebted to Andrew Gurr for this suggestion.
88. Galloway, *REED: Norwich*, pp. 72, 73, 75.
89. Galloway, *REED: Norwich*, pp. 73, 75.
90. Galloway, *REED: Norwich*, p. 378.
91. Galloway, *REED: Norwich*, p. 381.

6 Playing at Schools and University Colleges

1. Most of the plays performed were 'classical' (that is written by classical authors or contemporary works modelled on ancient Greek or Roman drama) and in Latin, although performances in English are occasionally recorded. See W. M. Hawkins, *Apollo Shroving*, ed. by Howard Garrett Rhoads (Philadelphia, PA: University of Pennsylvania Press, 1936), written for Hawkins's students at Hadleigh Grammar School, 1626; and Richard Edwardes, *Damon and Pythias*, ed. by D. Jerry White (New York and London: Garland, 1980), p. 7, performed at Merton College, 1567–68. Plays in Greek were also performed at the universities. See Frederick S. Boas, *University Drama in the Tudor Age* (Oxford: Clarendon, 1914), p. 386.
2. Jane Cowling, 'An Edition of the Records of Drama, Ceremony and Secular Music in Winchester City and College, 1556–1642' (unpublished doctoral thesis, Southampton University, 1993), p. 62. *REED: Cambridge*, ed. by Alan H. Nelson, 1 (London and Toronto: University of Toronto Press, 1989), p. 319. Scott McMillin and Sally-Beth MacLean, *The Queen's Men and their plays* (Cambridge: Cambridge University Press, 1998), p. 78.
3. *REED: Bristol*, ed. by Mark C. Pilkinton (London and Toronto: University of Toronto Press, 1997), p. 209.
4. Paul Whitfield White, *Theatre and Reformation: Protestantism, Patronage, and Playing in Tudor England* (Cambridge: Cambridge University Press, 1993), p. 105.

5. *VCH: A History of the County of Buckinghamshire*, ed. by William Page, 2 (London: Constable, 1908), p. 163.

6. Information kindly provided by L. J. Rich, Bursar of Boston Grammar School.

7. Play-acting had flourished in Renaissance schools as the performance of classical plays was widely adopted as a means of training pupils in Latin, rhetoric and oratory. See T. H. Vail Motter, *The School Drama in England* (London: Longman, 1929), p. 86.

8. See Motter, pp. 259–60. *VCH: A History of Hampshire and The Isle of Wight*, ed. by Arthur Doubleday, 2 (London: Constable, 1903), 250–408 (p. 312).

9. Cowling, pp. 17, 64.

10. Pilkinton, *REED: Bristol*, pp. 135–6.

11. *REED: Dorset/Cornwall*, ed. by Rosalind Conklin Hays and C. E. McGee, Sally L. Joyce and Evelyn S. Newlyn (Toronto: University of Toronto Press, 1999), p. 218.

12. Nottingham, Nottinghamshire Archives, Newark Corporation Minutes DC/NW 3/1/1, f45.

13. 'Records of Plays and Players in Lincolnshire, 1300–1585', ed. by Stanley J. Kahrl, *MSC*, 8 (Oxford: Oxford University Press, 1969 [1974]), p. 5.

14. *VCH: A History of Hampshire and The Isle of Wight*, ed. by William Page, 5 (London: Constable, 1912; repr. Folkestone: Dawsons, 1973), pp. 16–18. Doubleday, *VCH: Hampshire*, 2, p. 312.

15. Page, *VCH: Hampshire*, 5, p. 17. *The Buildings of England: Hampshire and the Isle of Wight*, ed. by Nikolaus Pevsner and David Lloyd (London: Penguin, 1967; repr. 1973), p. 702.

16. Page, *VCH: Buckinghamshire*, 2, p. 163.

17. T. F. Kirby, *The Annals of Winchester College* (London: Henry Frowde; Winchester: P. and G. Wells, 1892), p. 44.

18. It is not certain whether the present screen is original. According to Kirby it was erected in 1820 (p. 43); but he does not give his source and it is possible that the original screen was simply renovated in the nineteenth century. There is certainly always thought to have been a screens passage at the hall. (Information kindly provided by Suzanne Foster, Deputy College Archivist, Winchester College.)

19. See Alan Nelson, 'Hall Screens and Elizabethan Playhouses' in *The Development of Shakespeare's Theater*, ed. by John Astington (New York: AMS Press, 1992), 57–76 (pp. 69–70).

20. Conklin Hays and McGee, Joyce and Newlyn, p. 218.

21. See *RCHM: An Inventory of the Historical Monuments in Dorset*, 1 (London: HMSO, 1952), p. 141. John Hutchins, *The History and Antiquities of the County of Dorset*, 2 (Westminster: Nicholls, 1863; repr. Trowbridge: Redwood, 1973), p. 69.

22. Cited in Conklin Hays and McGee, Joyce and Newlyn, p. 350.

23. *RCHM: Dorset*, 1, p. 141.

24. The site has not served as a school for some time and has been almost entirely rebuilt. See Roger Price, *Excavations at St. Bartholomew's Hospital Bristol* (Bristol: Redcliffe Press, 1979), pp. 21, 23.

25. Price, p. 5. Walter Adam Sampson, *A History of Bristol Grammar School* (Bristol: Arrowsmith, 1912), pp. 29–30, 51–2.

26. Pilkinton, *REED: Bristol*, p. 117. See Mark C. Pilkinton, 'Entertainment at the Free School of St. Bartholomew, Bristol', *REED: Newsletter*, 13:2 (1988), 9–13 (p. 11) for further information about the school's use for plays.
27. Pilkinton, 'Entertainment at the Free School', p. 12.
28. The Magnus School abandoned the site in 1909. *VCH: A History of Nottinghamshire*, ed. by William Page, 2 (London: Constable, 1910; repr. Folkestone: Dawsons, 1970), p. 202.
29. *The Buildings of England: Nottinghamshire*, ed. by Nikolaus Pevsner, revised by Elizabeth Williamson (London: Penguin, 1951; repr. 1979), p. 194.
30. *The Buildings of England: Lincolnshire*, ed. by Nikolaus Pevsner and John Harris, revised by Nicholas Antram, 2nd edn (London: Penguin, 1964; repr. 1995), p. 168. L. J. Rich (School Bursar) kindly provided the information about the schoolhouse's dimensions.
31. Kahrl, p. 5.
32. Page, *VCH: Buckinghamshire*, 2, p. 312.
33. Motter, p. 34. Richard Southern, 'The "Houses" of the Westminster play', *TN*, 3 (1949), 46–52 (p. 48).
34. E. K. Chambers, *The Elizabethan Stage*, 1 (Oxford: Clarendon, 1923), p. 229.
35. William Tydeman, *Four English Comedies* (London: Penguin, 1984), p. 34.
36. See Chambers, *The Elizabethan Stage*, 1, p. 229.
37. See Andrew Gurr, *Playgoing in Shakespeare's London* (Cambridge: Cambridge University Press, 1989), p. 129.
38. Gurr estimates that an average Elizabethan spectator required 18 ins. × 18 ins. of space. See Alan B. Somerset, ' "How chances it they travel?": Provincial Touring, Playing Places, and the King's Men', *ShS*, 47 (1994), 45–60 (p. 59). Given the dimensions of the Winchester hall, and allowing a third of the space for a stage, approximately 533 people might have been accommodated in the hall.
39. Cowling, p. 16.
40. James McConica, 'The Rise of the Undergraduate College', in *The History of the University of Oxford*, ed. by James McConica, 3 (Oxford: Clarendon, 1986), 1–68 (pp. 1–2).
41. See *REED: Cambridge*, ed. by Alan H. Nelson, 2 (London and Toronto: University of Toronto Press, 1989), pp. 706–7.
42. See Nicholas Tyacke, 'Introduction', in *The History of the University of Oxford*, ed. by Nicholas Tyacke, 4 (Oxford: Clarendon, 1997), 1–25 (p. 2) and Nelson, *REED: Cambridge*, 2, p. 707.
43. Nelson, *REED: Cambridge*, 2, p. 707. Tyacke, 'Introduction', p. 2.
44. Nelson, *REED: Cambridge*, 2, p. 706. The universities exercised control over many aspects of local social and economic life. See, for example, *Club Law*, ed. by G. C. Moore Smith (Cambridge: Cambridge University Press, 1907), p. xiv.
45. See Boas, *University Drama*, pp. 3–4, 25 and John R. Elliott, Jr, 'Drama', in *The History of the University of Oxford*, ed. by Nicholas Tyacke, 4 (Oxford: Clarendon, 1997), 641–58 (p. 641).
46. See Nelson, *REED: Cambridge*, 2, p. 712. Boas, *University Drama*, p. 17.
47. John R. Elliott Jr, 'Drama at the Oxford Colleges and the Inns of Court, 1520 and 1534', in John C. Coldewey, 'English Drama in the 1520s: Six perspectives', *RORD*, 31 (1992), 64–6 (p. 64).

48. 'The Academic Drama in Oxford: Extracts from the Records of Four Colleges', ed. by R. E. Alton, *MSC*, 5 (Oxford: Oxford University Press, 1958 [1960]), (pp. 60, 69). The players rewarded by Magdalen could have been musicians, rather than actors.
49. Nelson, *REED: Cambridge*, 1, p. 319.
50. Ben Jonson, *Volpone* in *Jonson: Four Comedies*, ed. by Helen Ostovich (London: Longman, 1997), p. 64.
51. Ostovich, p. 64.
52. See Nelson, *REED: Cambridge*, 2, p. 986.
53. See Nelson, *REED: Cambridge*, 2, p. 985. The *Oxford City* Collection, ed. by Alexandra F. Johnston, and the *Oxford University* Collection, ed. by John R. Elliott Jr, both forthcoming in the REED series.
54. Gamini Salgado, *Eyewitnesses of Shakespeare* (London: Chatto & Windus, 1975), p. 30.
55. Translated by Salgado, p. 30. Jackson's Latin account is transcribed fully in G. Tillotson, '*Othello* and *The Alchemist* at Oxford in 1610', *Essays in Criticism and Research* (Cambridge: Cambridge University Press, 1942), 41–5 (pp. 41–2).
56. Tillotson, pp. 41, 44.
57. Tillotson, p. 43.
58. See Boas, *University Drama*, p. 220.
59. Nelson, *REED: Cambridge*, 2, p. 723.
60. Elliott, *Oxford University*, forthcoming in the REED series.
61. Andrew Gurr, *The Shakespearian Playing Companies* (Oxford: Clarendon, 1996), p. 164.
62. Nelson, *REED: Cambridge*, 1, p. 349. Elliott, *Oxford University*, forthcoming in the REED series.
63. Elliott, *Oxford University*, forthcoming in the REED series.
64. Nelson, *REED: Cambridge*, 1, pp. 71, 381.
65. See Nelson, *REED: Cambridge*, 1, pp. 365, 378. Tillotson, p. 43.
66. Elliott, *Oxford University*, forthcoming in the REED series. Boas, *University Drama*, p. 226.
67. Elliott, *Oxford University*, forthcoming in the REED series.
68. Elliott, *Oxford University*, forthcoming in the REED series.
69. Nelson, *REED: Cambridge*, 1, pp. 291, 311, 332, 338, 369.
70. See, for example, Nelson, *REED: Cambridge*, 1, p. 404.
71. *Oxford Council Acts, 1583–1626*, ed. by H. E. Salter (Oxford: Clarendon, 1928), p. 26. Alexandra F. Johnston lists nearly fifty payments to visiting players in the city accounts (1559–1617) (*Oxford City*, forthcoming in the REED series).
72. There appear to be thirty-nine civic payments to visiting players (1559–97), although the payment to Lord North's Men (1591–92) could be a payment to some of the nobleman's retainers. Nelson, *REED: Cambridge*, 1, pp. 206–369.
73. See, for example, Nelson, *REED: Cambridge*, 1, p. 319.
74. Alan H. Nelson, *Early Cambridge Theatres* (Cambridge: Cambridge University Press, 1994), p. 88.
75. Nelson, *REED: Cambridge*, 1, p. 338. Nelson, *Early Cambridge Theatres*, p. 99.

76. Nelson, *REED: Cambridge*, 1, p. 340.
77. Nelson, *REED: Cambridge*, 1, p. 341.
78. The recent problems at Chesterton explain its special mention in the 1593 Privy Council letter. Nelson, *REED: Cambridge*, 1, p. 349.
79. Elliott, *Oxford University*, forthcoming in the REED series.
80. Elliott, *Oxford University*, forthcoming in the REED series.
81. Nelson, *REED: Cambridge*, 2, p. 723.
82. One of the most famous critics of student drama was John Rainolds who engaged in a 'prolonged pamphleteering duel on the subject of academic performances with Gager at the end of the century'. See Boas, *University Drama*, p. 232.
83. See Boas, *University Drama*, p. 235.
84. *The Second Part of The Return From Parnassus*, in *The Three Parnassus Plays*, ed. by J. B. Leishman (London: Nicholson & Watson, 1949), 1.2.300.
85. *The Second Part of The Return From Parnassus*, 4.3.1766. References to the play will be cited in the text hereafter.
86. Boas, *University Drama*, pp. 387–8, 112. Nelson, *REED: Cambridge*, 2, p. 713.
87. Anonymous, *The Tragedy of Caesar's Revenge*, ed. by F. S. Boas and W. W. Greg (Oxford: Oxford University Press, 1911), p. ii. Christopher Marlowe, *Tamburlaine, Part I* in *The Complete Works*, ed. by J. B. Leishman (London: Penguin, 1984), 2.3, pp. 124–5.
88. Boas, *University Drama*, p. 100.
89. See Boas, *University Drama*, p. 255, and Alton, p. 81.
90. Nelson, *Early Cambridge Theatres*, p. 5.
91. Nelson, 'Hall Screens and Elizabethan Playhouses', p. 74.
92. Robert Willis and John Willis Clark, *The Architectural History of the University of Cambridge*, 2 (Cambridge: Cambridge University Press, 1886; repr. 1988), p. 468. Nelson, *Early Cambridge Theatres*, p. 68.
93. Nelson, *Early Cambridge Theatres*, p. 68.
94. *RCHM: An Inventory of Historical Monuments in the City of Oxford* (London: HMSO, 1939), p. 73. Alton, pp. 60, 59. The hall has not entirely escaped alteration. See *VCH: A History of the County of Oxford*, 3, ed. by H. E. Salter and Mary D. Lobel (Oxford: Oxford University Press, 1954; repr. London: Dawsons, 1965), p. 207.
95. *RCHM: Oxford*, p. 73.
96. Nelson, *Early Cambridge Theatres*, p. 39. *The Buildings of England: Cambridgeshire*, ed. by Nikolaus Pevsner, 3rd edn (London: Penguin, 1954; repr. 1977), p. 170.
97. Willis and Willis Clark, 2, p. 475. Michaelhouse was one of three institutions amalgamated to form Trinity in 1546. See Nelson, *Early Cambridge Theatres*, p. 67.
98. Pevsner, *Cambridgeshire*, p. 170.
99. Pevsner, *Cambridgeshire*, p. 170. See Nelson, *Early Cambridge Theatres*, pp. 43, 64.
100. *RCHM: Oxford*, p. 33. McMillin and MacLean, p. 78.
101. McMillin and MacLean, p. 79.
102. Nelson, 'Hall Screens and Elizabethan Playhouses', p. 68. Boas, *University Drama*, pp. 99–100.
103. See McMillin and MacLean, pp. 71, 74, 79.

104. Nelson, *REED: Cambridge*, 1, p. 170.
105. See, for example, Alton, p. 67. Nelson, *REED: Cambridge*, 1, p. 318.
106. Nelson, *Early Cambridge Theatres*, pp. 68–9.
107. Nelson, *REED: Cambridge*, 2, p. 717.
108. Nelson, *Early Cambridge Theatres*, p. 16.
109. Nelson, *REED: Cambridge*, 1, p. 319.
110. Nelson, 'Hall Screens and Elizabethan Playhouses', pp. 68–70.
111. Nelson, 'Hall Screens and Elizabethan Playhouses', pp. 69–70.
112. Jean Wilson, *The Archaeology of Shakespeare: The Material Legacy of Shakespeare's Theatre* (Stroud: Alan Sutton, 1995), p. 136.
113. See Nelson, *REED: Cambridge*, 2, p. 1147. Nelson, *REED: Cambridge*, 1, pp. 280, 212.
114. Tillotson, pp. 41–2.
115. Playhouses such as the second Blackfriars theatre could accommodate between 500–1000 people, while Trinity's Jacobean hall apparently held an audience of 2000 on one occasion. Keith Sturgess, *Jacobean Private Theatre* (London: Routledge & Kegan Paul, 1987), p. 48. Nelson, *REED: Cambridge*, 1, p. 539.
116. See, for example, Nelson, *REED: Cambridge*, 1, p. 305.

7   Playing in Markets and Game Places

1. *REED: Shropshire*, ed. by J. Alan B. Somerset, 1 (London and Toronto: University of Toronto Press, 1994), pp. 238, 247.
2. See Chapter 8 for a discussion of theatres in the Elizabethan and Jacobean provinces.
3. The actual number of 'playing places' may have been greater. See O. J. Padel, 'Ancient Parishes with possible examples of the Plain-an-gwary', *REED: Dorset/Cornwall*, ed. by Rosalind Conklin Hays and C. E. McGee, Sally L. Joyce and Evelyn S. Newlyn (Toronto: University of Toronto Press, 1999), pp. 559–63. See Jane A. Bakere, *The Cornish Ordinalia: A Critical Study* (Cardiff: University of Wales Press, 1980), p. 26 and Treve Holman, 'Cornish Plays and Playing Places', *TN*, 4 (1949–50), 52–4 (p. 52) for information on the 'rounds' at St Just and Pirran and their modification since the seventeenth century.
4. In the sixteenth century, the terms 'play' and 'game' could both be used to refer to theatrical entertainment, but they also had a range of other meanings relating to recreation. The words only appear to have become more specialised in their meanings with regards to theatre at the end of the sixteenth century, with 'play' tending to be used after this date as an alternative to 'interlude', and 'game' only being used to describe 'recreations of a non-dramatic character'. See Glynne Wickham, *Early English Stages, 1300 to 1600*, 2:ii (London: Routledge & Kegan Paul, 1972), p. 41.
5. 'Playing places' were not necessarily used for theatrical plays. See Padel, p. 559.
6. J. A. B. Somerset, 'Local Drama and Playing Places at Shrewsbury: New Findings from the Borough Records', *MRDE*, 2 (1985), 1–31 (p. 9).
7. Cited in Holman, p. 53.

8. Cited in Bakere, p. 27.
9. Kenneth M. Dodd, 'Another Elizabethan Theater in the Round', *SQ,* 21 (1970), 125–56 (pp. 126, 135). The site no longer survives having been partly built over by Willow Court (information kindly supplied by Colin Pendleton, Sites and Monuments Record Officer, Suffolk County Council).
10. Somerset, 'Local Drama', p. 25. Thomas Churchyard, *The Worthiness of Wales* (1587), cited in Arthur Freeman, 'A "Round" outside Cornwall', *TN,* 16 (1962), 10–11 (p. 10).
11. David Galloway, The "Game Place" and "House" at Great Yarmouth, 1493–1595', *TN,* 31 (1977), 6–9 (p. 7).
12. Archaeological excavations at the Castilly Henge monument indicate that 'the present form' of this site 'represents a remodelling of the original Neolithic henge' to form a *plen-an-gwarry* in the thirteenth or fourteenth century. *The Buildings of England: Cornwall*, ed. by Nikolaus Pevsner, revised by Enid Radcliffe (London: Penguin, 1951; repr. 1970), p. 110.
13. Dodd, p. 126. Galloway, 'The "Game Place"', pp. 7–8.
14. The Priory was granted 'to the Dean and Chapter of Norwich Cathedral' in 1538 after the Dissolution of the Monasteries but the town appears to have exercised 'some authority' over the Priory Garden and may have set aside a portion for use as the 'game place'. See A. Stuart Brown, 'The Theatre in Yarmouth', *TN,* 4 (1950), 54–7 (p. 54).
15. The Friary (founded in Shrewsbury in 1254–55) owned a 'fourteen-acre piece of land' outside the town walls in the area now known as Quarry Park, in which the 'quarry' was located. *REED: Shropshire*, ed. by J. Alan B. Somerset, 2 (London and Toronto: University of Toronto Press, 1994), p. 364.
16. Padel, p. 559.
17. David Dymond, 'God's Disputed Acre', *Journal of Ecclesiastical History*, 50:3 (1999), 464–97 (p. 481).
18. Galloway, 'The "Game Place"', p. 7.
19. Galloway, 'The "Game Place"', p. 7.
20. Galloway, 'The "Game Place"', pp. 6–7.
21. David Galloway, 'Records of Early English Drama in the Provinces and what they may tell us about the Elizabethan theatre', *The Elizabethan Theatre*, 7 (1981), 82–110 (p. 95).
22. Cited in *Shakespeare's Globe Rebuilt*, ed. by J. R. Mulryne and Margaret Shewring (Cambridge: Cambridge University Press, 1997), pp. 178–9.
23. 'Records of Plays and Players in Norfolk and Suffolk, 1330–1642', ed. by John M. Wasson and David Galloway, *MSC,* 11 (Oxford: Oxford University Press, 1980–81), p. 14. There are no records of plays at the 'game place'.
24. Wasson and Galloway, p. 15.
25. Somerset, 'Local Drama', pp. 25–6.
26. Translated from Latin in Somerset, *REED: Shropshire*, 2, p. 603. A further possible reference to a building at the 'quarry' may occur in 1492–93 when there is a payment '"pro masione dictorum ludentum" [for the structure of the said players]' in a production for the Prince of Wales. Somerset, 'Local Drama', p. 26.
27. Dodd, p. 126.
28. Galloway and Wasson, p. 132.

29. Somerset, *REED: Shropshire*, 1, p. 220. Somerset, *REED: Shropshire*, 2, p. 664.
30. Somerset, 'Local Drama', p. 7.
31. E. K. Chambers, *The Medieval Stage*, 2 (Oxford: Oxford University Press, 1903; repr. 1963), p. 390.
32. Somerset, *REED: Shropshire*, 1, p. 205.
33. Galloway, 'The "Game Place"', p. 7. Wasson and Galloway record only one corporate payment to players between 1559 and 1625, the Queen's players receiving twenty shillings in 1572–73 (p. 14).
34. In 1505–06 there is a payment 'to Walsham game at Gyslyngham' in the Thetford Priory accounts. Richard Beadle, 'Plays and Playing at Thetford and Nearby, 1498–1540', *TN*, 32 (1978), 4–11 (p. 5).
35. Somerset, 'Local Drama', p. 7.
36. Alan Everitt, 'The Market Towns', in *The Early Modern Town: A Reader*, ed. by Peter Clark (London: Longman, 1976), 168–204 (p. 168).
37. Everitt, p. 186.
38. Mark Girouard, *The English Town* (London and New Haven, CT: Yale University Press, 1990), p. 18.
39. John Marston, *Histrio-mastix* in *The Plays of John Marston*, ed. by H. Harvey Wood, 3 (London: Oliver & Boyd, 1939), 2.1, p. 258.
40. See Pamela King, 'Morality Plays', *The Cambridge Companion to Medieval English Literature*, ed. by Richard Beadle (Cambridge: Cambridge University Press, 1994), 240–64 (p. 247).
41. Girouard, p. 18.
42. Everitt, p. 180.
43. Everitt, p. 180.
44. B. Champion, *Everyday Life in Tudor Shrewsbury* (Shrewsbury: Shropshire Books, 1994), p. 34.
45. Champion, p. 32.
46. Girouard, p. 21.
47. *REED: Chester*, ed. by Lawrence M. Clopper (London: Manchester University Press; Toronto: University of Toronto Press, 1979), p. 156.
48. 'Records of Plays and Players in Kent, 1450–1642', ed. by Giles Dawson, *MSC*, 7 (Oxford: Oxford University Press, 1965), p. 150.
49. Somerset, *REED: Shropshire*, 1, p. 247.
50. In 1590 Norwich's Chamberlain's accounts include a payment to the Queen's Men when 'the Turke went vponn Roppes at newhall'; and at Bristol the corporation rewarded the Queen's Players that tumbled at the Free School where 'there was tumblinge shewen also by a Turcke vpon a Rope'. Hungary was part of the Turkish Empire at this time. The Turkish rope-dancer referred to in these records and the Hungarian rope-dancer mentioned at Shrewsbury are therefore likely to be the same person. See Andrew Gurr, *The Shakespearian Playing Companies* (Oxford: Clarendon, 1996), p. 205. The Bristol performance was possibly an open-air production, staged in the school's courtyard. (*REED: Bristol*, ed. by Mark C. Pilkinton (London and Toronto: University of Toronto Press, 1997), p. xxxvi.) The troupe also appears to have performed outdoors at Gloucester, receiving a civic reward for playing in the Cathedral churchyard in 1589–90. *REED: Cumberland, Westmorland, Gloucestershire*, ed. by Audrey Douglas and

Peter Greenfield (London and Toronto: University of Toronto Press, 1986), p. 311.
51. Dawson, p. 41. 'Records of Plays and Players in Lincolnshire, 1300–1585', ed. by Stanley J. Kahrl, *MSC*, 8 (Oxford: Oxford University Press, 1969 [1974]), p. 84.
52. Somerset, *REED: Shropshire*, 1, p. 238.
53. Somerset, *REED: Shropshire*, 1, p. 238.
54. Somerset, *REED: Shropshire*, 1, p. 238. Somerset, *REED: Shropshire*, 2, p. 669.
55. Somerset, *REED: Shropshire*, 2, p. 702. Gurr, *The Shakespearian Playing Companies*, p. 170.
56. Gurr, *The Shakespearian Playing Companies*, pp. 170, 179. Dawson, p. 62.
57. Wallace MacCaffrey, *Elizabeth I* (London: Edward Arnold, 1993), p. 393.
58. Gurr, *The Shakespearian Playing Companies*, pp. 178–9. *REED: Somerset*, ed. by James Stokes (with Bath, ed. by Robert J. Alexander), 1 (London and Toronto: University of Toronto Press, 1996), p. 13. Pilkinton, *REED: Bristol*, p. 126.
59. Somerset, *REED: Shropshire*, 2, pp. 381, 369, 381.
60. Somerset, *REED: Shropshire*, 2, p. 375.
61. Somerset, *REED: Shropshire*, 1, pp. 206–308.
62. Somerset, *REED: Shropshire*, 2, p. 382.
63. Somerset, *REED: Shropshire*, 1, p. 247.
64. The main market days were Wednesday and Saturday (Champion, p. 32). The players performed on Friday. See *Handbook of Dates*, ed. by C. R. Cheney (London: Royal Historical Society, 1991), p. 141.
65. Somerset, *REED: Shropshire*, 1, p. 238.
66. The cornmarket was licensed as the town's new market *c*.1261. Richard K Morris and Paul Stamper, 'A Structural Survey and Documentary History of the Market House, Shrewsbury', Shropshire County Council Archaeological Service, Report Number 81 (Shrewsbury: Shropshire County Council, 1996), p. 1.
67. Somerset, *REED: Shropshire*, 2, p. 669.
68. Information kindly provided by Bill Champion.
69. Champion, p. 32.
70. Part of this reward may have been for the players' assistance at the fire. Somerset, *REED: Shropshire*, 1, p. 238.
71. Cheney, p. 141. Champion, p. 32.
72. Somerset, *REED: Shropshire*, 2, p. 370.
73. Thomas Churchyard, *The Worthiness of Wales* (1587), cited in Freeman, p. 10.
74. Somerset, *REED: Shropshire*, 1, p. 242.

8 Provincial Playhouses in Renaissance England, 1559–1625

1. John H. Astington in *The Development of Shakespeare's Theater*, ed. by John H. Astington (New York: AMS Press, 1992), p. 6. In this chapter 'playhouses' are defined as 'buildings built solely or mainly, for the purpose of playing'.

David Galloway, 'Records of Early English Drama in the Provinces and what they may tell us about the Elizabethan Theatre,' *The Elizabethan Theatre*, 7 (1981), 82–110 (p. 93).

2. Claims for the existence of a number of other provincial Renaissance playhouses have been made, but subsequent research has revealed them to be unsubstantiated or erroneous. See, for example, David George, 'Early Playhouses at Liverpool', *TN*, 43 (1989), 9–16.

3. There is evidence of at least one further provincial playhouse, owned by Sir John Deane's grammar school, Northwich (Cheshire), but this appears to post-date 1625 and is not considered therefore in the main text. The only records of the playhouse's existence appear to be two tantalisingly brief allusions in the school's 1637 accounts. See Marjorie Cox, *History of Sir John Deane's Grammar School* (Manchester: Manchester University Press, 1975), p. 59.

4. *REED: Bristol*, ed. by Mark C. Pilkinton (London and Toronto: University of Toronto Press, 1997), pp. 242–3.

5. Andrew Gurr, *The Shakespearean Stage, 1574–1642*, 3rd edn (Cambridge: Cambridge University Press, 1970; repr. 1992), p. 213. Robert Tittler, *Architecture and Power: The Town Hall and the English Urban Community, c.1500–1640* (Oxford: Oxford University Press, 1991), p. 19.

6. Gurr, *The Shakespearean Stage*, p. 213.

7. Tittler, p. 40.

8. Alfred Harvey, *Bristol: A Historical and Topographical Account of the City* (London: Methuen, 1906), p. 247.

9. Kathleen Barker, 'An Early Seventeenth Century Provincial Playhouse', *TN*, 29 (1975), 81–4. Mark C. Pilkinton, 'The Playhouse in Wine Street, Bristol', *TN*, 37 (1983), 14–21 and 'New Information on the Playhouse in Wine Street, Bristol', *TN*, 42 (1988), 73–5. The contemporary material relating to the playhouse is now gathered in the *REED: Bristol* collection edited by Pilkinton (1997).

10. Pilkinton, 'The Playhouse', p. 16. Pilkinton, *REED: Bristol*, p. 224.

11. Pilkinton, 'The Playhouse', pp. 14, 19. Pilkinton, *REED: Bristol*, p. 205.

12. Pilkinton, *REED: Bristol*, p. 292.

13. Pilkinton, *REED: Bristol*, p. 161.

14. Pilkinton, *REED: Bristol*, p. 164.

15. Pilkinton, *REED: Bristol*, pp. 196–7.

16. Pilkinton, REED: Bristol, pp. 212–14.

17. Pilkinton, *REED: Bristol*, p. xxxvii.

18. See Jean Wilson, *The Archaeology of Shakespeare: The Material Legacy of Shakespeare's Theatre* (Stroud: Alan Sutton, 1995), p. 9 on the life of the Rose theatre, for example.

19. Pilkinton, *REED: Bristol*, p. xxxviii.

20. Wilson, pp. 9, 59.

21. Irwin Smith, *Shakespeare's Blackfriars Playhouse* (London: Peter Owen, 1966), pp. 134–5. Keith Sturgess, *Jacobean Private Theatre* (London: Routledge & Kegan Paul, 1987), p. 38.

22. Pilkinton, *REED: Bristol*, pp. 196–7.

23. Pilkinton, *REED: Bristol*, p. 129.

24. Pilkinton, 'The Playhouse', p. 17.

25. Kathleen Barker, *Bristol at Play* (Bradford-upon-Avon: Moonraker Press, 1976), p. 3. This property is shown as No. 7 in Roger Leech's reconstruction of the street's early modern topography (Roger H. Leech, *The Topography of Medieval and Early Modern Bristol*. Part I, Bristol Record Society, 48 (Bristol: Bristol Record Society, 1997), p. xxii). Woolfe also appears to have leased a small shop on Wine Street, subsequently bequeathing his interest in it to Isaac Woolfe. This is presumably the 'shop late of Isaac Wolfe cutler' identified as No. 2 Wine Street in 1661 (Leech, p. 171). Woolfe could have owned or leased a third property in the street as well, although its location remains unknown. Margaret Woolfe spoke of her husband having two Bristol properties at his death: a dwelling house (in which she and Nicholas lived) and a house in Wine Street known as the playhouse. Woolfe's will, likewise, mentions the playhouse and a dwelling house. The property leased from Christ Church in 1598 could have been the playhouse or dwelling house mentioned by Woolfe and his wife. If it was their dwelling house it would suggest the playhouse was in a third Wine Street property, unless the two were part of the expanded 1598 tenement. Pilkinton, *REED: Bristol*, pp. 212, 196–7.
26. Pilkinton, 'The Playhouse', p. 14. Leech, p. 172.
27. Pilkinton, 'The Playhouse', p. 16.
28. Pilkinton, *REED: Bristol*, pp. 164, 161, 164. He may have been using the term 'Roomes' as a general synonym for the property. There are precedents for this. See Smith, p. 172.
29. Pilkinton, *REED: Bristol*, p. 214.
30. See Smith, p. 139.
31. Harold Newcomb Hillebrand, *The Child Actors: A Chapter in Elizabethan Stage History* (New York: Russell & Russell, 1964), p. 90.
32. Pilkinton, *REED: Bristol*, pp. 202–3.
33. Pilkinton, *REED: Bristol*, p. 203.
34. Pilkinton, *REED: Bristol*, p. 209.
35. There appear to be no records of the troupe performing in London but they did perform in other provincial towns. See Gurr, *The Shakespearian Playing Companies*, p. 391.
36. The playhouse appears to have been used temporarily as a residential playhouse by earlier players. See Pilkinton, *REED: Bristol*, p. 198.
37. See Gurr, *The Shakespearian Playing Companies*, pp. 35, 296.
38. Pilkinton, *REED: Bristol*, p. 203.
39. In similar fashion, a number of London theatres and companies appear to have used contributions to the local poor as a way of reducing opposition to their establishments. See E. K. Chambers, *The Elizabethan Stage*, 4 (Oxford: Clarendon, 1923; repr. 1945), p. 316.
40. See Pilkinton, *REED: Bristol*, pp. 216–17, 232.
41. *REED: Lancashire*, ed. by David George (London and Toronto: University of Toronto Press, 1991), pp. 77, 331.
42. George, *REED: Lancashire*, p. 80.
43. George, *REED: Lancashire*, p. 81.
44. Translated in George, *REED: Lancashire*, pp. 304–5. Mercer's request was granted.
45. F. A. Bailey, 'The Elizabethan Playhouse at Prescot, Lancashire', *Transactions*

of the Historic Society of Lancashire and Cheshire, 103 (1952), 69–81 (pp. 77, 71).

46. No Richard Harrington is listed in the records of students matriculating at Oxford or Cambridge in the appropriate period. *Alumni Oxoniensis*, ed. by John Foster, 3 (London and Oxford: Parker & Co., 1891). *Alumni Cantabrigiensis*, ed. by John Venn and J. A. Venn, 3 (Cambridge: Cambridge University Press, 1922).
47. Bailey, p. 71.
48. See Bailey, p. 71, for further details.
49. Bailey, p. 71.
50. Bailey, p. 79.
51. George, *REED: Lancashire*, p. xliv.
52. Cited in J. J. Bagley, *Lancashire Diaries: Three Centuries of Lancashire Lives* (London: Philimore, 1975), pp. 11–12.
53. In 1535 Leland described the town as lying within a mile of Knowsley. John Leland, *Leland's Itinerary in England and Wales*, ed. by Lucy Toulmin Smith, 5 (London: Centaur, 1964), p. 42.
54. See Bailey, p. 77.
55. Peter Thomson, *Shakespeare's Professional Career* (Cambridge: Cambridge University Press, 1992), p. 46. Barry Coward, *The Stanleys: Lords Stanley and Earls of Derby, 1385–1672*, Chetham Society, 30 (Manchester: Manchester University Press, 1983), p. 113. Unfortunately, none of his plays survive and we do not know if they were performed.
56. Translated from Latin in George, *REED: Lancashire*, pp. 304, xlv.
57. George, *REED: Lancashire*, p. xlv.
58. Bailey, p. 77.
59. See, for example, Sturgess, pp. 38–9.
60. Smith, pp. 135–6.
61. Bailey, p. 79.
62. George, *REED: Lancashire*, p. 80.
63. At some point between 1603 and 1609, Elizabeth Harrington appears to have remarried, probably becoming the wife of Thomas Malbon. See Bailey, p. 75.
64. See Bailey, p. 77. George, *REED: Lancashire*, p. 83.
65. George, *REED: Lancashire*, p. 304. Bailey, p. 76.
66. Bailey, p. 77.
67. Bailey, p. 77.
68. Information kindly provided by Tom Hughes, Knowsley Museum.
69. *REED: York*, ed. by Alexandra F. Johnston and Margaret Rogerson, 1 (London: Manchester University Press; Toronto: University of Toronto Press, 1979), p. 530.
70. Johnston and Rogerson, 1, p. 530.
71. See Gurr, *The Shakespearian Playing Companies*, p. 121 and Chambers, *The Elizabethan Stage*, 4, pp. 342–3 for information about the Porter's Hall theatre.
72. Johnston and Rogerson, 1, p. 530.
73. See Eileen White, 'People and Places: The Social and Topographical Context of Drama in York, 1554–1609' (unpublished doctoral thesis, Leeds University, 1984), p. 437.

74. Foster, p. 1010.
75. White, p. 442. The discussion of Middleton in this chapter is much indebted to White's detailed research in York's early modern archives.
76. See White, pp. 444–5.
77. White, p. 449.
78. See *A Transcription of the Registers of the Company of Stationers of London, 1554–1640*, ed. by Edward Arber, 3 (London: privately printed, 1876; repr. Gloucester, MA: Peter Smith, 1967), p. 167.
79. *Miscellanea: Recusant Records*, ed. by Clare Talbot, Catholic Record Society, 53 (Newport: R. H. Johns, 1960), p. 233.
80. As White notes, the references 'present a plausible picture of one man's life' (p. 442).
81. White, p. 437.
82. Foster, p. 1010. Arber, p. 167.
83. See White, p. 448.
84. See White, p. 447.
85. If the Oxford matriculant was the author of the 1608 poems and the apparently Catholic Middleton living in York (1613–15), his university background and religion could have contributed to his having an interest in theatre. There was a Catholic tradition of using drama for religious and moral instruction, and plays were regularly staged in the colleges of the Renaissance universities, performances providing an opportunity for students to improve their oratorical and rhetorical skills. See Frederick S. Boas, *University Drama in the Tudor Age* (Oxford: Clarendon, 1914), pp. 386–90. (If Middleton was a Catholic, theoretically, he would have been obliged to conform to the established church before matriculating at Oxford; but these orders were not rigidly enforced. See James McConica, 'The Rise of the Undergraduate College', in *The History of the University of Oxford*, ed. by James McConica, 3 (Oxford: Clarendon, 1986), 1–68 (p. 51).) However, the apparently Catholic sympathies of the poet could also point to his identification with George Middleton's son, rather than the Oxford matriculant, as George's family is known to have had Catholic connections. See White, p. 442.
86. Cited in White, p. 447.
87. See Johnston and Rogerson, 1, pp. 381–568.
88. Johnston and Rogerson, 1, p. 530.
89. Johnston and Rogerson, 1, p. 530.
90. Johnston and Rogerson, 1, p. 531.
91. It took about six months to build the Fortune Theatre, for instance, in 1600. See Gurr, *The Shakespearean Stage*, p. 136.
92. Johnston and Rogerson, 1, p. 531.
93. Johnston and Rogerson, 1, p. 531.
94. Pilkinton, *REED: Bristol*, p. xxxvii, p. 242.
95. 'Sara Barker widdo' was buried on 7 August 1637 (Bristol, BRO, FCP/St. MR/R/1 (a) 2). *City Chamberlain's Accounts in the Sixteenth and Seventeenth Centuries*, ed. by D. M. Livock, Bristol Record Society, 24 (Bristol: Bristol Record Society, 1966), p. 158.
96. Pilkinton, *REED: Bristol*, p. lix.
97. Pilkinton, *REED: Bristol*, p. 242. BRO, FCP/St. MR/R/1 (a) 2.

98. Pilkinton, *REED: Bristol*, p. xl.
99. *Documents Illustrating the Overseas Trade of Bristol in the Sixteenth Century*, ed. by Jean Vanes, Bristol Record Society, 31 (Kendal: Titus Wilson, 1979), p. 55. *Records Relating to the Society of Merchant Venturers of the City of Bristol in the Seventeenth Century*, ed. by Patrick McGrath, Bristol Record Society, 27 (Bristol: Bristol Record Society, 1952), p. 3.
100. Pilkinton, *REED: Bristol*, p. 242. *Atlas of Historic Towns: Bristol*, ed. by M. D. Lobel and E. M. Carus-Wilson (London: Scolar Press, 1975), p. 17.
101. Speed shows only seven properties on the west side of Redcliffe Hill. (*The Counties of Britain: A Tudor Atlas by John Speed*, ed. by Nigel Nicolson and Alasdair Hawkyd (London: Pavillion, 1988), p. 83.) This is unlikely to be an exact representation, but other contemporary maps also show a small clustering of housing on the hill, suggesting that there were few houses in Jacobean Redcliffe. See John E. Pritchard, 'Old Plans and Views of Bristol', *Transactions of the Bristol and Gloucestershire Archaeological Society*, 48 (1926), 323–53.
102. Pilkinton, *REED: Bristol*, p. 242.
103. Pilkinton, *REED: Bristol*, p. 242.
104. Pilkinton, *REED: Bristol*, p. xl.

9 The Decline of Professional Touring Theatre

1. *REED: Coventry*, ed. by R. W. Ingram (London: Manchester University Press; Toronto: University of Toronto Press, 1981), p. 439.
2. *REED: Devon*, ed. by John M. Wasson (London and Toronto: University of Toronto Press, 1986), p. 51.
3. The fifteen REED collections published to date are: *REED: Bristol*, ed. by Mark C. Pilkinton (London and Toronto: University of Toronto Press, 1997); *REED: Cambridge*, ed. by Alan H. Nelson, 2 vols (London and Toronto: University of Toronto Press, 1989); *REED: Chester*, ed. by Lawrence M. Clopper (London: Manchester University Press; Toronto: University of Toronto Press, 1979); Ingram, *REED: Coventry* (1981); *REED: Cumberland, Westmorland, Gloucestershire*, ed. by Audrey Douglas and Peter Greenfield (London and Toronto: University of Toronto Press, 1986); Wasson, *REED: Devon* (1986); *REED: Dorset/Cornwall*, ed. by Rosalind Conklin Hays and C. E. McGee and Sally L. Joyce and Evelyn S. Newlyn (Toronto: University of Toronto Press, 1999); *REED: Herefordshire/Worcestershire*, ed. by David N. Klausner (London and Toronto: University of Toronto Press, 1990); *REED: Lancashire*, ed. by David George (London and Toronto: University of Toronto Press, 1991); *REED: Newcastle-upon-Tyne*, ed. by J. J. Anderson (London: Manchester University Press; Toronto: University of Toronto Press, 1982); *REED: Norwich*, ed. by David Galloway (London and Toronto: University of Toronto Press, 1984); *REED: Shropshire*, ed. by J. Alan B. Somerset, 2 vols (London and Toronto: University of Toronto Press, 1994); *REED: Somerset*, ed. by James Stokes (with Bath, ed. by Robert J. Alexander), 2 vols (London and Toronto: University of Toronto Press, 1996); *REED: Sussex*, ed. by Cameron Louis (Toronto: University of Toronto Press, 2000); *REED: York*, ed. by Alexandra F. Johnston and Margaret Rogerson, 2 vols

(London: Manchester University Press; Toronto: University of Toronto Press, 1979).

4. Any generalisations of this kind are necessarily tentative. Early modern England's surviving dramatic records cannot provide a complete picture of touring theatre: many records have been lost or imperfectly preserved. But the body of surviving evidence is sufficiently large and detailed for us to begin tracing patterns in the history of travelling theatre, as REED editors and scholars such as Andrew Gurr, *The Shakespearian Playing Companies* (Oxford: Clarendon, 1996), and Scott McMillin and Sally-Beth MacLean, *The Queen's Men and their plays* (Cambridge: Cambridge University Press, 1998) have demonstrated in their recent respective studies.

5. Gurr, *The Shakespearian Playing Companies*, p. 38.

6. See Patrick Collinson, *The Birthpangs of Protestant England: Religious and Cultural Change in the sixteenth and seventeenth centuries* (London: Macmillan, 1988), p. 49.

7. Only payments made to patronised and/or licensed playing companies have been counted. (Payments not to perform have been included.) Payments made to unnamed 'players' have not been counted unless the records or other contemporary evidence make it clear that the troupe was a patronised or licensed professional company. Unnamed players could be amateurs.

8. Peter Greenfield, 'Touring', in *A New History of Early English Drama*, ed. by John D. Cox and David Scott Kastan (New York: Columbia University Press, 1997), 252–68 (p. 265).

9. See Nelson, *REED: Cambridge*, 1, pp. 291, 311, 332, 338, 369.

10. Nelson, *REED: Cambridge*, 1, pp. 212, 216, 222–3, 226, 246, 249, 253, 257, 259, 262, 264, 266, 273, 311, 313, 323, 338, 355, 369; and pp. 276–7, 348–9.

11. Alan B. Somerset, ' "How chances it they travel?": Provincial Touring, Playing Places, and the King's Men', *ShS*, 47 (1994), 45–60 (p. 51).

12. See Table 9.2 and Ingram, pp. 355–447.

13. Of forty-nine civic theatrical regulations that I know of in the Elizabethan and Jacobean provinces, twenty-one were enforced in southern or East Anglian communities: Cambridge (1574, 1575, 1593, 1600, 1604), Great Yarmouth (1595–96), King's Lynn (1594), Hadleigh (1598), Ipswich (1608, 1614), Sudbury (1606–07), Norwich (1588, 1600, 1614, 1623), Southampton (1620, 1623), Abingdon (1624), Canterbury (1595), Hythe (1615) and Salisbury (1624). See Nelson, *REED: Cambridge*, 1, pp. 271, 276–7, 348, 381, 395; 'Records of Plays and Players in Norfolk and Suffolk, 1330–1642', ed. by John M. Wasson and David Galloway, *MSC*, 11 (Oxford: Oxford University Press, 1980–81), pp. 15, 66, 163, 183–4, 198; Galloway, *REED: Norwich*, pp. 91, 117, 140, 177; C. E. Burch, 'Minstrels and Players in Southampton, 1428–1635', *Southampton Papers*, 7 (1969), pp. 35–6; *REED: Berkshire*, ed. by Alexandra F. Johnston, forthcoming; James Gibson, 'Stuart Players in Kent: fact or fiction?', *REED: Newsletter*, 20:2 (1995), 1–12 (pp. 7, 5–6); Trowbridge, Wiltshire and Swindon Record Office, Salisbury City Ledger Book, SH/DB/CR 72 Misc. 7/128.

14. Sally-Beth MacLean, 'Touring Routes: "Provincial Wanderings" or Traditional Circuits?', *MRDE*, 6 (1993), 1–14 (p. 10).

15. Wasson, *REED: Devon*, (Exeter, 1580s) pp. 158–60, 162–6, (Barnstaple, 1600s) pp. 47–9.
16. MacLean, 'Touring Routes', p. 14.
17. See MacLean, 'Touring Routes', p. 14.
18. Only payments explicitly requiring companies not to perform and/or to leave a community or household are included. There are occasional records of companies receiving rewards without performing but these have not been counted unless there is direct evidence that the payments were made to prevent performance(s).
19. See Somerset, ' "How chances it they travel?" ', p. 50.
20. Cited in Margot Heinemann, *Puritanism and Theatre* (Cambridge: Cambridge University Press, 1980), p. 34.
21. Somerset, ' "How chances it they travel?" ', p. 50.
22. *Tudor Royal Proclamations: The Later Tudors (1553–1587)*, ed. by Paul L. Hughes and James F. Larkin, 2 (London and New Haven, CT: Yale University Press, 1969), pp. 115–16.
23. See Gurr, *The Shakespearian Playing Companies*, p. 56.
24. See Gurr, *The Shakespearian Playing Companies*, p. 38. There is certainly evidence of players performing and being encouraged to play at inns rather than civic halls in the early seventeenth century (see Chapter 5).
25. Gibson, 'Stuart Players', p. 3.
26. See Gibson, 'Stuart Players', pp. 3, 7, 5–6, 11.
27. Hughes and Larkin, 2, pp. 115–16.
28. See Gurr, *The Shakespearian Playing Companies*, pp. 37–8.
29. Not all acting companies observed the terms of the new act. See Chapter 1 for a discussion of Sir Walter Waller's players, a troupe that faced prosecution after attempting to perform without sufficient licence in Kent in 1583. London, PRO, State Papers, 12/163/44 (Microfilm).
30. See Gurr, *The Shakespearian Playing Companies*, p. 38.
31. I have encountered at least fifty-three orders regulating dramatic activity in individual regional towns and cities (1559–1642): Bristol (1585, 1595–96, 1613), Cambridge (1574, 1575, 1593, 1600, 1604, 1632), Chester (1596–97, 1615), Gloucester (1580–81, 1590–91), Exeter (1609), Worcester (1622, 1626, 1635–36, 1640–41), Liverpool (1572), Norwich (1589, 1601, 1614, 1623), Bridgnorth (1570–71, 1601–02), Shrewsbury (1594), York (1578, 1582, 1592), Canterbury (1595), Hythe (1615), Boston (1578), Great Yarmouth (1595–96), King's Lynn (1594), Hadleigh (1598), Ipswich (1608, 1614), Sudbury (1606–07), Abingdon (1624), Durham (1608), Leicester (1566–67, 1582–83, 1606–07), Newark (1568), Oxford (1579–80, 1584, 1593), Hull (1599), Salisbury (1624), Stratford-upon-Avon (1602, 1612) and Southampton (1620, 1623). See Pilkinton, *REED: Bristol*, pp. 128–9, 148, 176; Nelson, *REED: Cambridge*, 1, pp. 71, 276–7, 348, 381, 395, 641; Clopper, pp. 184, 292–3; Douglas and Greenfield, pp. 306–7, 311; Wasson, *REED: Devon*, p. 183; Klausner, pp. 413–14, 455, 457–8; George, *REED: Lancashire*, p. 39; Galloway, *REED: Norwich*, pp. 91, 117, 140, 177; Somerset, *REED: Shropshire*, 1, pp. 19, 21, 281; Johnston and Rogerson, 1, pp. 384, 399, 464–5; Gibson, 'Stuart Players', pp. 7–8, 5–6; 'Records of Plays and Players in Lincolnshire, 1300–1585', ed. by Stanley J. Kahrl, *MSC*, 8 (Oxford: Oxford University Press, 1969 [1974]), p. 5; Wasson and Galloway,

pp. 15, 66, 163, 183–4, 198; Johnston, *REED: Berkshire*, forthcoming; Durham, Durham Record Office, Order Book of the City of Durham, DU 1/4/4, f15v; *REED: Leicestershire*, ed. by Alice B. Hamilton, forthcoming; Nottingham, Nottinghamshire Archives, Newark Corporation Minutes, DC/NW/3/1/1, f45; *Oxford City* Collection, ed. by Alexandra F. Johnston, and the *Oxford University* Collection, ed. by John R. Elliott, forthcoming in the REED series; Edward Gillett and Kenneth MacMahon, *A History of Hull* (Oxford: Oxford University Press, 1980), p. 121; Trowbridge, Wiltshire and Swindon Record Office, Salisbury City Ledger Book, SH/DB/Cr 72 Misc. 7/128; Stratford-upon-Avon, SBTRO, Stratford-upon-Avon Council Minutes 1593–1628, BRU2/2, pp. 95, 220; Burch, pp. 35–6. More regulatory orders are likely to be discovered as research continues. Of the fifty-three regulations identified above, twenty-five relate partly or entirely to the use of civic halls.
32. See David Dymond, 'God's Disputed Acre', *Journal of Ecclesiastical History*, 50:3 (1999), 464–97 (p. 484).
33. SBTRO, BRU2/2, pp. 95, 220.
34. Johnston and Rogerson, 1, p. 399.
35. Heinemann, p. 33. Night-time play performances were restricted in cities such as Gloucester (1580–81, 1590–91), Shrewsbury (1594) and Worcester (1622, 1626, 1640–41). Sunday playing was also prohibited at Gloucester (1590–91), and Shrewsbury (1594). See Douglas and Greenfield, pp. 306, 311; Somerset, *REED: Shropshire*, 1, p. 281; Klausner, pp. 453, 455, 458.
36. Douglas and Greenfield, pp. 306–7.
37. Nelson, *REED: Cambridge*, 1, p. 348. Gurr, *The Shakespearian Playing Companies*, p. 14.
38. Nelson, *REED: Cambridge*, 1, p. 403. G. Tillotson, '*Othello* and *The Alchemist* at Oxford in 1610', in *Essays in Criticism and Research* (Cambridge: Cambridge University Press, 1942), 41–5.
39. See Elliott, *Oxford University*, forthcoming in the REED series and Nelson, *REED: Cambridge*, 1, pp. 71, 381.
40. Galloway, *REED: Norwich*, p. 91.
41. See Galloway, *REED: Norwich*, pp. 148, 161.
42. Cited in Gillett and MacMahon, p. 121.
43. Somerset, *REED: Shropshire*, 1, p. 19.
44. Clopper, p. 184.
45. Clopper, p. 184.
46. See Conklin Hays and McGee, Joyce and Newlyn, pp. 127, 272; Stokes (with Alexander), 1, pp. 73, 26, 219.
47. Gurr, *The Shakespearian Playing Companies*, p. 38.
48. The opponents of public theatre were not necessarily Puritans in or outside London. Neither Protestants nor Puritans were automatically opposed to theatre. See Collinson, p. 103, and Heinemann, p. 21.
49. Clopper, pp. 292–3.
50. Galloway, *REED: Norwich*, p. 65.
51. Pilkinton, *REED: Bristol*, p. 176.
52. Johnston and Rogerson, 1, p. 449.
53. Wasson and Galloway, p. 198.

54. Robert Tittler, *Architecture and Power: The Town Hall and the English Urban Community, c.1500–1640* (Oxford: Oxford University Press, 1991), p. 147.
55. Wasson and Galloway, p. 198.
56. See Heinemann, pp. 33–4.
57. Christopher Hill, *Society and Puritanism in pre-Revolutionary England* (London: Penguin, 1986), p. 160.
58. Heinemann, p. 239.
59. Heinemann, p. 6.
60. Heinemann, p. 33.
61. See Heinemann, p. 34.
62. Conklin Hays and McGee, Joyce and Newlyn, p. 47.
63. See Heinemann, p. 34.
64. Galloway, *REED: Norwich*, p. 177.
65. Galloway, *REED: Norwich*, p. 177.
66. Galloway, *REED: Norwich*, p. 223.
67. Heinemann, p. 35.
68. Heinemann, pp. 35, 31.
69. Heinemann, p. 35.
70. Greenfield, 'Touring', p. 265.
71. See Gurr, *The Shakespearian Playing Companies*, pp. 56 and 37.
72. See Peter Greenfield, 'Professional Players at Gloucester: Conditions of Provincial Performing', in *The Elizabethan Theatre*, 10 (1988), 73–92 (p. 83).
73. Mary A. Blackstone, 'Patrons and Elizabethan Dramatic Companies' in *The Elizabethan Theatre*, 10 (1988), 112–32 (p. 125). The respect commanded by royal and noble patrons' names did not decline in all regions. Perhaps unsurprisingly, the Stuart towns that were 'receptive to players' were often 'those that also remained sympathetic to the Crown', although there are exceptions (see Greenfield, 'Touring', p. 267). Coventry rewarded players until the 1640s but sided with the Parliamentarians in the Civil War. See Philip Tennant, *The Civil War in Stratford-upon-Avon* (Stroud: Alan Sutton, 1996), p. 21.
74. Blackstone, p. 129. There are exceptions to this pattern. See Ingram, pp. 431 and 439 for examples.
75. Conklin Hays and McGee, Joyce and Newlyn, p. 47.
76. Greenfield, 'Touring', p. 252.
77. See Gurr, *The Shakespearian Playing Companies*, p. 29.
78. Gurr, *The Shakespearian Playing Companies*, p. 44.
79. Gurr, *The Shakespearian Playing Companies*, pp. 36, 44.
80. McMillin and MacLean, p. 6.
81. See Gurr, *The Shakespearian Playing Companies*, p. 44.
82. See Gurr, *The Shakespearian Playing Companies*, p. 40.
83. McMillin and MacLean's research suggests that the specially formed royal company often divided 'into branches in order to tour more widely', adopting the practice from their first year of travelling, 1583 (pp. xii, 44). But the divided troupes did not specialise respectively in touring and metropolitan playing as the later royal troupes appear to have done (p. 44). See Gurr, *The Shakespearian Playing Companies*, p. 50 for a discussion of 'duplicate' royal companies in the Stuart period.
84. Gurr, *The Shakespearian Playing Companies*, p. 44.

Select Bibliography

Manuscripts and microfilms

Bristol, BRO, FCP/St. MR/R1 (a) 1–4.
Chelmsford, ERO, Maldon Chamberlains' Accounts, D/B3/3/287–9.
Chelmsford, ERO, Archdeacon's Court Records, D/AEA 8 and 11.
Chelmsford, ERO, Hornchurch Churchwardens' Accounts, D/P/115/5/1.
Durham, Durham Record Office, The Order Book of the City, DU 1/4/4.
London, Lambeth Palace Library, MS 654, n°167.
London, PRO, Star Chamber 8 12/11.
London, PRO, Star Chamber 8 19/10.
London, PRO, State Papers 12/103/44.
London, PRO, State Papers 12/160/48.
Nottingham, Nottinghamshire Archives, Newark Corporation Minutes, DC/NW/ 3/1/1.
Stratford-upon-Avon, SBTRO, Stratford-upon-Avon Council Minutes 1593–1628, BRU2/2.
Trowbridge, Wiltshire and Swindon Record Office, SH/DB/CR 72 Misc. 7/128.

Secondary sources

Alton, R. E. (ed.). 'The Academic Drama in Oxford: Extracts from the Records of Four Colleges', *MSC*, 5 (Oxford: Oxford University Press, 1958 [1960]), 29–95.
Anderson, J. J. (ed.). *REED: Newcastle-upon-Tyne* (London: Manchester University Press; Toronto: University of Toronto Press, 1982).
Astington, John H. (ed.). *The Development of Shakespeare's Theater* (New York: AMS Press, 1992).
Atherton, Ian *et al.* (eds). *Norwich Cathedral, Church, City and Diocese, 1096–1996* (London: Hambledon Press, 1996).
Bailey, F. A. 'The Elizabethan Playhouse at Prescot, Lancashire', *Transactions of the Historic Society of Lancashire and Cheshire*, 103 (1952), 69–81.
Bakere, Jane A. *The Cornish Ordinalia: A Critical Study* (Cardiff: University of Wales Press, 1980).
Barker, Kathleen. 'An Early Seventeenth Century Provincial Playhouse', *TN*, 29 (1975), 81–4.
Barker, Kathleen. *Bristol at Play* (Bradford-upon-Avon: Moonraker Press, 1976).
Bentley, Gerald Eades. *The Profession of Player in Shakespeare's Time, 1590–1642* (Guildford and Princeton, NJ: Princeton University Press, 1984).
Berry, Herbert. *The Boar's Head Playhouse* (London and Toronto: Associated University Press, 1986).
Betjeman, John (ed.). *Collins Guide to English Parish Churches* (London: Collins, 1958).
Blackstone, Mary A. 'Patrons and Elizabethan Dramatic Companies', *The Elizabethan Theatre*, 10 (1988), 112–32.

Blandamer, Anne. 'The Duke of Buckingham's House at Burley-on-the-Hill', *Rutland Record*, 18 (1998), 349–60.

Boas, F. S. *University Drama in the Tudor Age* (Oxford: Clarendon, 1914).

Boddy, G. W. 'Players of Interludes in North Yorkshire in the early seventeenth century', *North Yorkshire County Record Office Publications*, Offprint from 7:3 (1976).

Bradbrook, Muriel. *The Rise of the Common Player* (London: Chatto & Windus, 1962).

Bradley, David. *From Text to Performance in the Elizabethan Theatre: Preparing the Play for the Stage* (Cambridge: Cambridge University Press, 1992).

Brannen, Anne (ed.). *REED: Cambridgeshire*, forthcoming.

Brinksworth, E. R. 'The Archdeacon's Court: Liber Actorum, 1584', *Oxfordshire Record Society*, 23 (1942), 124–5.

Brownstein, O. L. 'A Record of London Inn Playhouses from *c*.1565–1590', *SQ*, 22 (1971), 17–24.

Burch, C. E. 'Minstrels and Players in Southampton, 1428–1635', *Southampton Papers*, 7 (1969).

Chambers, E. K. *The Elizabethan Stage*, 4 vols (Oxford: Clarendon, 1923).

Champion, Bill. *Everyday Life in Tudor Shrewsbury* (Shrewsbury: Shropshire Books, 1994).

Cherry, Bridget and Nikolaus Pevsner (eds). *The Buildings of England: Devon*, 2nd edn (London: Penguin, 1953; repr. 1991).

Clark, Andrew. 'Maldon Records and the Drama', *N&Q*, 10th series, 7 (1907), 181–3, 342–3, 422–3.

Clark, Andrew. 'Maldon Records and the Drama', *N&Q*, 10th series, 8 (1907), 43–4.

Clark, Andrew. 'Players Companies on Tour', *N&Q*, 10th Series, 12 (1909), 41–2.

Clark, Peter. *The English Alehouse: A Social History, 1200–1830* (London and New York: Longman, 1983).

Clark, Peter (ed.). *The Early Modern Town: A Reader* (London: Longman, 1976).

Clopper, Lawrence M. (ed.). *REED: Chester* (London: University of Manchester Press; Toronto: University of Toronto Press, 1979).

Cocks, Alfred Heneage. 'The Parish Church of All Saints, Great Marlow', *Records of Buckinghamshire*, 6 (1887–91), 326–40.

Coldewey, John C. 'English Drama in the 1520s: Six perspectives', *RORD*, 31 (1992), 57–78.

Coldewey, John C. 'Playing Companies at Aldeburgh, 1566–1635', *MSC*, 9 (Oxford: Oxford University Press, 1977), 16–23.

Coldewey, John C. (ed.). *REED: Nottinghamshire*, forthcoming.

Collinson, Patrick. *The Birthpangs of Protestant England: Religious and Cultural Change in the sixteenth and seventeenth centuries* (London: Macmillan, 1988).

Cowling, Jane. 'An Edition of the Records of Drama, Ceremony and Secular Music in Winchester City and College, 1556–1642' (unpublished doctoral thesis, University of Southampton, 1993).

Cox, J. Charles, *Churchwardens' Accounts from the fourteenth century to the close of the seventeenth century* (London: Methuen, 1913).

Cox, John D. and David Scott Kastan (eds). *A New History of Early English Drama* (New York: Columbia University Press, 1997).

Craik, T. W. *The Tudor Interlude: Stage, Costume and Acting*, 3rd edn (Leicester: Leicester University Press, 1958; repr. 1967).

Crossley, Alan (ed.). *VCH: A History of the County of Oxford*, 11 (Oxford: Oxford University Press, 1983).

Dawson, Giles (ed.). 'Records of Plays and Players in Kent, 1450–1642', *MSC*, 7 (Oxford: Oxford University Press, 1965).

Dodd, Kenneth M. 'Another Elizabethan Theater in the Round', *SQ*, 21 (1970), 125–56.

Douglas, Audrey and Peter Greenfield (eds). *REED: Cumberland, Westmorland, Gloucestershire* (London and Toronto: University of Toronto Press, 1986).

Dunning, R. W. (ed.). *VCH: A History of the County of Somerset*, 3 (London: Oxford University Press, 1974).

Dunning, R. W. (ed.). *VCH: A History of the County of Somerset*, 6 (Oxford: Oxford University Press, 1992).

Dymond, David. 'God's Disputed Acre', *Journal of Ecclesiastical History*, 50:3 (1999), 464–97.

Elliott Jr, John R. (ed.). The *Oxford University* Collection, forthcoming in the REED series.

Emmison, F. G. *Elizabethan Life: Morals and the Church Courts* (Chelmsford: Essex County Council, 1973).

Emmison, F. G. *Tudor Secretary: Sir William Petre at Court and Home* (London: Longman, 1961).

Everitt, Alan. 'The Market Towns', in *The Early Modern Town: A Reader*, ed. by Peter Clark (London: Longman, 1976), 168–204.

Farrer, William and J. Brownbill (eds). *VCH: A History of the County of Lancashire*, 7 (London: Constable, 1912; repr. Folkestone: Dawsons, 1992).

Feuillerat, Albert (ed.). *Documents relating to the Office of the Revels in the time of Queen Elizabeth* (London: David Nutt, 1908).

Fletcher, Anthony and Peter Roberts (eds). *Religion, Culture and Society in Early Modern Britain: Essays in Honour of Patrick Collinson* (Cambridge: Cambridge University Press, 1994).

Foakes, R. A. and R. T. Rickert (eds). *Henslowe's Diary* (Cambridge: Cambridge University Press, 1968).

Galloway, David. 'The "Game Place" and "House" at Great Yarmouth, 1493–1595', *TN*, 31 (1977), 6–9.

Galloway, David. 'Records of Early English Drama in the Provinces and what they may tell us about the Elizabethan Theatre', *The Elizabethan Theatre*, 7 (1981), 82–110.

Galloway, David (ed.). *REED: Norwich* (London and Toronto: University of Toronto Press, 1984).

George, David. 'Shakespeare and Pembroke's Men', *SQ*, 32 (1981), 305–23.

George, David. 'Jacobean Actors and the Great Hall at Gawthorpe, Lancashire', *TN*, 37 (1983), 109–21.

George, David (ed.). *REED: Lancashire* (London and Toronto: University of Toronto Press, 1991).

Gibson, James. 'Stuart Players in Kent: Fact or Fiction?', *REED Newsletter*, 20:2 (1995), 1–12.

Gillett, Edward and Kenneth A. MacMahon. *A History of Hull* (Oxford: Oxford University Press, 1980).

Girouard, Mark. *Life in the English Country House* (London: Penguin, 1980).

Girouard, Mark. *Robert Smythson and the Elizabethan Country House* (London: Country Life, 1983).

Girouard, Mark. *The English Town* (London and New Haven, CT: Yale University Press, 1990).

Greenfield, Peter. 'Professional Players at Gloucester: Conditions of Provincial Performing', *The Elizabethan Theatre*, 10 (1988), 73–92.

Greenfield, Peter. 'Touring' in *A New History of Early English Drama*, ed. by John D. Cox and David Scott Kastan (New York: Columbia University Press, 1997), 252–68.

Greenfield, Peter and Jane Cowling (eds). *REED: Hampshire*, forthcoming.

Greg, W. W. (ed.). *The True Tragedy of Richard Duke of York*, 1595, Shakespeare Quarto Facsimiles, 11 (Oxford: Oxford University Press, 1958).

Gurr, Andrew. *The Shakespearean Stage, 1574–1642*, 3rd edn (Cambridge: Cambridge University Press, 1970; repr. 1992).

Gurr, Andrew. *The Shakespearian Playing Companies* (Oxford: Clarendon, 1996).

Hadfield, John (ed.). *Shell Guide to England* (London, 1970).

Hamilton, Alice B. (ed.). *REED: Leceistershire*, forthcoming.

Harbage, Alfred (ed.). *Annals of English Drama, 975–1700*, 2nd edn revised by S. Schoenbaum, 3rd edn revised by Sylvia S. Wagonheim (London: Methuen, 1964; repr. New York: Routledge, 1989).

Hays, Rosalind Conklin. 'Dorset Church Houses and the Drama', *RORD*, 31 (1992), 13–23.

Hays, Rosalind Conklin and C. E. McGee, Sally L. Joyce and Evelyn S. Newlyn (eds). *REED: Dorset/Cornwall* (Toronto: University of Toronto Press, 1999).

Heinemann, Margot. *Puritanism and Theatre* (Cambridge: Cambridge University Press, 1980).

Herbert, N. M. (ed.). *VCH: A History of the County of Gloucester*, 4 (Oxford: Oxford University Press, 1988).

Heywood, Thomas. *An Apology for Actors* (1612; London and New York: Johnson Reprint Company repr. 1972).

Hill, Christopher. *Society and Puritanism in Pre-Revolutionary England* (London: Penguin, 1986).

Hillebrand, Harold Newcomb. *The Child Actors: A Chapter in Elizabethan Stage History* (New York: Russell & Russell, 1964).

HMC: Report on the MSS of the Earl of Ancaster preserved at Grimsthorpe (Dublin: HMSO, 1907).

Holderness, Graham and Bryan Loughrey (eds). *A Pleasant Conceited Historie, Called The Taming of a Shrew* (Hemel Hempstead: Harvester Wheatsheaf, 1992).

Holland, Elizabeth. 'The Earliest Bath Guildhall', *Bath History*, 2 (1988), 163–80.

Holman, Treve. 'Cornish Plays and Playing Places', *TN*, 4 (1949–50), 52–4.

Hughes, Paul L. and James F. Larkin (eds). *Tudor Royal Proclamations: The Later Tudors (1553–1587)*, 2 (London and New Haven, CT: Yale University Press, 1969).

Hutchins, John. *The History and Antiquities of the County of Dorset*, ed. by W. Skipp and J. N. Hodson, 4 vols (Westminster, 1865–74; repr. Trowbridge, 1973).

Ingram, R. W. (ed.). *REED: Coventry* (London: University of Manchester Press, Toronto: University of Toronto Press, 1981).

Ingram, William. 'The Costs of Touring', *MRDE*, 6 (1993), 57–62.

Johnston, Alexandra F. (ed.). *REED: Berkshire*, forthcoming.

Johnston, Alexandra F. (ed.). The *Oxford City* Collection, forthcoming in the REED series.

Johnston, Alexandra F. and Wim Husken (eds). *English Parish Drama* (Amsterdam, Atlanta, 1996).

Johnston, Alexandra F. and Margaret Rogerson (eds). *REED: York*, 2 vols (London: Manchester University Press; Toronto: University of Toronto Press, 1979).

Jonson, Ben. *Poetaster* in *The Works of Ben Jonson*, ed. by C. H. Herford and Percy Simpson, 4 (Oxford: Clarendon, 1932; repr. 1954).

Kahrl, Stanley J. (ed.). 'Records of Plays and Players in Lincolnshire, 1300–1585', *MSC*, 8 (Oxford: Oxford University Press, 1969 [1974]).

Klausner, David N. (ed.). *REED: Herefordshire/Worcestershire* (London and Toronto: University of Toronto Press, 1990).

Knutson, Roslyn Lander. *The Repertory of Shakespeare's Company, 1594–1613* (Fayetteville, AR: University of Arkansas Press, 1991).

Lancashire, Ian (ed.). *Dramatic Texts and Records of Britain: A Chronological Topography to 1558* (Toronto: University of Toronto Press, 1984).

Leech, Roger H. *The Topography of Medieval and Early Modern Bristol*, Part I, Bristol Record Society, 48 (Bristol: Bristol Record Society, 1997).

Le Hardy, William. 'Elizabethan Players in Winslow Church', *TN*, 12 (1957–58), 107.

Leishman, J. B. (ed.). *The Three Parnassus Plays* (1598–1601) (London: Nicholson & Watson, 1949).

Livock, D. M. (ed.). *City Chamberlain's Accounts in the Sixteenth and Seventeenth Centuries*, Bristol Record Society, 24 (Bristol: Bristol Record Society, 1966).

Louis, Cameron (ed.). *REED: Sussex* (Toronto: University of Toronto Press, 2000).

MacCaffrey, Wallace. *Elizabeth I* (London: Edward Arnold, 1993).

MacLean, Sally-Beth. 'Touring Routes: "Provincial Wanderings" or Traditional Circuits?', *MRDE*, 6 (1993), 1–14.

Mann, David. *The Elizabethan Player* (London: Routledge, 1991).

Marston, John. *The Plays of John Marston*, ed. by H. Harvey Wood, 3 vols (London: Oliver & Boyd, 1939).

McConica, James (ed.). *The History of the University of Oxford*, 3 (Oxford: Clarendon, 1986).

McGrath, Patrick (ed.). *Records Relating to the Society of Merchant Venturers of the City of Bristol in the Seventeenth Century*, Bristol Record Society, 17 (Bristol: Bristol Record Society, 1952).

McMillin, Scott and Sally-Beth MacLean. *The Queen's Men and their plays* (Cambridge: Cambridge University Press, 1998).

Middleton, Thomas. *A Mad World, My Masters*, ed. by Standish Henning (London: Edward Arnold, 1965).

Motter, T. H. Vail. *The School Drama in England* (London: Longman, 1929).

Mowl, Timothy. *Elizabethan and Jacobean Style* (London: Phaidon, 1993).

Murray, John Tucker. *English Dramatic Companies, 1558–1642*, 2 vols (London: Constable, 1910).

Nashe, Thomas. *The Works of Thomas Nashe*, ed. by Ronald B. McKerrow, revised by F. P. Wilson, 5 vols (London, 1904–10; repr. Oxford: Basil Blackwell, 1958).

Nelson, Alan H. *Early Cambridge Theatres* (Cambridge: Cambridge University Press, 1994).

Nelson, Alan H. (ed.). *REED: Cambridge*, 2 vols (London and Toronto: University of Toronto Press, 1989).

Page, William (ed.). *VCH: A History of the County of Buckinghamshire*, 2 (London: Constable, 1908).

Page, William (ed.). *VCH: A History of the County of Hampshire and the Isle of Wight*, 5 (London: Constable, 1912; repr. Folkestone: Dawsons, 1973).

Page, William (ed.). *VCH: A History of the County of Nottinghamshire*, 2 (London: Constable, 1910; repr. Folkestone: Dawsons, 1970).

Page, William (ed.). *VCH: A History of the County of Rutland*, 2 (London: St Catherine Press, 1935).

Pevsner, Nikolaus (ed.). *The Buildings of England: Cambridgeshire*, 3rd edn (London Penguin, 1954; repr. 1977).

Pevsner, Nikolaus (ed.). *The Buildings of England: Cornwall*, revised by Enid Radcliffe (London: Penguin, 1951; repr. 1970).

Pevsner, Nikolaus (ed.). *The Buildings of England: S. Devon* (London: Penguin, 1952).

Pevsner, Nikolaus (ed.). *The Buildings of England: Nottinghamshire*, revised by Elizabeth Williamson (London: Penguin, 1951; repr. 1979).

Pevsner, Nikolaus and John Harris (eds). *The Buildings of England: Lincolnshire*, revised by Nicholas Antram, 2nd edn (London: Penguin, 1964; repr. 1995).

Pevsner, Nikolaus and David Lloyd (eds). *The Buildings of England: Hampshire and the Isle of Wight* (London: Penguin, 1967).

Pilkinton, Mark C. 'The Playhouse in Wine Street, Bristol', *TN*, 37 (1983), 14–21.

Pilkinton, Mark C. 'Entertainment and the Free School of St Bartholomew's, Bristol', *REED Newsletter*, 13:2 (1988), 9–13.

Pilkinton, Mark C. 'New Information on the Playhouse in Wine Street, Bristol', *TN*, 42 (1988), 73–5.

Pilkinton, Mark C. (ed.). *REED: Bristol* (London and Toronto: University of Toronto Press, 1997).

Price, Roger. *Excavations at the St Bartholomew's Hospital, Bristol* (Bristol: Redcliffe Press, 1979).

RCHM: An Inventory of Historical Monuments in Dorset, 1 (London: HMSO, 1952).

RCHM: An Inventory of Historical Monuments in Essex, 2 (London: HMSO, 1921).

RCHM: An Inventory of Historical Monuments in Essex, 4 (London: HMSO, 1923).

RCHM: An Inventory of Historical Monuments in the City of Oxford (London: HMSO, 1939).

RCHM: An Inventory of Historical Monuments in the City of Salisbury, 1 (London: HMSO, 1980).

Rothwell, W. F. 'Was there a typical Elizabethan Stage?' *ShS*, 12 (1959), 15–21.

Rowan, D. F. 'The Players and Playing Places of Norwich', in *The Development of Shakespeare's Theater*, ed. by John H. Astington (New York: AMS Press, 1992), 77–94.

Salgado, Gamini. *Eyewitnesses of Shakespeare* (London: Chatto & Windus, 1975).

Salter, H. E. (ed.). *Oxford Council Acts, 1583–1626* (Oxford: Clarendon, 1928).

Salter, H. E. and Mary D. Lobel (eds). *VCH: A History of the County of Oxford*, 3 (Oxford: Oxford University Press, 1954; repr. London: Dawsons, 1965).

Shakespeare, William. *The Norton Shakespeare*, ed. by Stephen Greenblatt *et al.* (London and New York: Norton, 1997).

Shakespeare, William. *The Riverside Shakespeare*, ed. by G. Blakemore Evans *et al.* (Boston, MA: Houghton Mifflin, 1974).

Shakespeare, William. *Titus Andronicus*, ed. by Jonathan Bate (London and New York: Routledge, 1991).

Sisson, C. J. 'Shakespeare's Quartos as prompt-copies. With some account of Cholmeley's Players and a new Shakespeare allusion', *RES*, 70 (1942), 129–43.

Smith, Irwin. *Shakespeare's Blackfriars Playhouse* (London: Peter Owen, 1966).

Somerset, J. Alan B. 'Local Drama and Playing Places at Shrewsbury: New Findings from the Borough Records', *MRDE*, 2 (1985), 1–31.

Somerset, J. Alan B. ' "How chances it they travel?": Provincial Touring, Playing Places, and the King's Men', *ShS*, 47 (1994), 45–60.

Somerset, J. Alan B. (ed.). *REED: Shropshire*, 2 vols (London and Toronto: University of Toronto Press, 1994).

Speed, John. *The Counties of Britain: A Tudor Atlas*, ed. by Nigel Nicolson and Alasdair Hawkyd (London: Pavillion, 1988).

Stokes, James (ed.). *REED: Somerset*, 2 vols (with Bath, ed. by Robert J. Alexander) (London and Toronto: University of Toronto Press, 1996).

Stone, Lawrence. *The Crisis of the Aristocracy, 1558–1641*, abridged edn (Oxford: Oxford University Press, 1967).

Stone, Lawrence (ed.). 'Companies of Players entertained by the Earl of Cumberland and Lord Clifford, 1607–39', *MSC*, 5 (Oxford: Oxford University Press, 1958 [1960]), 17–28.

Stoppard, Tom. *Rosencrantz and Guildenstern are dead* (London: Faber & Faber, 1967).

Sturgess, Keith. *Jacobean Private Theatre* (London: Routledge & Kegan Paul, 1987).

Styles, Philip (ed.). *VCH: A History of the County of Warwick*, 3 (London: Oxford University Press, 1945).

Thomson, Peter. *Shakespeare's Professional Career* (Cambridge: Cambridge University Press, 1992).

Tittler, Robert. *Architecture and Power: The Town Hall and the English Urban Community, c.1500–1640* (Oxford: Oxford University Press, 1991).

Tyacke, Nicholas (ed.). *The History of the University of Oxford*, 4 (Oxford: Clarendon, 1997).

Ungerer, Gustav. 'Shakespeare in Rutland', *Rutland Record*, 7 (1987), 242–48.

Vanes, Jean (ed.). *Documents Illustrating the Overseas Trade of Bristol in the Sixteenth Century*, Bristol Record Society, 31 (Kendal: Titus Wilson, 1979).

Wasson, John M. 'Elizabethan and Jacobean Touring Companies', *TN*, 42 (1988), 51–7.

Wasson, John M. (ed.). *REED: Devon* (London and Toronto: University of Toronto Press, 1986).

Wasson, John M. 'The English Church as Theatrical Space', in *A New History of Early English Drama*, ed. by John D. Cox and David Scott Kastan (New York: Columbia University Press, 1997), 25–37.

Wasson, John M. and David Galloway (eds). 'Records of Plays and Players in Norfolk and Suffolk, 1330–1642', *MSC*, 11 (Oxford: Oxford University Press, 1980–81).

Wasson, John M. and Barbara D. Palmer. 'Professional Players in Northern England, Parts I and II', a paper given at the Annual Conference of the Shakespeare Association of America at Washington DC, 1997, 1–22.

Welander, David. *The History, Art and Architecture of Gloucester Cathedral* (Stroud: Alan Sutton, 1991).

White, Eileen. 'People and Places: The Social and Topographical Context of Drama in York, 1554–1609' (unpublished doctoral thesis, Leeds University, 1984).

Whitfield White, Paul. *Theatre and Reformation: Protestantism, Patronage, and Playing in Tudor England* (Cambridge: Cambridge University Press, 1993).

Whitfield White, Paul. ' " Drama in the Church": Church-playing in Tudor England', *MRDE*, 6 (1993), 15–36.

Wickham, Glynne. *Early English Stages, 1300–1600*, 4 vols (London: Routledge & Kegan Paul, 1959–81).

Willis, Robert and John Willis Clark. *The Architectural History of the University of Cambridge*, 4 vols (Cambridge: Cambridge University Press, 1886; repr. 1988).

Wilson, Jean. *The Archaeology of Shakespeare: The Material Legacy of Shakespeare's Theatre* (Stroud: Alan Sutton, 1995).

Index

in Gloucester, 4, 21, 22, 36, 37, 39, 40, 61, 194
in Great Yarmouth, 132, 134
in Hadleigh, 33
in Leicester, **2**, **6**, 19, 21, 27, 28, 36, 37
in Linton, 24
in Norwich, 12, 28, 216
in Nottingham, 21
in Oxford, 25, 118
performances at, 1, 4, 12, 15, 17, 19, 20, 21, 22, 24–5, 27, 28, 29, 30, 33, 35–8, 39–43, 44, 140, 148, 156, 177, 178; regulation of, 24–5, 33–5, 36, 44, 92, 118, 132, 134, 148, 173–4, 177, 178, 225
in Shrewsbury, 17, 27, 37, 140, 141, 142
in Southampton, 92
in Stratford-upon-Avon, **4**, **5**, 28, 33, 173–4
in Sudbury, 35, 178
symbolism of, 26, 27
in Worcester, 33, 36
in York, 17, 28, 33, 35, 156, 174, 178
see also mayors' parlours and court rooms
Tragedy of Caesar's Revenge, The, 121
transport, *see* carts and wagons
travelling, by playing companies, *see* touring
Travels of the Three English Brothers, The, 75, 202
Trinity College (Cambridge), *see* Cambridge University
Trinity College (Oxford), *see* Oxford University
Troublesome Reign of King John, The, 208
True Tragedy of Richard III, The, 208–9
True Tragedy of Richard Duke of York, The, 38
trumpets, 15, 16, 35
see also musical instruments
tumblers and tumbling, 1, 12–13, 27, 54, 61, 108, 110, 111, 128, 137, 216

Ungerer, Gustav, 203, 204
universities and university colleges, *see* Cambridge University; Oxford University
University College (Oxford), *see* Oxford University

Vaux, Lord Edward, 75
Vaux's Men, 75
Vere, Edward de, Earl of Oxford, 9
Vere, de, family of, 9
vicarages, *see* churches and cathedrals, architectural and topographical features of
Villiers, George, Duke of Buckingham, 79
visitation articles, 62–3, 199
Volpone, 115

wagons, *see* carts and wagons
Waller, Sir Walter, 2, 5–6, 224
Waller's Men, 2, 5–6, 224
Walsham-le-Willows (Suffolk), 129, 130, 132, 134
Walsingham, Sir Francis, 5, 6, 8, 46
Wambus, Francis, 31
war, *see* Civil War
Warrington (Lancashire), 89, 96, 153
Warwick, earl of, *see* Dudley, Ambrose
Warwick's Men, 12, 25, 47
Wasson, John, 10, 11, 24, 216
weapons, *see* military equipment
West Ham (Essex), 49, 51, 56, 59
Westminster School (London), *see* schools
Westmorland, county of, 166, 167, 168, 170, 171
Weymouth (Dorset), 179
Wharton, Lord Philip, 71, 72
Wharton's Men, 71, 72
What mischief worketh in the mynd of man, 13
White, Eileen, 157, 221
White Horse Inn (Norwich), *see* inns
Whitehall (London), 192
Whiteway, William, 25
Wickham, Glynne, 207
Wilkins, George, 202

DATE DUE
Fecha Para Retornar

STORE #47-0100